UNDER ONE ROOF

The Story of the Extraordinary Growth
of American Family Insurance

ISBN 0-9658469-0-3

Printed in the United States of America

Research, writing, design, and layout by
Hakala Communications Inc., St. Paul, Minnesota
Project director: William Hakala
Research and writing: Tom Teigen
Designer: Victoria Hakala
Layout: Beth Zell
Copy editor: Ellen Green

Production/Color Separations and Electronic Image Assembly: Four Lakes Colorgraphics Inc., Madison, Wisconsin

Printing: Universal Lithographers Inc., Sheboygan, Wisconsin

Binding: Midwest Editions, Inc., Minneapolis, Minnesota

CONTENTS

Acknowledgments

Foreword

Milestones

Appendix

Index

ACKNOWLEDGMENTS

Under One Roof, the history of the American Family Insurance Group, could not have been told without the help of many people and organizations. We are particularly grateful to Dale Mathwich, American Family chairman and chief executive officer, who saw the need to tell American Family's story and devoted an extraordinary amount of time to the project. As the primary reader, Mathwich brought a depth of understanding that comes from more than forty years with the company. We also owe a debt of gratitude to public relations director Rick Fetherston and corporate communications manager Mary Vertacic, who shepherded the project along; they spent many hours planning, reading, finding facts and photographs, and juggling the seemingly endless details inherent in producing a corporate history.

More than eighty people shared their recollections, insights, and opinions about the company, its founders, and development. A list of interview participants and other contributors can be found in the appendix. Most notable on the list are the four surviving chairmen of American Family, Irving Maurer, John O. "Pete" Miller, W. Robert Koch, and Dale Mathwich, and current president Harvey Pierce.

Much of the written information and most of the photographs used to tell this story were found in American Family's publications and archives, under the care of archives custodian Pat Peirce. Special thanks to Irving Maurer, whose informal histories of the company provided an excellent framework for identifying key events that shaped the company's early years. A number of individuals, organizations, books, and publications provided insight and historical context. These are listed in the appendix.

—Hakala Communications

FOREWORD

When a company becomes as successful and large as ours, it is easy to forget our humble beginning. This company was founded seventy years ago by people with an entrepreneurial spirit and sense of optimism that helped them overcome some serious challenges over the years.

Under One Roof brings their story to life. You will meet some remarkable men and women who turned hopes and dreams into extraordinary success not even they could have imagined. Their story is our story, and it is worth telling and remembering. That is the primary reason I commissioned this book.

As the years pass, it becomes increasingly difficult to research and produce an accurate corporate history. Important records are thrown out, and many of the company pioneers pass away. And, as is true with all history, more is left out than can be included. Many important contributions must be summarized, while others are excluded altogether. Some stories conflict with memories or even the written record, forcing difficult choices.

Nevertheless, I believe *Under One Roof* is an accurate portrayal of our history, which is essential because this book will become the basis for all subsequent history of this company. It is the unvarnished truth: successes and failures, the good and the bad. And finally, this book is highly entertaining because it is, above all else, a story about people.

And just as it helps us to understand where we came from, I think it helps us know where we need to go and what we need to do to build on our success into the twenty-first century.

Dale F. Mathwich

—Dale F. Mathwich
Chairman and Chief Executive Officer

October 1997

MILESTONES
1927-1962

H.L. Wittwer

1927

Farmers Mutual Automobile Insurance Company founded October 3.

1930

National Mutual Automobile Insurance Company established to sell to nonfarmers.

1933

Farmers Mutual and National Mutual merge.

Farmers Mutual enters Minnesota.

1932

Farmers Mutual adopts semi-annual, semi-direct plan, sending renewal notices directly to policyholders.

1935

Farmers Mutual establishes State Farm Mutual of Madison, Wisconsin to sell windstorm insurance.

Farmers Mutual moves into the Boyd mansion.

1938

Both premiums and assets surpass $1 million.

1939

Farmers Mutual News gives information to policyholders.

Farmers Mutual enters Missouri.

1940

Farmers Mutual is licensed in Nebraska, North and South Dakota.

Farmers Mutual issues nonassessable policies.

1943

Farmers Mutual is licensed in Indiana and Kansas.

1948

State Farm Mutual of Madison is renamed Farmers Mutual Insurance Company of Wisconsin.

1949

Farmers Mutual sells life insurance and sickness and accident coverage for the Union Mutual Life Insurance Co.

Farmers Mutual introduces agent bonuses.

FM provides the field and home office with monthly news.

Farmers Mutual is licensed in Iowa.

1950

Annual premiums exceed $10 million.

1951

Farmers Mutual moves into its East Washington Avenue office in December.

1952

District managers become full time and give up personal sales.

Farmers Mutual sales begin in Illinois.

1955

The board of directors sets exclusive agent representation as a goal for the company.

1956

The first Leading Career Agent convention is held in Chicago.

Two hundred agents sign exclusive representation agreements.

Farmers Mutual introduces an advanced compensation plan for new agents.

1957

The first sales school is held at the home office.

Farmers Mutual offers its own sickness and accident insurance.

1958

American Family Life Insurance Company opens July 1, logging $1 million in sales.

Farmers Mutual establishes four regions led by regional vice presidents (RVPs).

The first regional office opens in St. Joseph, Missouri.

Homeowners insurance is introduced.

1959

Farmers Mutual enters the computer age with the RAMAC 305.

Agents and the company share advertising costs through a cooperative program.

1960

Farmers Mutual buys Farmers Mutual Managers, the management company, and ends its management agreement.

1961

The Central Region is dissolved.

American Standard Insurance Company (ASIC) begins sales September 30.

Farmers Mutual unveils major medical insurance.

1962

Life insurance sales reach $100 million.

Home Office, Madison, Wisconsin

MILESTONES

1963-1997

1966

American Family sales begin in Colorado.

1967

All-lines applications exceed 200,000.

1969

American Family Financial Services (AFFS) opens on May 26.

1970

All-lines policies in force exceed 1 million.

Both premiums and assets surpass $100 million.

1971

American Family pays agents more than $1 million in bonuses.

1972

Life insurance in force reaches $1 billion.

1963

March 5, policyholders give final approval to change the company's name to American Family Mutual Insurance Company.

1965

American Family jingle is copyrighted July 9.

Co-op television advertising begins.

The agent cooperative office program starts.

The AmPlan monthly billing system is introduced.

1973

American Family Financial Services loans in force exceed 10,000.

1975

American Family grows to be the fifth largest mutual auto insurer.

1976

Policyholders' surplus totals $100 million.

1977

Northwest Region moves to Eden Prairie, Minnesota.

American Family celebrates its fiftieth anniversary.

1978

Annual life sales surpass $1 billion for the first time, with more than $3 billion in force.

American Family Financial Services loans in force exceed 20,000.

1979

Policyholders' surplus tops $200 million.

1980

Wisconsin Region moves into new building.

American Family breaks into the nation's top twenty auto insurers.

1981

American Family becomes the fourth largest mutual auto insurance company.

Assets surpass $1 billion.

All-lines policies total more than 3 million.

1983

Fourteen agents test the DEFACTO computer system.

1986

Premiums hit $1 billion mark. All-lines apps exceed 1 million.

American Family posts its first $100 million operating gain.

Policyholders' surplus tops $500 million, assets top $2 billion.

Sales begin in Arizona on March 1.

1987

All-lines policies surpass 4 million.

1990

Ground is broken for the national headquarters.

1991

The Wisconsin Region is renamed the Great Lakes Region.

1992

National headquarters construction completed.

Policyholders' surplus exceeds $1 billion.

1993

Assets total $5 billion.

The board of directors travels to St. Joseph, Missouri, for its first meeting outside of Madison.

1994

The State Capitol Credit Union becomes the first occupant of the American Center Office Park.

American Family rolls out its one-of-a-kind catastrophe trailer.

American Family ranks as the eleventh largest property/casualty insurer.

1995

American Family forms the Mountain and Valley regions.

Sales begin in Ohio on January 1.

Life insurance in force surpasses $32 billion.

Assets surpass $6 billion.

First urban service center opens in Kansas City in December.

1996

Policies in force total more than 6 million.

Policyholders' surplus exceeds $2 billion.

Spanish language radio commercials begin in select markets.

1997

RVP role restructured as RVP of sales.

Spanish language television commerical and multi-line brochure introduced.

Chapter One

*All history resolves itself very easily into the
biography of a few stout and earnest persons.*

—RALPH WALDO EMERSON

TILLING THE SOIL, PLANTING THE SEED

HOTEL CHARLES, MARSHFIELD, WISCONSIN

On this unseasonably warm day in mid-March, Herman Wittwer gripped the steering wheel with both hands, struggling to keep the wheels straight as a farmer with a team of mules pulled his car toward the clean, dry blacktop of Highway 13. It was the third time this trip that he'd been stuck in the mud, and he was down to his last pair of trousers. At least he'd be on his way home tomorrow.

"Thank you for your help," Wittwer said, standing on the side of the road. "I'm sorry to have troubled you."

"No trouble," the old farmer replied and nodded toward Wittwer's mud-caked automobile. "I've got one of those myself, but she's not worth a darn this time of year."

Wittwer smiled and scraped the mud from his shoes before climbing back into the Chrysler "50." Heading south toward Marshfield, Wittwer pushed his car past the 30-mph speed limit and checked his pocket watch. Four o'clock. He'd still have time to clean up at the Charles before the meeting.

The year was 1927, and Marshfield, a central Wisconsin lumber town turned bustling regional hub, had become a common stop for traveling salesmen. Many of them stopped at the Charles, Marshfield's newest hotel. Billed as the "traveling man's mecca," the Charles featured comfortable rooms, soft beds, and fine cuisine. On weekends, its elegant, seven-course dinners typically began with blue points on the half-shell and progressed through such entrees as beef tenderloin in bordelaise sauce or roasted milk-fed spring duckling to chocolate *blancmange* and strong black coffee.

Just a few years before, when Wittwer first traveled to Marshfield, horse-drawn wagons outnumbered cars and finding gasoline was sometimes difficult. But these days, many of the business and pleasure travelers who stayed at the Charles arrived by automobile, and service stations lined the main highway nearby.

In the 1920s, Americans embraced the automobile— among them Warren G. Harding, who in 1921 became the first president to arrive at his inauguration in an autocar. As postwar depression gave way to prosperity under Harding's successor, Calvin Coolidge, cars became faster, flashier, more reliable—and most important, "closed." In 1919, nine of ten automobiles were open-air touring vehicles. By 1927, more than 80 percent of the nation's automobiles were closed sedans that could be driven year-round.

Mass production also made the car more affordable. When Ford introduced the Model T in 1908, it sold for $850. Eight years later, the price of a new "Tin Lizzie" was less than $300. The installment plan also made motorcars easier to buy. Five dollars down bought a coupon book from the local dealer, and with payments of five dollars a week, you could drive a new Model T off the lot in just over a year. By the end of the 1920s, the American public was

State Historical Society of Wisconsin

buying more than 4 million cars annually, and nearly half the nation's consumer debt was tied up in auto financing.

By 1927, the car was so popular that the year's biggest story was not Charles Lindbergh's solo flight across the Atlantic Ocean, or Calvin Coolidge not running for reelection, or even Alvin "Shipwreck" Kelly's twenty-three days and seven hours atop a flagpole. The biggest story was that the Ford Motor Company had reclaimed the top slot among automakers by introducing the new Model A roadster.

Enthusiasm and expertise did not necessarily go hand in hand. Driver's education was informal at best. A new car owner might know someone who could provide a few pointers—mainly about how to crank the engine without breaking your arm. Otherwise, drivers simply got behind the wheel and drove, learning along the way. As millions of novices took to the road, accidents increased—and so, inevitably, did the demand for insurance.

Auto insurance had been around since 1898, when Travelers Insurance

A country road near Madison, Wisconsin, in the 1920s.

In 1916, Congress appropriated $75 million for road construction over five years. Three years later, Maj. Dwight D. Eisenhower led a convoy of U. S. Army vehicles from New York to San Francisco to dramatize the link between better roads and national security. Congress responded in 1921 with the Federal Highway Act, sharing with the states the cost of road construction and resurfacing.

First coupe built in Wisconsin in 1905 by Gus Wilke, fire chief of Sheboygan.

State Historical Society of Wisconsin

wrote the first policy using a standard "horse-drawn carriage" form with a special endorsement. By 1905, an auto owner could get liability, fire, and theft coverage. These early policies covered only damage for accidents with a moving object, based on the assumption that in a collision with an immobile object, the driver was obviously at fault. Coverage for personal injury to the driver or his passengers wasn't available until the 1930s.

Lacking meaningful statistics, insurers could only experiment with underwriting, which involves classifying acceptable risks and selecting those the company will insure. Using such characteristics as a car's weight, horsepower, and number of cylinders, the industry established the first automobile

Wisconsin: The Auto State

In the American lexicon, *Detroit* is synonymous with the automobile. Mammoth factories churning out millions of automobiles a year have made the city and its satellites the car capital of the world. But in the early days of the automobile, when invention, not mass production, was the driving force, Wisconsin was among the leaders.

Charles and Frank Duryea, a couple of Ohio boys living in Peoria, typically receive credit for launching the American automobile industry with the first autocar to come off the production line. The brothers built thirteen two-cylinder Duryeas in 1896. But any Wisconsin auto-buff will tell you that Dr. J. W. Carhart, a Racine, Wisconsin,

physician, built the first successful steam-powered car in 1872, and Gottfried Schloemer, a Milwaukee barrel-maker, built the first practical gasoline-powered car in 1889—four years before the Duryeas even tested their invention.

Although the Duryea brothers were the first to "mass produce" the automobile for sale, a Wisconsin man sold the first automobile. In 1895, the same year the Duryeas set up their first factory, A. W. Ballard, a bicycle repairman from Oshkosh, built an autocar for a physician living in Wausau.

The Wisconsin legislature sponsored the world's first automobile race in 1878, offering a $10,000 prize for the first practical, self-propelled highway vehicle. Two steam wagons participated, with the winner completing the 150-mile trip from Green Bay to Madison at the average speed of 6 mph.

By the time Herman Wittwer and Richard Kalbskopf started Farmers Mutual Automobile Insurance Company, Wisconsin factories had built more than four million motorcars. The state was home to the Nash, the Rambler, the Jeffery, the Case, the Mitchell of Racine, the Kissel Kar of Hartford, and the Lafayette of Milwaukee and Kenosha. There was the Hayberg, the Monarch, the Merkel (later the Merkel motorcycle), the Superior, the Kunz, the Pierce-Racine, the Earl, the four-wheel-drive motorcars built in Clintonville, the Petrel friction-drive car, the Ogren, the Badger "30", the Vixen Cyclecar, the Johnson Steamer, and many more.

The Great Depression, two world wars, and the successful mass production of other makes drove these and other car companies out of business. And Wisconsin settled contentedly for being the nation's dairy state.

classifications—W, X, Y, Z, with the Model T in a class of its own. To attract lower risks, some companies gave discounts to people who drove often, figuring practice made them better drivers.

But policies favoring the experienced driver worked against farmers. At the time, most country roads were dirt paths that became muddy rivers in the spring and fall. The Model T, the farmer's car of choice, was useless in the snow, and farmers typically put them up on blocks for half the year. When farmers were able to drive, it was on empty country roads and small-town streets. Accidents were few. Nevertheless, farmers paid the same premiums for car insurance as city dwellers—twenty-five dollars a year for a new Ford sedan.

This practice seemed unfair, particularly because most farmers hadn't shared in the general American prosperity of the 1920s. The government dropped price supports following World War I, and farm prices plunged. During the 1920s, more than four million discouraged farmers abandoned their land and moved to cities and suburbs to find work in the nation's expanding industrial economy.

Herman Wittwer, who grew up in southern Wisconsin's dairy country, understood the plight of farmers. And as a special agent for the Wisconsin Automobile Insurance Company, he traveled the state meeting regularly with farmers who sold auto insurance on the side. Small and soft-spoken, Wittwer earned the respect of these farmer-agents through his honest, easy manner as he recruited and trained, answered questions, and settled disputes.

Wittwer, it was said, was a man to whom you could talk straight, a man who would listen. As these farmer-agents complained to him about the unfairness of auto insurance rates, he found that he agreed with them. More and more, as he traveled Wisconsin's back roads, Wittwer decided it was a cause worth pursuing. Finally, he had found a mission that would bring some focus to his wandering, rudderless career.

Lord knows, he'd been looking since he left Monticello.

Minnesota Historical Society

Poor country roads forced farmers to store their cars during the winter and spring. Because Wisconsin farmers drove their cars only half the year, Herman Wittwer believed they deserved better insurance rates.

In the late 1920s, state legislatures and insurance commissioners, frustrated by the time required to review policies and rates, considered mandating uniform auto insurance policies. To derail government intrusion, the American Mutual Alliance began work on a uniform policy. The National Bureau of Casualty Underwriters, representing the for-profit insurance companies owned by stockholders, joined the effort in 1933. With the help of the American Bar Association, the groups developed the first standard provisions of the Basic Automobile Liability Policy, effective January 1, 1936.

Searching for the Right Note

Born January 6, 1889, Herman Louis Wittwer grew up in Monticello, a small cheese and lumber town at the intersection of two busy railroads in south-western Wisconsin. His father and uncle owned the Grand Central Hotel, where the two men and their families lived and worked. Wittwer's parents were of Swiss descent—his father was an immigrant—as were most residents of Monticello. Known to non-Swiss as Switzers, they tended to be industrious, earnest, and forbearing people, for whom fun must be preceded by work. From them, Herman developed a sense of decorum and propriety that shaped both his personal and business relationships. Friendly without being too familiar, confident without being arrogant, he grew to be a popular though somewhat reserved young man.

A view of Monticello in 1907. Below: Young Herman Wittwer (second row, second from right, behind bass drummer) played the alto horn in Monticello's Messenger Band.

Usually surrounded by strangers at the hotel, he learned to listen attentively, making people feel he was interested—not only in what they were saying but in them personally.

In Monticello, young Wittwer also discovered his first passion—music. A dance hall attached to the hotel often hosted traveling shows, dance bands, high school plays, and community performances. As a junior member of the Monticello Messenger Band, Herman played the alto horn. Later, he took up the clarinet and in high school earned extra money playing in area dance bands. Years later,

The University of Wisconsin Regimental Band appeared in the Badger yearbook in 1911. Wittwer (seated in the first row, third from right) played first chair clarinet.

an in-law recounted how he and Herman one night—spirits high from an evening of merrymaking—walked the dozen miles of train tracks between Monroe and Monticello, playing their clarinets as they went.

Music helped to mold Wittwer's personality. In learning the fundamentals of musicianship, he acquired the discipline of practice that carried into every aspect of his life. Playing in various bands, he learned to blend his musical voice with others. Taking the lead to perform a solo, he elaborated on the melody, then stepped back to support others in carrying the main theme. Sensitive to the moods of others, he knew when to step in and when to lay back, trusting his own intuition and that of those around him.

Wittwer brought along his clarinet and his love of music when he left Monticello for Madison and the University of Wisconsin in 1906. As a member of the university's regimental band, he was first chair clarinet for the first public performance of "On Wisconsin" in 1909.

Wittwer's clarinet carried him beyond the world of classical music and fight songs and into the vaudeville house, landing him a spot in the pit orchestra at the old Orpheum Theater on Monona Avenue (now Martin Luther King Boulevard). Several nights a week, he sat in the pit, playing popular songs such as "Meet Me in St. Louis Louis" and "In My Merry Oldsmobile" to earn money for school.

At the Orpheum, Herman Wittwer met Barbara Hickey, a fiery, young

*Herman Wittwer
Class of 1911
University of Wisconsin
Madison*

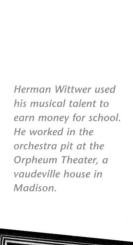

Herman Wittwer used his musical talent to earn money for school. He worked in the orchestra pit at the Orpheum Theater, a vaudeville house in Madison.

woman of Irish descent who grew up near Madison's "bloody 4th ward," the railroad district around West Washington Avenue. Barbara attended the Wisconsin School of Music and the Four C Business College before becoming a secretary at the theater. Her saucy spirit and cutting wit contrasted sharply with Herman's polite if not formal demeanor. She gave him the pet name "Pootsy," playfully violating his sense of propriety.

Wittwer's friends at the university called him "Witty." An enjoyable companion, he liked poker, brandy Manhattans, and good cigars—although true to his upbringing, good times always followed studying. Majoring in German, he took courses in Spanish and English as well. His senior thesis, "A Study of the New York Central Stocks and Bonds in Relation to the Money Market," belied an interest in business.

After graduation, Wittwer, like many young men of the era, drifted. Unsure what to do with his life, he enrolled in graduate school and stayed on at the Orpheum. He recalled later that he "stumbled" into the insurance business in 1913, when he became an agent in New Glarus. His career as a field man was lackluster. His only boast from those days was that he introduced the brandy Manhattan to that small Wisconsin town.

Wittwer was more enthusiastic about dating Barbara Hickey. In 1915—perhaps on a whim for Barbara but after careful consideration on Herman's part—the two eloped, catching a night train to Crown Point, Indiana, where they married on November 23. Married life appealed greatly to Wittwer, but his future as an insurance man did not. In 1917, the year America joined the Great War in Europe, Wittwer returned to graduate school and the old Orpheum Theater—though he continued to sell insurance on the side.

A year later, he enrolled in dental school at Marquette University, playing his clarinet part-time at the Empress, a Milwaukee burlesque house. But dentistry disappointed Herman, too. "Damn tooth carpentry," he called it. Spiraling inflation made it difficult to keep up with bills. In March 1919, Barbara gave birth to their first daughter, Jane. Later that year, Herman dropped out of Marquette and packed the family up for the return trip to Madison. The day they left, Barbara salvaged a set of plaster-cast teeth from a box destined for the trash bin. Time and again when Herman's spirits were low, she pulled out the plaster teeth to remind him that things could be worse.

Herman Wittwer (first row, far right) with a group of his university pals.

Back in Madison, Herman Wittwer joined the Wisconsin Automobile Insurance Company of Monroe, Wisconsin, as a special agent. Again, he immersed himself in the insurance business—this time with a sense of urgency spurred by having a family to support.

The Wittwers rode out the postwar recession and, with the rest of the country, turned onto Prosperity Street in 1922. When he was not on the road, Herman became an active city and cultural booster. In 1926, he was one of the founding members and treasurer of the Madison Civic Symphony Orchestra. At a time when Prohibition was an occasionally observed law, Herman and Barbara also found time to duck into speakeasies in her old neighborhood and attend cocktail parties with superior court judge Roy Proctor and society writer Alexius Baas. On weekends, Herman hit the golf course in a pair of baggy plus-fours and checkered knee socks, emulating the great Bobby Jones.

At 38, Wittwer's life seemed full, yet he could not shake an underlying sense of dissatisfaction. Secretary of Commerce Herbert Hoover was preaching the gospel of small business, and new ventures were sprouting up all around. Wittwer often bumped into Phil Snodgrass, a fellow employee at Wisconsin Auto who had left to help launch General Casualty, a new insurance company. Snodgrass talked enthusiastically of the company's plans for the future. When he asked how Wittwer's job was going, Herman smiled thinly and said little. His career seemed stuck in the deep ruts of a muddy Wisconsin byway.

Monday mornings were especially difficult. While Herman packed his bags into the back of the Chrysler, Barbara would be up early making breakfast. She seemed cheerful and optimistic, but Herman knew she wasn't happy to have

Top: Herman Wittwer holding his daughter Jane.
Bottom: Barbara Wittwer.

Movie houses and live theater added luster to Madison life in 1927.

In 1927, traffic accidents killed 592 Wisconsin residents, a six-fold increase in ten years. The following year, the Wisconsin legislature required all automobile drivers to be licensed and gave the state authority to revoke someone's license if found to be incompetent, reckless, physically handicapped, or otherwise a menace to the public.

him gone so often. Their daughters were growing up between his visits home. Jane had turned eight early in March. Herman hadn't missed her birthday, but car troubles made it a close call. Joyce, their second daughter, was already three. He had to get off the road.

One possibility involved offering special auto insurance rates for farmers. A young Illinois company called State Farm Mutual Insurance Company was growing rapidly by giving farmers a preferred rate. No company was doing that for Wisconsin farmers, who owned roughly half of the 560,000 automobiles in the state. Wittwer spent several weeks in early 1927 studying the files, finding that farmers did indeed have fewer accidents than people in small towns and cities.

Barbara encouraged him to take his analysis to the company. "Catch their eye," she said. "Then ask for a promotion that will keep you in the office."

He did. And when management said no—standing by the conventional wisdom that farmers presented greater risk—Barbara said, "To hell with them, Pootsy! Do it on your own."

In March 1927, Wittwer followed his wife's advice and arranged a meeting with an old friend at the Charles Hotel in Marshfield.

Laying the Foundation

Smartly dressed in a Hickey-Freeman suit and freshly polished Florsheim shoes, Herman Wittwer nodded to a couple of familiar faces in the spacious lobby of the Charles. Walking into the restaurant, he heard the man he'd come to meet from a table near the back, gesturing wildly to a waiter. "Borrow the money," he bellowed. "Buy on margin. Hell, rob a bank if you have to. But get in now. Prices are going up, and you'll be a millionaire in a few years."

As Wittwer approached the table, a bit apprehensively, Richard Kalbskopf jumped to his feet. "Herman!" he shouted.

"Nice to see you again, Richard," Wittwer said.

Kalbskopf slapped the waiter's shoulder. "I was just telling my good friend here that the stock market is a racket to get into," he said. "You'd agree, wouldn't you?"

"I don't know," Wittwer said, the typical voice of caution that at times irritated Kalbskopf. "Some say prices are inflated. Could be a correction coming."

"The same gloom-and-doom prophets who can't accept the fact that prosperity is here to stay," Kalbskopf said, with a dismissive wave. "You need to act before it's too late." Wittwer's smile at the waiter showed he disagreed with his friend.

In contrast to the guarded Wittwer, Kalbskopf held little back. The son of a traveling salesman who settled in Marshfield, he was an imposing figure, over six feet tall and weighing more than 200 pounds. Boisterous, with a shock of black hair greased to his head, Kalbskopf had a firm handshake and a slap on the back for everyone in Marshfield. He joined his father's insurance agency after a stint as an army private during World War I.

Kalbskopf was a self-promoter, unafraid to mention that he was the best insurance man in Wood County, whether it was

The Fortunate Reimbursing the Unfortunate

The roots of America's mutual insurance movement stretch back to 1752, when Benjamin Franklin organized the Philadelphia Contributorship for the Insurance of Houses from Loss by Fire. This and countless other mutual companies helped the capital-scarce economy distribute among many people the risk of losses caused by fire.

In 1857, New York State codified the formation of town mutuals with legislation allowing twenty-five or more people living in a township (thirty-six square miles) to establish a mutual fire insurance company. Wisconsin enacted a similar law two years later. The rise of the Grange, an activist farmers' association that often claimed conspiracy between for-profit insurance companies and big railroads, fostered the spread of town mutuals. By 1920, more than a thousand of these small mutuals had formed in the nation. The vast majority wrote fire and lightning insurance, but many sold windstorm and other coverage as well. Over time, town mutuals expanded to serve larger areas, and by the middle of the twentieth century many had become commercial ventures.

Most town mutuals were assessment companies that charged a small policy fee to pay the secretary for typing up the policy and managing the company's few affairs. At the end of the year, losses were tallied and a member assessment levied to cover the losses. One early Farmer's Mutual agent described the arrangement as "the fortunate reimbursing the unfortunate."

In the 1920s, more than two hundred Wisconsin town mutuals served farmers primarily. Town mutual secretaries often sold auto insurance on the side, providing a ready-made sales force for Farmers Mutual.

true or not. He was also wealthy, having married Esther Lang, the daughter of a well-to-do industrialist with a hand in many profitable ventures. Over the years, Kalbskopf had often boasted about his wife's inheritance, offering many times to become Wittwer's business partner. Wittwer was about to take him up on it.

Farmers Mutual founders Richard Kalbskopf and Herman Wittwer.

But first Kalbskopf had to tell Wittwer about the Feds padlocking the Marshfield Brewery. "The near beer was a bit nearer than it should have been," he said.

"I hear the legislature is going to debate a resolution calling on Congress to repeal Prohibition," Wittwer said.

"At least bring back beer," Kalbskopf asserted. "I don't drink the stuff myself, but we've got a perfectly good brewery just sitting there."

After dinner, the waiter brought ice, and Wittwer pulled a flask of brandy from his vest, discreetly pouring its contents into their teacups. "Richard," Wittwer began with an uncertainty he was not accustomed to, "I have a proposition for you."

Slowly, over several trips to the flask, Wittwer laid out his plan for a company selling auto insurance to Wisconsin farmers only. He told Kalbskopf about how State Farm was doing the same thing in Illinois. "Herman Ekern. You remember him—former Wisconsin insurance commissioner. He's their attorney," Wittwer said. "I think we could get him to help us."

Kalbskopf was sold long before Wittwer finished. "Sounds like a good racket," he said. "Count me in."

Now came the hard part. Selling a good idea was one thing; asking for money was another. Wittwer was still imbued with the sense of decorum and propriety he'd learned in his youth, particularly concerning finances. "I've saved a few thousand dollars to help us get started," he said slowly, letting the sentence trail off into the restaurant din.

"If we're going to do this, Herman, let's do it right," Kalbskopf said, a bit loudly for Wittwer's comfort. "I'll kick in $50,000."

Wittwer shifted uncomfortably in his chair. Fifty thousand dollars allowed a new commercial insurance company to charge a premium while reserving the right to make assessments. But Wittwer preferred starting a mutual company, which required 200 charter members, not a specific sum of money. Wittwer agreed to accept Kalbskopf's contribution, but only as a startup loan to the new corporation. Unwilling to live off Esther Kalbskopf's inheritance, Wittwer also insisted on keeping his job with Wisconsin Auto until he and Kalbskopf were ready to start selling policies for their new company.

"You're a stubborn man, Herman," Kalbskopf said. "Have it your way. You got a name for this company of ours?"

"Farmers Mutual Automobile Insurance Company," Wittwer said.

"I like it. Says exactly what we're all about."

That settled, they laid out a plan for developing a field force. Wittwer thought Farmers Mutual should work with town mutual secretaries. Wisconsin had more than 200 of these locally based insurance organizations insuring farmers against fire and windstorm damage. Often town mutual secretaries, farmers themselves, also sold auto insurance, many of them for Wisconsin Auto, and Wittwer met regularly with these agent-farmers during his weekly travels.

Wittwer occasionally asked questions to which he already knew the answer as a way of measuring the listener by his response. "So who do we need to support our little venture?" he asked Kalbskopf.

"August Rammer," Kalbskopf said. "Big farmer from Sheboygan. He's secretary of the Wisconsin Association of Mutual Insurance Companies. There's Ben Lang at McMillan Mutual, Charles Klevene at Seneca, Henry Ott at Plymouth Farmers, a few others I can't think of offhand. Harvey Spriggs is another. Down by Racine. If we can get letters of support from these fellows, we should have no trouble recruiting agents and members, and getting approval from the insurance commissioner."

Wittwer was impressed. Kalbskopf even mentioned a few names he hadn't thought of. They would begin by contacting these men. Then while Wittwer made his rounds for Wisconsin Auto, he'd raise the subject with other town mutual secretaries. When someone showed interest, Wittwer would pass the name along to Kalbskopf, who would follow up, working out an individual agreement with each agent. It was an arrangement that would come back to haunt the company.

By the time the two men finished, the restaurant was empty. On the dark

At the turn of the century, the era of the Progressives, state governments wrestled with their role as regulators of the insurance industry. In 1889, the Wisconsin legislature debated the first bill proposing state control of accident insurance rates. In 1906, Gov. Robert La Follette launched an investigation of life insurance companies. In 1911, the legislature held fourteen weeks of hearings on the role of rating bureaus in fire insurance.

Farmers Mutual's first office consisted of two rooms and a broom closet above Breitenbach's Shoe Store in the old Tenney Building.

street outside, they shook hands. "I may be crazy, Richard," Wittwer said, in what seemed for him a display of wild optimism, "but this could be a million-dollar company some day."

Two Rooms and a Broom Closet

Herman Ekern, the Chicago attorney Wittwer had mentioned, was supportive of the plan and offered some helpful advice, but declined to serve as Farmers Mutual's attorney because of his ties to State Farm, which was seeking a Wisconsin license.

Wittwer turned to William J. P. Aberg, a Madison attorney with Sanborn, Blake, and Aberg. As the local counsel for the Chicago, Milwaukee, St. Paul, and Pacific Railroad, Aberg had little background in insurance law. But he was a capable attorney with a sound reputation and was a familiar face in the halls of the Wisconsin State Capitol. An avid conservationist, Aberg was instrumental in crafting the Conservation Act of 1927.

Aberg turned over much of the legal legwork to Ernest Pett, a junior partner. Like Wittwer, Pett was interested in the arts. He'd traveled in France during the war with an "old-fashioned minstrel show" and produced similar shows in Madison. Pett and Wittwer hit it off immediately.

In April, Farmers Mutual filed articles of organization, bylaws, a plan of operation, and letters of support from town mutual secretaries around the state with the Wisconsin Department of Insurance. With minor changes, Commissioner M. A. Freedy approved the plan, allowing the company to incorporate and begin the challenging task of recruiting agents and selling the 200 charter policies required to receive an insurance charter in the state.

Wittwer quit his job at Wisconsin Auto, and Kalbskopf moved his family to Madison. The partners rented space in the old Tenney Building, a three-story, white brick structure at the corner of Pinkney and East Main on Capitol Square. The office consisted of two second-story rooms and a broom closet above Julius Breitenbach's shoe store. Wittwer and Kalbskopf worked at opposite ends of a long, wooden table at one side of the office. Hazel Jacobson, the receptionist/secretary, sat at a desk near the door. For meetings, they borrowed chairs from a neighbor, the law firm of Hall, Baker, and Hall.

In addition to Farmers Mutual Automobile Insurance Company, the directory in the lobby listed the Wittwer, Kalbskopf Insurance Agency. To make ends meet, both men continued to write insurance, not only for Farmers Mutual but also for several other companies. This enabled them to sell insurance to drivers who did not meet Farmers Mutual's strict qualifications.

To launch Farmers Mutual, Aberg suggested Wittwer and Kalbskopf follow common practice and form a management company. That summer, they incorporated Farmers Mutual Managers, Inc., capitalized by fifty shares of common stock and 200 shares of preferred stock, with shares valued at $100.

Wittwer and Kalbskopf each invested $3,500 in cash, credited themselves $1,000 for three months of promotional services, and took seventeen shares of common stock and seventy-five shares of preferred stock valued at $9,200. In return for his legal services, Pett received a single share of common stock, making him the third voting member of the management company. The management firm held the remaining fifteen shares of common stock in reserve.

Kalbskopf took on the role of chief salesman and recruiter, selling most of the preferred stock for Farmers Mutual to new district agents, who were required to purchase at least $500 worth of stock. The stock didn't carry voting rights, but offered an 8 percent annual return.

Sale of fifty shares of common stock and two hundred shares of preferred stock generated the initial capital for Farmers Mutual Managers, the management company which operated Farmers Mutual Automobile Insurance Company.

August Rammer was one of the first town mutual secretaries to become a district agent for Farmers Mutual. When Wittwer called on him, Rammer was the secretary of the Wisconsin Association of Mutual Insurance Companies, a title he would hold for twenty-four years. Like Kalbskopf, Rammer had a husky frame and hearty laugh, but he was more statesman than salesman, and

August J. Rammer

Herman L. Wittwer

Richard J. Kalbskopf

less rough around the edges. Wittwer approached him about signing a letter of support. After hearing Wittwer's plans and judging him sincere, Rammer signed on.

Rather than wait for Wittwer to approach him, Harvey Spriggs, a sheep farmer from Racine, traveled to Madison to get in on the ground floor of the new company. Small and thin, with an angular face, Spriggs wore a black suit and black hat in the mode of an aging Wyatt Earp. "Where is this man Wittwer?" he asked the startled Hazel Jacobson, as he strode into the Farmers Mutual office.

"Right here," Wittwer said, rising from the back table.

Spriggs surveyed the barren room as he crossed the wooden floor. "Thought for a minute there I walked into the governor's office," Spriggs said through his heavy, soup-strainer mustache.

The old farmer's wry sense of humor wasn't wasted on Wittwer. "Nothing but the best for Wisconsin's farmers," he responded, covering a half-eaten Limburger cheese sandwich with yesterday's *Wisconsin State Journal*.

Spriggs signed on immediately as a district agent.

Charter Agents, Charter Members

Wittwer, Kalbskopf, and a dozen district agents spent the spring and summer of 1927 signing up charter members. The task required determined salesmanship. Wisconsin—as was the case

Herman Wittwer's handwritten draft of an early Farmers Mutual promotional letter.

with all states but Massachusetts—did not require insurance on private automobiles. Thus an agent's first challenge was to sell the prospect on the importance of insuring his car. Complicating the sale was the requirement that each application be accompanied by a check for the first year's premium—though the coverage wouldn't go into effect and provide protection until all 200 policies were sold and the company received its charter.

On May 17, 1927, the Jagodzinski brothers, who farmed near Marshfield, bought the first Farmers Mutual policy, paying Joseph Radtke $15.22. Radtke's commission: $2.28. When the brothers renewed the policy, Radtke received $1.52. Other early members, such as Gustav Schultz, a farmer near Poy Sippi, were more frugal, buying just fire, theft, and tornado coverage, with an annual premium of $4.80.

On Friday, August 19, Farmers Mutual presented to the insurance commissioner more than 200 applications. The following Monday, Farmers Mutual Managers, Inc., held its first meeting at the office of Sanborn, Blake, and Aberg.

The three shareholders, Wittwer, Kalbskopf, and Pett, met in Pett's office, conducting business over a desk covered with papers and coffee cups. The brief, uneventful meeting was dominated by details and formalities. The group named Kalbskopf president of the management company, Pett vice president, and Wittwer secretary/treasurer.

The next week, state insurance commissioner M. A. Freedy threw an unexpected curve at Farmers Mutual. Previously, the insurance department required a new company to show 200 charter applications, but Freedy now interpreted the law as requiring 200 policies per line. Farmers Mutual offered five separate coverages for automobiles—liability, property damage, fire, theft, and tornado. There were more sales to be made.

Because farmers best understood fire and theft insurance, Farmers Mutual

OF APPLICANT	DATE REC'D	DATE DEP. AT BANK OF WIS.	PREMIUM PD.	SECURED BY
Jagodzinski Bros.,	May 17	May 17	$15.22 Pd	Radtke
Gustav A. Schultz	17	17	16.00 "	Radtke
Clarence Brett	17	17	6.66 "	Kalbskopf
John Radtke	17	17	9.47 "	Radtke
Herman Stecker	23	23	27.50 "	Radtke
Henry Stecker	23	23	23.80 "	Radtke
Clarence Brett	23	23	14.00 Pd.	Kalbskopf
Peter Peterson	23	23	9.60 Pd.	Radtke
Gustav Wunrow	23	23	21.20 "	Radtke
Casper Gallatin	23	23	5.07 "	Radtke
Mrs. Ida Berdan	23			
Peter Kalbskopf	23			
Oscar A. Sommer	24			
Louis W. Hipke	25			
Malcolm Gallatin	26			
Samual Bauwerdink	31			
Ralph Whitehead	31			
John Manlick	June 2			
Geo. Kieffer	2			
Geo. Baltus	3			
W. C. Garten	6			
Bernard J. Brechtrup	6			
Henry Knorr	6			
Ben Lang	7			
Albert Schiferl	8			
O. K. Anderson	8			
Joseph Banscher	8			
Edward Marty	8			
J. Moritz	9			
Jacob Stauffer	9			
Stauffacher Bros	9			
Wm. Dhein Jr	11			
F. E. Roderick	10			
Geo. W. Eaton	10			

APPLICATION
Combination Policy — *HOME OFFICE COPY*
Farmers' Mutual Automobile Insurance Company
Madison, Wisconsin

In the summer of 1927, Farmers Mutual enrolled 346 charter members. Shown are a partial list and copy of the first issued policy. Although the Jagodzinski brothers were the first to buy a Farmers Mutual policy, Garfield Caley, a farmer near Waterford, was issued Policy No. 1 on October 3, 1927, the day the company received its charter. Caley, like many farmers, was reticent about buying a policy from a company not yet licensed. "I had to guarantee [the policy] personally before the applicant would accept it," Harvey Spriggs recalled. The policy on the 1925 Ford roadster provided liability coverage of $10,000 per person, $20,000 per accident, and $1,000 for property damage. Impressed with the company, Caley himself became a Farmers Mutual agent.

The Importance of Being Earnest

Herman Wittwer earnestly believed that members paid their premiums in good faith, and the company had a duty to pay legitimate claims quickly. But Farmers Mutual's low premiums—based on the firm belief that its members were careful, conscientious drivers—depended on paying legitimate claims only.

When a railroad line submitted a $47 bill for damages to a crossing gate, Wittwer was tenacious in investigating his company's ninth claim. He discovered that an inexperienced gate operator had neglected to sound the warning bell and lowered the gate just moments before the train passed. To avoid being hit by the oncoming train, a farmer whose truck stalled on the tracks had to drive through the gate.

The railroad company disputed Wittwer's findings and demanded payment from Farmers Mutual or the farmer himself. After some negotiation, Wittwer agreed to pay half the claim; the railroad accepted responsibility for the other half. Considering that Farmers Mutual paid claims totaling $45.85 in 1927, a $23.50 savings was significant.

charter sales were strongest in these lines. To boost liability and property damage sales, Farmers Mutual Managers launched the company's first sales contest in late August. The three-week contest recognized only combination policies—liability and property damage combined with fire, theft, or tornado coverage. The grand prize was an all-expenses-paid trip to Madison for the first policyholders' meeting.

The contest produced the needed sales, and Wittwer sent letters to the company's 346 charter members, inviting them to the first policyholders' meeting on October 3, 1927, at the offices of Sanborn, Blake, and Aberg on the eighth floor of the Gay Building on North Carroll Street.

Birth of a Company

As Wittwer and Kalbskopf walked into the Gay Building an hour before the policyholders' meeting, several farmers were gathered in the lobby. Some spent the night in Madison, taking their wives to the Strand to see Ramon Novarro in *Ben Hur*. But their conversation focused on the insurance company they'd joined.

At ten o'clock, twenty-five men crammed into the eighth-floor conference room, but it was so crowded that some members had to stand with their backs against the walls. Wittwer decided to move the gathering to the Green Room of the Loraine Hotel. There he called the meeting to order. "We started this company," he said, "because farmers deserve a lower premium for their auto insurance. It's being done in other states, but not here in Wisconsin—at least not until today! There are those who say such a company cannot succeed. To them I say, 'Watch us grow, and grow with us.'" The room, filled with men who had sold policies for and bought policies from a company that did not yet exist, echoed with applause.

The policyholders elected seven members to the first board of directors of Farmers Mutual Automobile Insurance Company: Aberg, Kalbskopf, Rammer, Spriggs, Wittwer, Albert Schiferl of Hewitt, and R. A. Baxter of Brodhead.

After lunch, Herman Ekern addressed the gathering. Ekern was well known in Wisconsin as a Progressive and staunch supporter of farmers during Robert La Follette's years as governor, and they were eager to hear what he had to say. Ekern complimented the men for their initiative and commitment to farmers, but cautioned them to set adequate rates for their coverage. "An

insolvent insurance company," said the man known for prudence, "is of no service to anyone."

The audience greeted Ekern's words with the thunderous applause Wittwer and Kalbskopf had hoped for, christening what would become a close, and occasionally tumultuous, relationship between Farmers Mutual and State Farm.

Watch Us Grow and Grow with Us

"Watch us grow and grow with us" served as Farmers Mutual's motto during those early years. Although the economy remained flat through 1927, and many speculated that the Big Bull Market was over, the company charged ahead. Just 39 applications arrived the first month but by year's end, largely due to Kalbskopf's recruiting efforts, Farmers Mutual had 14 district agents, 236 local agents, and 486 policyholders paying $8,130 in premiums.

The first claim arrived on October 13. A policyholder had crashed his 1926 Nash into an Overland Whippet, badly damaging the Whippet's fender and bumper. Total cost: $14. By the end of the year, Farmers Mutual incurred a mere $45.85 in losses, proving that farmers were preferred risks.

Other Wisconsin insurers noted the early success of Farmers Mutual. By the time the company held its annual policyholders' meeting on January 17, 1928, several competitors had issued "special farm rates."

While Wittwer and Kalbskopf felt vindicated by the advent of these special farm rates, Farmers Mutual was not yet a moneymaker. At this point, Kalbskopf, Wittwer, and Pett proved that their management company, Farmers Mutual Managers, did not exist to milk the insurance company of its profits—as some similar firms had done. At the close of 1927, after paying

Ten days after receiving its charter, Farmers Mutual incurred its first claim. The company paid fourteen dollars to repair an Overland Whippet's fender and bumper. Above left: An early promotion for Farmers Mutual Insurance.

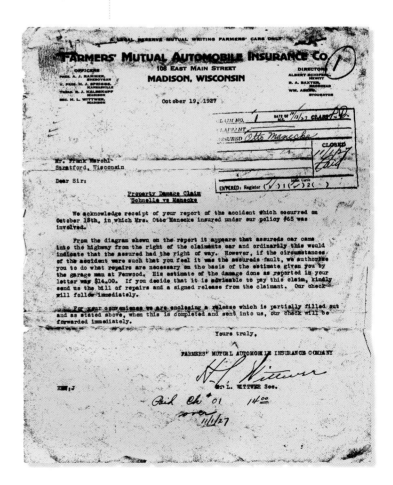

commissions, the insurance company owed the managers $450. To help Farmers Mutual build its reserves, the managers waived the entire amount. The managers followed this precedent time and again, waiving tens of thousands of dollars by the early 1930s; the figure approached $200,000 annually after World War II.

The year 1928 was a roller-coaster ride for the country and the company. As the stock market rallied in March only to fall again in June, Farmer's Mutual grew tenfold. By the end of 1928, a sales force of almost 700 agents had sold more than 4,500 policies and collected $81,000 in premiums. But the management company, again turning back thousands of dollars to Farmers Mutual, lost money.

When Harold Frank joined the company on May 8—replacing the first accountant James Nugent—Farmers Mutual employees numbered four, excluding Wittwer and Kalbskopf. The staff doubled within a year. Alex Opgenorth and Harold Koerner handled claims, Harold Frank and his wife Maybelle took care of accounting and office management, Hazel Jacobson was the receptionist, and Clarice Doane Every, Eldora Campbell, and Gertrude Coffey Koltes— the clerical staff—did everything else.

In the fall of 1928, Herbert Hoover, promising continued prosperity, defeated Alfred Smith in a landslide, and rode down Pennsylvania Avenue in the rain to take the oath of office. No one then could have recognized the rain as an omen. At the January 1929 policyholders' meeting, the bullish but conservative members of Farmers Mutual debated lowering premiums as opposed to building a surplus that eventually would enable the company to pay dividends. Remembering Ekern's warning at the first policyholder's meeting, caution ruled as they chose to build the tiny company's surplus.

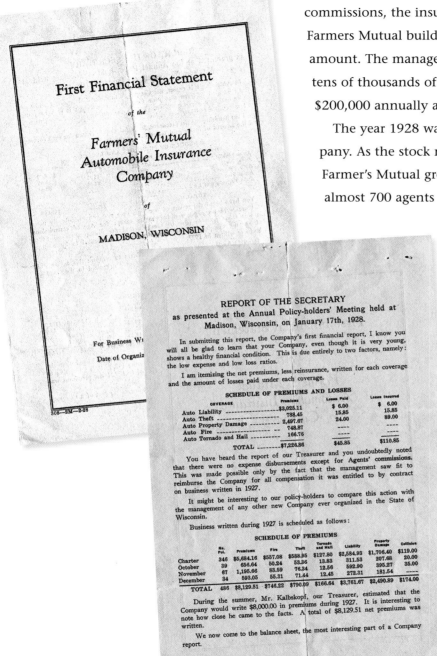

First financial statement of Farmers Mutual Automobile Insurance Company, October 3, 1927, to December 31, 1927.

Chapter Two

*We are the first nation in the history of the world
to go to the poor house in an automobile.*

—WILL ROGERS

TURBULENT TIMES
AT HOME AND ABROAD

Herman Wittwer walked out of the Tenney
Building on a mild autumn afternoon,
gave a newsboy three cents and carried the *Capital Times*
to a park bench on the square. It was October 3, 1929.
Farmers Mutual turned two years old that day, and Wittwer
basked in his sense of accomplishment. As he unfolded the
newspaper, Joseph Boyd, a well-known Madison businessman who'd opened the state's first brokerage firm,
approached. Wittwer rose to greet him, but Boyd merely
nodded. Wittwer wrote it off as a hard day at Boyd's investment firm. He didn't understand how hard until he got to
the financial pages. The stock market had taken a beating.

*Completed in 1929, the new Tenney Building was one
of the most prestigious office addresses of the 1930s.*

THREE SECTIONS IN THIS EDITION

The Wisconsin State Journal

A Fact-Finding AMERICAN Newspaper

HOME FINAL

PRICE THREE CENTS

MADISON, TUESDAY, OCTOBER 29, 1929

TWENTY-FOUR PAGES

More Billions Slashed From Stock Values

Stock Crash Aids Real Business, Assert Heads of Madison Firms

Bankers End Slump Just Before Close

Drowned, 6 Saved in Shipwreck

T. E. Burton, Ohio G.O.P. Leader, Dies

Dr. J. R. Straton, Noted Fundamentalist, Dies

Plane Lost in Mountain Snow Storm

Schmedeman Vetoes Mack Truck Purchase

Move to Rid Lake Mendota of Sewage

Grundy Hits Tariff Role of Midwest

Now Is Time to Get That Doll, Children

Union Needs Only $323 in Campaign

Peterson Guilty of Killing Sister

Mistrial Ends Case Against Ex-Governor

Poor Pa

Weather

Woman Lies in Car Wreck 2 Hours; Dies

West Point Head Talks Navy Cadic With Good

Budget Body Hears All Requests Tonight

Daladier Gives Up Cabinet Attempt

Aunt Het

Cautious stewards of its policyholders' money, Farmers Mutual didn't lose a dime in the crash of 1929. The company had all its money in double-and triple-A bonds, utility and municipal bonds, investment certificates, and savings accounts.

Final quotations weren't available for the afternoon edition because the ticker tape couldn't keep pace.

Wittwer and Kalbskopf were extremely careful with Farmers Mutual's money—too careful for Kalbskopf's tastes. Everything was in high-grade bonds, investment certificates, or the bank. But at Kalbskopf's urging, the management company invested some of its money in the market. Despite the sudden downturn, Kalbskopf remained bullish. After calling the company's Chicago brokerage firm the following morning, he told Wittwer, "Hold pat. Prices will bounce back."

The bounce never came. When Wittwer unfolded the *Wisconsin State Journal* on Tuesday, October 29, the banner headline read, "More Billions Slashed from Stock Values." To give traders a chance to catch up, the market closed Thursday noon and didn't reopen until the following Monday.

Several Madison business leaders, toeing President Hoover's optimistic line, asserted that the drop in stock prices was good for the economy. In a statement that appealed to Wittwer, Leo Crowley, president of the Bank of Wisconsin, blamed the crash on "folks who were playing [the market] for speculation and not for investment." The crash would purge speculators from the market, Crowley said, and redirect investments to other areas.

Few Midwesterners took the crash seriously. The hottest topic of conversation at Madison hotels booked for Wisconsin's homecoming game against undefeated Purdue focused on federal agents coming in to enforce Prohibition during homecoming weekend. The Baron's store manager best expressed the local view of Wall Street's turmoil: "For a community like Madison to take seriously the crash of the stock market seems very foolish."

Wittwer and Kalbskopf were too preoccupied to worry about the crash. Premiums increased 122 percent to just over $180,000 in 1929, and the company's surplus jumped from $6,000 at the end of 1928 to more than $23,000.

Farmers Mutual had also moved into the eighth floor of the new Tenney Building built on the same site as its namesake. The lavish, ten-story, steel and glass structure quickly became the most prestigious office address of its day. The art deco design featured a marble lobby and corridors and a bank of elevators, each with its own attendant. Hall, Baker, and Hall, Farmers Mutual's neighbors from the old building, moved into the new office tower. So did the barber and the shoe-shine man. One of the new tenants was R. G. Dun & Company, which later merged with Bradstreet.

After settling into the new office, Wittwer reorganized the fifteen employees into nine departments—accounting, underwriting, policy writing, statistical, mailing, supplies and purchases, agency, stenographic, and claims. He also appointed three department heads: Harold Frank as director of accounting, Alex Opgenorth director of claims, and a brash young man named Irving Maurer director of underwriting.

Underwriters at that time not only classified and selected risks but set the corresponding premiums. For two years, Farmers Mutual had survived without this essential position by insuring one class—farmers. It set premiums by simply shaving 25 percent off those posted by the rating bureaus most companies used. But in the fall of 1929, Farmers Mutual Managers decided to sell insurance to nonfarmers and needed an underwriter. Harold Frank knew Maurer from his days at Hardware Mutual Insurance Company (later Sentry Insurance) in Stevens Point, Wisconsin, and recommended him.

Maurer, the son of German immigrants, was born in Marshfield in 1905 and raised in Stevens Point. With dreams of becoming a lawyer, he enrolled at Stevens Point Normal School and took a night job with the railroad. But in 1925, Carl Jacobs, a family friend and head of Hardware Mutual, offered Maurer an assistant underwriting job. At that time, assistant underwriters typically were women, and the job paid only $75 a month, less than Maurer made as a night clerk with the

State Historical Society of Wisconsin

Unemployed people in Wisconsin's Winnebago County line up at a relief station for a ration of rough fish.

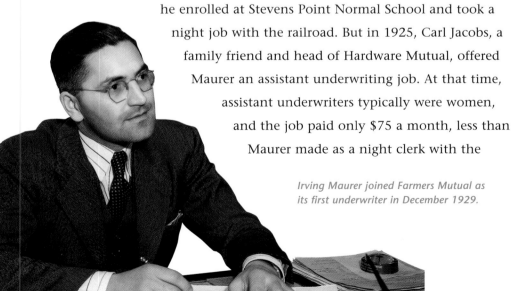

Irving Maurer joined Farmers Mutual as its first underwriter in December 1929.

railroad. But Jacobs sold Maurer on the prospect of learning the insurance business from the ground up, and the young man left school. Maurer advanced steadily at Hardware Mutual, learning both underwriting and sales. But he was still interested in earning a law degree, and when he heard about the position at Farmers Mutual, he jumped at the chance—not because he was interested in the fledgling company but because he might be able to enroll at the University of Wisconsin. He joined Farmers Mutual in late 1929. The job demanded long hours, and Maurer again put his schooling on hold.

Maurer's workload reflected the company's success. Optimism dominated the 1930 annual meeting where there was no talk of the depression, save for a couple of jokes from Harvey Spriggs and Kalbskopf. "This broker friend of Dick's checked into a Chicago hotel and the clerk asked if he wanted a room for sleeping or jumping," Spriggs deadpanned.

Kalbskopf, his face red with laughter, added, "I knew a fellow and his wife who jumped together because they had a joint account."

Other than patting themselves on the back, the only significant business was to elect Bernard Gehrmann, a farmer and state assemblyman from Mellen, to the board. A leader in the state's co-op movement, Gehrmann was well known to the mutual members who elected him unanimously. A large man given to long speeches about the plight of farmers and, in true Progressive form, the need for cooperative action, Gehrmann was a Republican legislator from 1927 to 1933. Elected to Congress as a Progressive in 1934, he represented the 10th District for ten years.

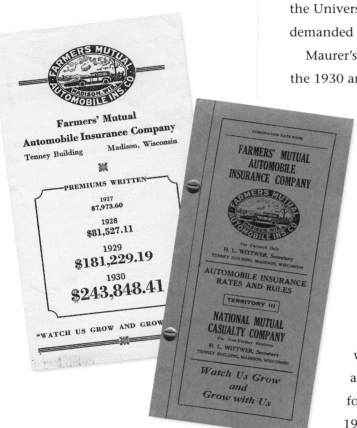

Farmers Mutual continued to grow even as the country entered the Great Depression.

No Bounce to the Recovery

When the market crashed in the fall of 1929, more than $30 billion evaporated from the nation's economy. To aid the expected recovery, the Federal Reserve loosened credit arrangements for business. Fixed investment trusts, which promised to buy only the best stocks and hold them "until hell freezes over," lured Americans back into the market. In the spring of 1930, the "Little Bull Market" set in, and "Happy Days are Here Again" was the most popular song on the radio.

Insurance companies, confident in the stock market, grew fat during the 1920s by underpricing policies and offsetting losses with investment income. But as the depression deepened, spreading across the country, many of those companies collapsed. In 1931 alone, fifty-six insurance organizations, including three in Wisconsin, closed their doors. Farmers Mutual, on the other hand, had been a cautious steward of its policyholders' money. At the time of the crash, it held $88,000 in double- and triple-A bonds issued by utility companies and municipal governments, $6,000 in investment certificates, and $18,000 in savings accounts. Others scoffed at Farmers Mutual's conservative investment approach—only to find themselves playing catchup.

The economic collapse took its toll on bonds as well as stocks. But Wittwer's inclination, and the company's policy, was to buy high-quality bonds and hold them to maturity. By 1932, only one bond in the company's portfolio had defaulted. Nevertheless, the sharp drop in bond values threatened Farmers Mutual's "A" rating. To avoid this downgrading, the company established in 1930 a $2,500 voluntary contingency fund to offset the lower market value of its bonds. A year later, the board increased that reserve to $40,000.

Some policyholders were critical of the action. Higher reserves meant the company showed only a small profit, delaying dividends for at least another year. But after a long discussion, members demonstrated their interest in the long-term health of the company by approving the action.

The home office also sacrificed. In 1930, Wittwer and Kalbskopf each took a 12.5 percent pay cut, bringing their monthly salaries down to $350. Three years later—in the midst of the Great Depression when jobs were scarce, competition fierce, and employees in many professions were afraid to take time off—Farmers Mutual staff accepted a 10 percent pay cut, and few took vacations, fearing to even raise the issue.

Farm Crisis and a Mutual Dilemma

The Hoover administration fought "deflation" with a sizable tax cut and a $400 million public works program. The federal government also bought surplus commodities in a vain attempt to stop the downward spiral of the farm economy, which dropped from $12 billion in 1929 to just over $5 billion in three years. But commodity prices continued to slide. For Wisconsin's dairy farmers, dairy fat used in cheese and other products fell from thirty cents per

A Man and His Cheese

The nephew of a man who owned a cheese factory, Herman Wittwer became a connoisseur of cheese. Unfortunately for those around him, Wittwer's cheese of choice was the malodorous Limburger. A favorite casual lunch for the Farmers Mutual executive was a Limburger cheese sandwich and bottle of Special Export, followed by an Upmann or Perfecto Garcia queen cigar. The combination prompted him to stash a supply of Wrigley's Spearmint Gum in his desk.

Wittwer's wife, Barbara, was not a Limburger enthusiast. One day, Herman came home for lunch to find her fumigating the house with air freshener. Unable to find the Limburger, he asked where it was. "Buried," she ranted. "Like all dead things should be!"

Driving Up Premiums

During the 1930s, the Wisconsin legislature passed numerous laws affecting drivers and insurance companies. While many of these laws offered greater protection for the man or woman behind the wheel, they also contributed to the rise in insurance premiums.

A 1931 bill enabled passengers in an accident to recover damages. By 1932, "guest" claims accounted for nearly one-third of all liability claims against Farmers Mutual. A 1933 law allowed victims to recover damages even if the person at fault was killed in the accident, extending liability beyond the death of the wrongdoer.

Perhaps the most significant 1930s-era law allowed plaintiffs to name insurance companies as defendants in personal injury and property damage cases, leading to a rash of law suits. "Not only is the average verdict higher as a result of this law, but the cost of each claim is materially enhanced because of an insurance company's inability to get a fair deal at the hands of a jury," Wittwer complained in 1936. The result was more out-of-court settlements "regardless of the merits of the case."

hundredweight to nineteen. The Farmers Holiday Association responded with milk strikes across the country, including Wisconsin. Farm foreclosures were epidemic, and clashes among farmers, bankers, and auctioneers became a regular occurrence.

Against this backdrop, Farmers Mutual faced one of its most difficult challenges. Across the industry, claims payments soared as the number of accidents rose and state legislatures mandated broader coverage. At Farmers Mutual, claims losses nearly doubled to $74,000 between 1930 and 1931.

To prevent a tide of red ink, insurance companies raised auto premiums in Wisconsin 30 to 50 percent. Farmers Mutual hadn't raised its annual seventeen-dollar premium since it began. Given the plight of farmers, it would not do so now. Instead, the company, led by underwriting director Irving Maurer, hammered out a new plan of operation that broke radically with the more conventional insurance companies.

To compensate for his lack of formal education, Maurer had become a dedicated student of insurance, devouring industry journals until he understood and could apply the most arcane concepts. After studying the situation with Wittwer and William Aberg, Maurer reasoned that Farmers Mutual could not continue to follow the orthodox methods of the insurance industry and expect to avoid rate increases. They would have to reduce costs.

First, instead of issuing complete renewal policies every year, which the policy writing department typed up at the rate of eight per hour, Farmers Mutual would issue a renewal certificate, produced at the rate of 1,000 per hour by a new business machine on which the company rented time. Second, instead of using an agent to deliver renewal certificates and collect premiums at a cost of about three dollars per policy, renewals would be handled through the mail at the cost of a first-class stamp—three cents.

But the most significant departure from orthodoxy was shifting to a semi-annual plan similar to that used by State Farm. Under this approach, members paid two six-month premiums rather than one annual premium. The approach would make it easier for cash-strapped farmers to pay the premium. The first six-month premium would be slightly higher, the additional revenue paying some of the cost of generating new business—primarily the agent's commission. The result: a lower renewal rate, helping retain members.

Getting state approval of the plan was sure to be difficult. Farmers Mutual proposed a similar plan in 1927 and again in 1931. But insurance commissioner M. A. Freedy rejected it, arguing the unlevel premiums violated the state's antidiscrimination law by applying different rates to the same class of business. He repeatedly rejected State Farm's application for related reasons.

Wisconsin's new insurance commissioner, Harry Mortensen, also rejected Farmers Mutual's semi-annual plan. But this time, Farmers Mutual's future depended on getting the plan approved. Wittwer, Maurer, and Aberg set up a series of meetings with Mortensen. After a week of intense discussions and compromises, he approved the plan.

The battle, however, didn't end there. In early April, Maurer packed his car for a week-long trip to sell the overall plan to the company's eight hundred agents. At that time, Farmers Mutual, like most companies, operated on the American Agency System, under which agents owned the policies and renewals. The agents, who usually sold for many different companies, often shifted policyholders from one insurance company to another, depending on which had the lower rate or was paying the higher commission. With the home office handling renewals by mail, agents would lose control over where to place those policies.

In one town after another, the agents gave Maurer a cool reception. Maurer's manner—formal, somewhat pedantic—didn't help. The meetings became long, ponderous discussions of the principles, history, and future of insurance. Maurer, however, was convincing when he talked about the commitment Farmers Mutual and the agents shared in supporting the farmer through a mutual company. Slowly, the agents began to understand that the company's future was at stake and that they were being asked to sacrifice their control over renewals for the good of the members. At the end of each meeting, Maurer took a vote. All but one man supported the change.

The new plan went into effect in April 1932. Farmers Mutual dropped its slogan "Watch us grow and grow with us" in favor of "The company with the low renewal rates."

When the economy crashed, so did the auto market. New car sales declined 75 percent between 1929 and 1932.

To help the fledgling company weather the Great Depression, Farmers Mutual employees accepted a 10 percent pay cut in the summer of 1933. The company restored a portion of that cut in December with its first holiday bonus—fifty dollars for married men, twenty-five dollars for all others.

The semi-annual plan not only solidified the company's position in the farm market but also benefited farmers who bought from competitors. Stock and mutual companies alike rolled back their rate increases to compete with Farmers Mutual.

The new plan wreaked havoc in the home office as staff scrambled to adopt new processes and procedures for this unusual approach. While many companies were cutting Saturday morning from the traditional five-and-a-half-day work week, Farmers Mutual staff worked overtime. The sacrifice paid off. Operating expenses dropped to $57,000 in 1932, an $8,000 reduction. And membership doubled over the next three years.

Going to Town

In 1930, Farmers Mutual entered the town market by way of the cattle pasture. Larger insurance companies had moved into the farm market with their own "special farm rates." Farmers Mutual Managers realized that as a matter of survival it needed to expand beyond the farm market. The company's bylaws, however, stipulated that it sell auto insurance to farmers only. Changing those bylaws required a three-fourth's majority vote, which would be difficult to obtain.

August Rammer, who replaced Aberg on the management company board, had the solution. Rammer was on the board of the Sheboygan County Cattle Owners Mutual Insurance Company, organized in 1928 to protect nearly a thousand farmers from cattle losses due to tuberculosis.

By early 1930, the Sheboygan company, which was forced to levy a 100-percent assessment in 1928 and 1929, was ready to close its operation—opening the door for Farmers Mutual Managers to buy its charter. On January 11, 1930—after forming a new management company, National Mutual Managers, Inc.—Wittwer, Kalbskopf, and Rammer met with the Cattle Owners' board, many of whom were members of Farmers Mutual. In exchange for $300 to settle outstanding claims, the Cattle Owners' board agreed to change the name of the company to the National Mutual Casualty

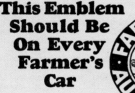

Farmers Mutual Automobile Insurance Company's charter limited membership to farmers. The metal emblem at the right was designed to attach to the insured's car radiator.

Company and amend its bylaws to authorize the sale of automobile and other kinds of insurance.

A month later, members of the Sheboygan County Cattle Owners' Mutual Insurance Company supported the change, then elected a new board, including Wittwer, Kalbskopf, Rammer, Bill Aberg, and Joseph Radtke of Marshfield.

But Farmers Mutual didn't find Wisconsin's small towns and cities as fertile as the farm market. One problem was that the company adopted premiums based on national-rating-bureau schedules, meaning it had little to distinguish itself from other insurance companies. More important was the lack of a field force. Farmers Mutual had a ready-made agency force for the farm market—the town mutual secretaries, who sold fire and windstorm insurance to farmers. National Mutual had no equivalent entrée into the nonfarm market.

As a result, National Mutual didn't generate enough charter policyholders to receive its license until July 30, 1930. Sales continued to lag, and over the next three years Wittwer, Kalbskopf, and Rammer contributed nearly $30,000 to National Mutual to keep the company solvent.

District agent Joseph Radtke (left) and Richard Kalbskopf talk in Kalbskopf's office.

To survive, National Mutual would have to merge with the financially robust Farmers Mutual. But such a merger would be politically difficult. The cultural gap between townspeople and farmers widened as regional and national economies undermined local self-sufficiency. Farmers Mutual exploited that gap by restricting membership to those who lived and worked on farms, arguing that the careful farmer should not be pooled with people who lived in towns or cities.

The situation was complicated by rumors—spread mainly by competitors—that Farmers Mutual was a farm company in name only. The rumors dumbfounded Wittwer, who was strongly committed to the mutual and co-op movements. Farmers Mutual lived up to Wittwer's commitment, developing working relationships with some of the state's largest farm organizations, including the Wisconsin State Grange. The Wisconsin Association

TWith the death toll on American roadways surpassing 36,000 by the mid-1930s, Farmers Mutual and other insurers exhorted the public to show some restraint behind the wheel. "Sometimes one wonders if it wouldn't be a good idea to quit improving roads and cars for awhile and concentrate on bringing out some new, late 1936 model drivers, with eight-cylinder brains and streamlined common sense," Irving Maurer said in one of Farmers Mutual's morning radio spots on WIBA Madison.

of Farm Mutual Companies even adopted Farmers Mutual as its official automobile insurance company. Still the rumors persisted, and merging the two companies might confirm them.

Wittwer, however, was willing to stake the company's reputation on a merger, which he knew to be the only solution. He listened to the arguments of those who disagreed, but Wittwer had a stubborn streak. Once convinced, he rarely was swayed.

In a May 1933 notice to Farmers Mutual agents, Wittwer announced the merger, placing it in the context of the classic farm co-op battle against "outside interests."

"Did you ever see it fail?" he wrote. "A farm cooperative organization does what it sets out to do, and the minute a certain degree of success is attained, outside interests step in, cut prices, and go to extremes to break up the membership. Your officers and directors unanimously decided to turn the trick and invade the membership of outside organizations for the benefit of the entire company and its members."

Farmers, frustrated by low commodity prices and the evolution of large corporations moving in as "the middle man" in the farm market, rallied behind Wittwer's David-and-Goliath appeal. When the merger was discussed at the 1934 annual policyholders' meeting, there was not one word of dissent.

Breaking New Ground

As Farmers Mutual employees sorted through the Monday mail early in March 1935, Harold Frank placed the premium checks in a small stack. He wasn't sure what he'd do with them. By order of the new president, Franklin D. Roosevelt, the banks were closed. They wouldn't reopen for several days—possibly longer. In Madison and many other communities, local merchants wouldn't accept checks until the banking crisis was over.

Wittwer had been on the phone with Leo Crowley, at the Bank of Wisconsin, who assured him that the bank would reopen later that week—in plenty of time to meet the March 15 payroll. Wittwer wasn't a man given to panic. If the bank didn't reopen, he knew there was enough cash in the Farmers Mutual safe to tide the company over. "There's nothing to fear but fear itself," Wittwer reassured the staff, echoing Roosevelt's inauguration speech given two days earlier.

Herman L. Wittwer
A Man of Means in Troubled Times

At the onset of the Great Depression, Herman Wittwer made $400 a month with Farmers Mutual Managers and $100 a month with National Mutual Managers—plus commissions and overwriting from his personal insurance sales through the Wittwer and Kalbskopf agency. He wasn't rich, but considering that three-fourths of American families were living on less than $3,000 a year, he was more than comfortable. Wittwer was, in fact, in a growing class of businessmen and entrepreneurs carving out successful careers in the nation's industrial and service economy.

An adroit businessman, Wittwer was well regarded within insurance circles. He served as secretary of the Association of Wisconsin Mutual Insurance Companies and the Wisconsin Mutual Insurance Alliance as well as chairman of the Casualty Section of the National Association of Mutual Insurance Companies. His warm, friendly nature, his quiet confidence, and his honesty and dependability made him many friends and few enemies. He was as comfortable playing bridge at the Madison Club as he was talking Badger football with Ray Sather, the company's longtime janitor.

The Wittwers weren't ostentatious; they held in disregard the newly affluent Madisonians who flaunted their wealth. Barbara, who knew many of these families, had little tolerance for those who forgot or ignored where they had come from. One evening, Barbara interrupted a woman talking endlessly of her lavish redecorating with a

Founder/Secretary 1927-1959
Board Chairman 1959-1968

H. L. Wittwer

simple question: "So, have your parents got a new roof on the outhouse?"

Despite the demands of business, Wittwer remained active with the Madison Civic Orchestra, serving as its president from 1937 to 1940 and as a playing member through 1946. He developed a close friendship with conductor Sigfrid Prager. At dinner parties, with Prager at the piano and Wittwer on clarinet, the two men entertained guests with popular and classical numbers. Wittwer did a passable imitation of Benny Goodman's swing style as well as Paul Whiteman's distinctive arrangement of "Rhapsody in Blue."

Herman and Barbara also hosted large family gatherings at their home. After dinner, the women cleared the dishes, and the men sat around the table to talk sports, politics, and religion. A generous host, Wittwer passed out cigars and filled glasses with Chivas Regal. An articulate conversationalist, he read *Fortune* magazine, the *Wall Street Journal*, and many insurance industry publications. But his personal library was filled with books on history, philosophy, music, and public affairs.

An ardent Republican, Wittwer gave grudging support to President Franklin Roosevelt in his bold steps to combat the depression. But as the economic malaise wore on and Roosevelt claimed increasing executive power, the tepid support of many businessmen such as Wittwer evaporated. He believed that the essential aspects of the New Deal should be handled through the states, charity through the churches, and employment through private enterprise.

The Wittwers themselves were generous, supporting several charities as well as taking care of family members. Wittwer was nevertheless uncomfortable with the awkwardness created by charity among family and friends, so Barbara handled most of it, sometimes creating more awkwardness. Once she gave one of Herman's suits to one of her brothers, down on his luck. When she and Herman met her brother on Capitol Square, Barbara worried about Herman's reaction to seeing his suit on someone else. "That was a nice suit your brother had on," Herman commented.

In 1935, Farmers Mutual Managers named its new windstorm company State Farm Mutual Insurance Company. The managers hoped the similarity of names would prevent its role model, Illinois-based State Farm Mutual, from entering Wisconsin.

While the nation struggled under the weight of the Great Depression, Farmers Mutual's premiums increased 50 percent in 1933 to more than $300,000. A fraction of that growth came from another state—Minnesota—where a new law required trucks to file insurance policies with the Minnesota Warehouse Commission. Because St. Paul was a common destination for farm trucks in northwestern Wisconsin, Farmers Mutual received a Minnesota license.

"Inasmuch as we are in there," Wittwer told the policyholders, "we might as well try to get some business."

Kalbskopf recruited Dan Gaumnitz, a former State Farm agent, to be the company's first "state agent." Kalbskopf and Gaumnitz worked together to develop business in Minnesota. Though premiums totaled just $23,000 in 1935, they jumped to $100,000 two years later and continued to grow, eventually making Minnesota one of the company's leading producers.

In 1935, Farmers Mutual branched out from automobile coverage to offer windstorm insurance to farmers in Wisconsin. Because insurance law prohibited companies from writing unrelated lines of insurance, Farmers Mutual Managers established State Farm Mutual Insurance Company of Madison, Wisconsin—with Erv Albrecht president, Wittwer secretary, and Kalbskopf treasurer—to write windstorm coverage. Using the traditional town mutual approach, the company collected an initial two-dollar policy fee to cover the agent's commission then levied an assessment in October to cover losses during the spring and summer storm season. The name State Farm Mutual erected yet another barrier keeping Illinois-based State Farm Mutual Automobile Insurance Company out of Wisconsin. The new company quickly became the fastest-growing windstorm company in the state. Adding burglary and theft coverage in 1937, State Farm's insurance in force rose to $48 million in 1938.

Farmers Mutual bought the Joseph Boyd mansion at 312 Wisconsin Avenue in 1935.

Moving Out

Throughout the depression, while other companies were laying off employees or closing their doors, Farmers Mutual added staff. By the mid-1930s, the company's nearly thirty employees filled half the eighth floor of the Tenney Building. With no room to expand, Farmers Mutual in March 1935 bought the Joseph Boyd mansion at 312 Wisconsin Avenue. (Now the site of the Bethel Lutheran Church.)

From the turn of the century, Boyd had been a widely respected man about Madison, becoming chairman of the Bank of Wisconsin and founder of the state's first authorized securities brokerage. But the stock market crash hit Boyd hard, and in 1931 the company went into receivership. Auditors uncovered improprieties in Boyd's operation, and in 1934, at age seventy-two, he was convicted on four counts of embezzlement and sentenced to the Wisconsin State Prison at Waupun for ten to twenty-five years.

Farmers Mutual bought Boyd's three-story colonial-style house and a rooming house next door for $27,500, just over half the estimated $50,000 value.

Farmers Mutual's thirty employees gather at the entrance of their new home office in 1935.

Above: Clarice Every (front desk) and Alex Opgenorth (seated in back office) handle claims for Farmers Mutual. Above right: The stenography department churns through hundreds of dictations every week.

Landscaping and renovations brought the total cost to $65,000.

"This will give Farmers Mutual a permanent home," Wittwer wrote Congressman Gehrmann. "After remodeling the house, we will have nearly double the office space we now have, and the cost of operating it will not be increased over present rentals."

The company's growth accelerated in 1935 after Wisconsin enacted its "Judgment Law." Since 1921, lawmakers had regularly introduced bills to require drivers to carry insurance. Insurance companies fought the legislation, fearing they would be required to accept all applicants. The "Judgment Law" was a compromise, which prohibited people found liable in an accident from driving until all claims against them were paid. To capitalize on the anticipated rush of new business, Farmers Mutual aimed its first direct-mailing campaign at drivers in small towns. The response was overwhelming, and premium income grew by 64 percent.

Farmers Mutual was unprepared for this rapid growth spurt. In the insurance industry, a large surge in new business drains a company's surplus. Although premiums are earned gradually over the course of a policy's term, the expense associated with new business—primarily agent commissions and issuance expense—must be paid immediately. Rapid growth left Farmers Mutual cash poor in 1936. To relieve the situation, the management company moved its $40,000 contingency fund to Farmers Mutual.

Meanwhile, underwriters with too little time to properly evaluate all the new applications let unqualified drivers slip in. The result was a 6 percent underwriting loss—the company's first. To correct the situation, Farmers Mutual tightened underwriting rules, discontinued unprofitable lines, and—for the first time in its nine-year history—raised its farm rates.

The "Roosevelt Recession" intensified the problem. Early in 1937, the Federal Reserve, troubled by the rising national debt, tightened credit, and Roosevelt slashed government spending. The economy collapsed, and the stock market plummeted 38 percent between August and October (compared to 45 percent in the crash of 1929). Farmers Mutual—without the cushion of its contingency fund—took a $53,000 loss on its investments.

As a result, A. M. Best Company was prepared to lower Farmers Mutual's financial rating from "A" to "B." To prevent this, the management company—Wittwer, Kalbskopf, and Rammer—again stepped in, contributing $50,000 to the mutual company's surplus.

Premiums surpassed $1 million in 1938. The following year, Maurer, recently promoted to agency director, spent much of his time on the road recruiting district agents in the company's third state—Missouri.

In 1940, Farmers Mutual issued its first nonassessable policies. Not only was this a tribute to the company's financial strength, but it was a boon to sales. Traditionally, many mutual companies charged a policy fee or token premium up front, then at the end of the year, charged members an assessment to cover losses. Although Farmers Mutual never issued an assessment on its auto policies, many prospects remained wary of the assessable coverage. Competitors exploited that fear, painting a bleak picture of Farmers Mutual and raising the specter of large year-end assessments.

In 1940, Farmers Mutual began issuing nonassessable auto insurance. The company proudly announced this landmark of financial strength by sending this card to policyholders.

And Now . . .
A NON-ASSESSABLE POLICY

As a climax to the greatest year in Farmers' Mutual history, policies now are given the added safety of a non-assessable clause---at the same low premiums.

When the premium to extend your policy is received, you will be given a special endorsement making your policy non-assessable.

FARMERS' MUTUAL AUTOMOBILE INSURANCE CO.

UNINTERRUPTED PROGRESS

	Assets	Legal Reserves	Surplus and Vol. Reserves
December 31, 1927	$ 6,959.47	$ 4,719.73	$ 2,239.74
December 31, 1928	47,722.69	41,582.14	6,140.55
December 31, 1929	121,499.53	97,871.44	23,628.09
December 31, 1930	228,161.78	177,955.13	50,206.65
December 31, 1931	285,556.78	193,410.90	92,145.88
December 31, 1932	280,238.33	164,179.77	116,058.56
December 31, 1933	305,592.15	174,712.99	130,879.16
December 31, 1934	389,923.59	234,915.58	155,008.01
December 31, 1935	501,018.19	341,908.32	159,109.87
December 31, 1936	739,385.90	520,118.80	219,267.10
December 31, 1937	835,019.48	601,827.95	233,191.53
December 31, 1938	1,093,698.69	733,401.45	360,297.24
December 31, 1939	1,308,563.98	834,505.63	474,058.35

FARMERS' MUTUAL AUTOMOBILE INSURANCE CO.
(Non-Assessable Protection for Farm and City Risks)
312 WISCONSIN AVENUE, MADISON, WISCONSIN   (OVER)

2422-50140

FARMERS' MUTUAL NEWS
Published by FARMERS' MUTUAL AUTOMOBILE INSURANCE CO.

Vol. 2 • 1938   Madison, Wisconsin   No. 1

One More Forward Step

PROMOTE SAFETY, BE "SAFETY-MINDED"
By H. J. Brennan, Vice-President

Extra! Extra!

Farmers Mutual prided itself on being a small, friendly insurance company providing personal service to its members. By 1937, the Farmers Mutual family had grown to 45,000 members. To keep them informed, the company produced *Farmers Mutual News*, becoming one of the first insurers to send promotional material with its renewal notices. First published in the summer of 1937, the newsletter featured a partial listing of members who filed claims and received payments during the first half of the year. In addition, the first issue carried an article placing the cause of most accidents squarely on the driver. A list of the causes for highway fatalities in 1936 showed 22 percent driving too fast, 16 percent on the wrong side of the road, 23 percent without the right of way, 10 percent off the road, 10 percent driving recklessly, 5 percent failing to signal properly, and 14 percent miscellaneous actions.

To mark the beginning of its nonassessable policies, Farmers Mutual adopted a new logo that boasted its nonassessable coverage.

Two words dominated the center of the new logo: Safe Driver. As more people took to the road and the number of accidents increased, Farmers Mutual, and other insurers, aggressively promoted safe, conscientious driving. Accident rates and claims payments continued to climb. Farmers Mutual responded in two ways. In 1941, the company refined its classification system, dividing city drivers into two classes—occupational and nonoccupational—raising rates for those who drove extensively for work. The following year, Farmers Mutual implemented its first field underwriting program, with district supervisors training agents to be more selective in their prospecting. The program offered increased commissions to supervisors with loss ratios below 45 percent and imposed penalties on those with loss ratios exceeding 55 percent.

War at Home and Abroad

While Roosevelt offered the New Deal as an answer to America's economic woes, across the Atlantic Adolf Hitler offered a different solution—expansion and conquest. By 1938, Hitler had rebuilt the German army from its defeat in World War I. Austria, Czechoslovakia, and Poland fell in rapid succession. In America, isolation versus intervention in the affairs of Europe dominated the 1940 elections. Bernard Gehrmann, an ardent

The Home Office Agency
Wittwer, Kalbskopf, & Webster, Inc.

When Herman Wittwer and Richard Kalbskopf founded Farmers Mutual Automobile Insurance Company, money was scarce and profits—if any—were to be shoveled back into the business. To help them through the lean years, the two insurance men formed the Wittwer & Kalbskopf Agency, through which each partner sold insurance for Farmers Mutual and a number of other insurance companies.

In 1933, they added Laudon Newell (Lod) Webster to the agency, forming Wittwer, Kalbskopf & Webster, Inc. Each man held fifty shares of common stock in the venture. Webster, one of Farmers Mutual's early agents, joined the company in 1928. He later accepted an offer from another company, working there several years before returning to Farmers Mutual in 1933. Webster was the "active manager" of Wittwer, Kalbskopf & Webster, which became known as the home office agency.

With exclusive rights to sell Farmers Mutual insurance in Madison, the agency grew steadily, and Webster became one of the company's leading producers.

When Kalbskopf left Farmers Mutual in 1944, Wittwer and Webster shared ownership of the agency. Lod's son, Chuck Webster—who as a boy shoveled Kalbskopf's sidewalk and as a young man worked briefly as an underwriter for Farmers Mutual—joined the agency in 1954. In 1963, he purchased Wittwer's stock in the corporation, forming Webster & Webster, Inc. Chuck Webster quickly became a leading salesman, and in 1967 he became the company's first million-dollar producer.

isolationist, missed Farmers Mutual's 1940 annual meeting to stay in Washington and fight Roosevelt's request for increased military funding to aid England. But after the Japanese bombed Pearl Harbor on December 7, 1941, Gehrmann was among 388 congressmen supporting the declaration of war. Nine men from the home office—Art Babler, P. K. Bruce, Charles Carman, Gordon Erdman, John Farnsworth, Newman Himley, Bob Kelliher, Les Ramiker, and Alfred Seidl—went on to serve in the U. S. military. Those left at home worked evenings and weekends through the end of the war. Even relatives came in to help.

To boost morale, Wittwer suggested the personnel committee publish a newsletter for the home office and field force. The first issue of *Coverall* appeared in July 1942. Carrying office and industry news, cartoons, and miscellaneous articles written by staff, *Coverall* ran for the duration of the war. The war affected the nation and the company in many other ways. Just as the automobile industry was picking up, the War Production Board commandeered its factories to produce planes, tanks, trucks, and jeeps. Except on a limited basis, factories didn't resume making private automobiles until 1945. Congress froze prices, wages, salaries, and rents throughout the country, and the Office of Price Administration rationed everything from canned goods to fuel oil.

On December 1, 1942, Americans began receiving gas rationing cards. In the Midwest, an "A" card entitled the holder to 16 gallons of gas each month, about 240 miles of driving. "B" cardholders received an additional 16 gallons, and "C" cardholders unlimited rations. Farmers Mutual revamped its classification of private cars to correspond with the rationing system. Its A-1 class included farmers and select "A" cardholders.

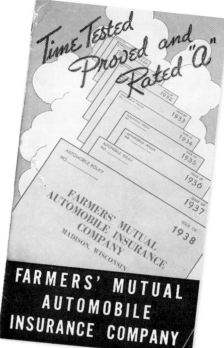

Farmers Mutual emerged from the Great Depression and entered the war years with a strong financial base.

State Historical Society of Wisconsin

IS YOUR TRIP NECESSARY?

NEEDLESS TRAVEL
interferes with the War Effort

Americans, encouraged by posters such as this, conserved gasoline for the war effort by reducing their dependence on automobiles.

With forty years of experimentation beneath its belt, the insurance industry modernized its rating system in 1939. Rather than focus on the cost or size of an automobile, it now rated cars based on how they would be used. Cars designated "A-1" had annual mileage under 7,500, were not used in business, and were driven by no more than two people, neither under age twenty-five. "A" was for all other individually owned automobiles not used in business, and "B" for all other automobiles. Three years later, the rating system was adapted to the national gas-rationing system.

City "A" included the remaining "A" and "B" cardholders. Class C, the highest premium, applied to all others.

Though inconvenient for Americans who'd grown dependent on their cars, gasoline rationing was a mixed blessing to Farmers Mutual and other auto insurance companies. The industry began adopting more liberal policies such as comprehensive coverage and personal bodily injury coverage, which, combined with ever-increasing accident rates, drove up claims payments. Gas rationing, along with a lower national speed limit (first 40 mph and later 35 mph) greatly reduced the number and severity of accidents. Farmers Mutual was among the first to cut premiums in the wake of gas rationing.

But rationing also discouraged agents, convincing many that people weren't interested in buying auto insurance. Farmers Mutual responded by mailing 43,000 letters to prospects offering a free ration book cover in exchange for information about their insurance coverage. The campaign provided agents with thousands of leads.

Rationing was more than a minor inconvenience for Jim Caskey, who joined Farmers Mutual in November 1939 as one of four field claims representatives. Shortly after the war started, Wittwer called Caskey to the home office to discuss Caskey's home state, Missouri.

Since the beginning of the war, Missouri agents had submitted almost one claim a day

State Historical Society of Wisconsin

Under federally imposed gas rationing, attendants at the Old Log Cabin Filling Station near Tomah, Wisconsin, handled more than money. Each coupon had to have the holder's name, license number, and home state written on the back.

Under gas rationing, claims director Alex Opgenorth saw the activity in his department slow down.

for cars destroyed by fire. Alex Opgenorth, Farmers Mutual claims director, discovered that some used-car dealers selling insurance for Farmers Mutual were making deals with draftees to get their cars paid off. "Don't worry about it, George," the agent would say with a wink. "You just go defend our country. But leave your car out on the road some night before you go, and we'll take care of it." That night, the car would mysteriously catch fire.

After talking with Opgenorth, Caskey met with Wittwer. "You're the only guy we know we can trust in Missouri," Wittwer told him. "Would you go down there and see what you can do to straighten the damn thing out?"

Wittwer convinced Caskey to transfer to Missouri as a state agent. The company provided a company car, moving expenses, and an expense account.

Caskey and his wife moved to Jefferson City, Missouri, that spring, and Caskey started cleaning house, firing all the used-car-dealer agents and many of the district agents, who should have dealt with the problem. "It was a hell of a lot of work for a long time," Caskey remembered.

Gas rationing made Caskey's job more difficult. Citizens' committees in each community determined which rationing card local residents received. Two committee members in Jefferson City were agents for competing insurance companies, and they decided Caskey should get an "A" card—four gallons a week. After talking with Wittwer and Kalbskopf, Caskey moved to Kansas City, where a Farmers Mutual agent served on the committee. There Caskey was able to get the gas he needed.

By the time the war ended, cars were in such high demand that Caskey was able to sell his 1941 Plymouth, driven more than 100,000 miles, for twice what the company paid. When Harold Frank, who handled the company's purchases, heard that, he bragged all over the company about his investment profit.

State Farm of Madison, vs. State Farm of Bloomington

The battle to keep State Farm Mutual Automobile Insurance Company of Illinois out of Wisconsin started before the birth of Farmers Mutual. State Farm, organized in 1922, applied for a Wisconsin license in 1925, 1926, 1927, and 1932, and was rejected by four different insurance commissioners because the company did not set up reserves against its "life membership fee," which the company charged all new policyholders to cover the cost of generating new business.

In 1931, State Farm attorney Herman Ekern, former Wisconsin insurance commissioner and attorney general, launched the Workman's Mutual Insurance Company of Milwaukee, using the State Farm plan. Commissioner Harry Mortensen, a former Progressive Party ally of Ekern's, ordered the company to cease operations. But Ekern ignored him. An alliance of Wisconsin mutuals took Workman's to court, forcing it to abandon the life membership fee.

Wittwer, Kalbskopf, and Maurer all looked to State Farm as a model, and developed personal as well as professional relationships with its executives. Nevertheless, Wittwer realized State Farm would be a formidable competitor of Farmers Mutual. So in 1935— with an eye to setting up another barrier to State Farm's entry into the state —Farmers Mutual dubbed its new

windstorm company State Farm Mutual Insurance Company of Madison, Wisconsin.

Late in June 1939, Mortensen, whose term as commissioner was about to expire, prepared to give the Illinois company a Wisconsin license. In a legal battle that played out on the front pages of the *Wisconsin State Journal* and the *Capital Times*, Farmers Mutual won an injunction preventing him from doing so. The circuit judge, however, vacated his own injunction, and Mortensen dropped the license in the mail before Bill Aberg, Farmers Mutual's attorney, could appeal.

The Wisconsin Mutual Insurance Alliance, representing 117 mutual insurance companies in the state, joined Farmers Mutual in its suit to force Mortensen to withdraw the license. The Wisconsin mutual companies dropped their case after the new insurance commissioner, Morvin Duel, a former insurance agent from Fond du Lac, refused to renew the Illinois company's license.

The battle continued, however, when State Farm filed suit, asking the courts to force Duel to renew the company's license. State Farm appealed the case to the State Supreme Court, which ruled against the Illinois company in 1940, 1942, 1943, and 1944.

Even during this period, relations between the two companies were

cordial. Often after arguing the case in court, Aberg, Erwin Meyers (State Farm's attorney), and Sterling Schallert (Meyers's nephew, a law student, and future Farmers Mutual employee) often went to lunch together.

The fight boiled over into the legislature in 1941, where bills allowing State Farm into Wisconsin failed. Republican leaders threatened to hold the legislature in session through the summer unless Commissioner Duel issued State Farm a license. Charges and counter charges spilled onto the front page of the daily papers. Even Julius Heil, governor of Wisconsin, was dragged into the controversy.

After ten years in court, State Farm changed its operation to comply with Wisconsin law. But not until 1950 did it receive a license. Injunctions during the court proceedings, however, allowed the Illinois company to operate in Wisconsin throughout the dispute.

The battle also seeped across state lines, creating hard feelings among Illinois legislators and bureaucrats. In 1945, Farmers Mutual inquired into obtaining an Illinois license. So much antagonism had built up between the states that Farmers Mutual didn't secure a license in Illinois until 1951.

War in the Office

As war raged in Europe and the Pacific, tempers flared and factions formed in Farmers Mutual's home office. Almost from the beginning, there was friction between Wittwer and Kalbskopf. While Wittwer ran the home office business, Kalbskopf was the promoter. More comfortable launching an idea than following through on the details, he spent much of his time on the road, meeting with the field force, promoting contests, and spreading good will—much of it in the form of scotch. Kalbskopf enjoyed nothing more than a good meal and a night at the bar with one of the company's field men, racking up hefty expenses that rankled Wittwer's frugal nature. For his part, Kalbskopf chaffed at Wittwer's conservative attitude and felt his contributions as a recruiter and financier were disregarded. The animosity eventually grew so strong that August Rammer spent most of his limited time in the office settling feuds.

Agency manager Irving Maurer was a third powerful personality in this volatile mix. Maurer, who had proven himself a master of the insurance business, expected much of himself and worked late most nights, leaving his wife, Kathryn, to care for their two young children. By nature introverted and insecure, Maurer compensated by being outwardly aggressive—some say intimidating—which enabled him to make difficult decisions but won him few friends among employees or agents.

The growing demands of managing Farmers Mutual frayed the relationship between founders Richard Kalbskopf (left) and Herman Wittwer.

Maurer's style rubbed Kalbskopf and Wittwer the wrong way as well. Maurer pushed for aggressive expansion, at times criticizing the Farmers Mutual leadership for being too cautious. At the 1940 policyholders' meeting, Wittwer took him gently to task, saying, "When discussing the company's growth, Mr. Maurer, our agency manager, made a rather pertinent comment. He said: 'When a company has entered the stabilization stage to such an extent that no new blood, no new ideas, no new markets, and no new ambitions are brought in, old age and death are around the corner.' I'm sure Mr. Maurer was making no reference to Farmers Mutual in his remarks." Wittwer then presented developments demonstrating the company's growth,

Madison's State Street in 1939. Reproduced courtesy of State Historical Society of Wisconsin.

including expansion into Minnesota and Missouri and application for licenses in North and South Dakota, Iowa, and Nebraska.

Aberg tried to put a happy face on the almost open hostility. "No group ever got together which could be unanimous in their opinions," he told policyholders. "We have differences on the board, and we contemplate having them in the future. It shows virility, and it shows that the company is not made up of a lot of stooges, but of men who think for themselves."

In 1940, at Aberg's suggestion, the company hired a management consultant

to iron out its problems. The consultant was an evangelist for a new generation of business machines that used punch cards to store information, and he spent most of his time with Bob Kelliher in accounting. While punch-card machines revolutionized the processing of applications and claims, they did little to ease the feuding among senior management.

The stress of the conflict eventually got to Maurer, who suffered a nervous breakdown and took a month's rest in Florida. When he returned, he found that he'd been replaced by his assistant, Ken Bruce, and demoted to underwriting director. Despite the demotion, Wittwer and Kalbskopf continued to lean heavily on Maurer, asking him to write bulletins, reports, and speeches. Yielding to his wife's advice, Maurer refused, insisting those tasks weren't in the job description of an underwriting manager.

Kalbskopf eventually took over as agency director, but the job was difficult and time-consuming, and the department floundered under his leadership. In 1944, he and Wittwer appointed state directors to head most of the nine states, placing them on commission and giving them authority to run their operations. They also wrote the company's first district manager agreements, formalizing their relationship with Farmers Mutual.

Maurer by this time was ready to leave the company unless he was given more authority, and he boldly approached Wittwer about purchasing stock in the management company. Wittwer listened, rolling an Upmann cigar between his fingers for a long time after Maurer presented his case. With more than $1 million in assets and annual premiums nearing $2 million, the company had already grown far beyond Wittwer's dreams. He needed an expert to help him manage the organization, and Maurer was far more qualified than Kalbskopf. Kalbskopf, of course, would never agree, but Rammer could be convinced. "I'll take it up with the board," Wittwer said.

Loudon "Lod" Webster and Peggy Kurnett keep busy at Wittwer, Kalbskopf, and Webster, Inc., the home office agency.

As Richard Kalbskopf left
Farmers Mutual, Allied armies
closed in on Berlin. Soon World
War II would be over, and
Farmers Mutual would find itself
in a challenging new world.

After hearing of Maurer's desire to buy common stock,
Kalbskopf and Rammer wondered whether other employees
should be given similar opportunities. In July, the board gave
Maurer a chance to make his pitch. Maurer detailed his con-
tributions to the company, implying he would leave Farmers
Mutual if he didn't receive the stock option.

Kalbskopf presented a letter from Harold Wilkie, attorney
for the Wisconsin Mutual Insurance Alliance, urging the
company to open up stock options to other employees.
Rammer proposed a compromise: sell Maurer the five
shares he requested, then develop a comprehensive
employee stock ownership plan. Rammer and Wittwer
voted for the resolution, Kalbskopf against it.

In August, the board issued five shares of common
stock to Maurer at $100 per share. Rammer and Wittwer
voted for the resolution, Kalbskopf against it. The in-
fighting intensified when Wittwer promoted Maurer to
assistant secretary and proposed putting him in charge
of a production department, overseeing agency, information, and sales promotion efforts. Kalbskopf fought the
appointment, but Rammer again sided with Wittwer.

During a bitter argument with Wittwer over Maurer's appointment,
Kalbskopf issued an ultimatum: "Either Maurer goes, or I do!"

Kalbskopf left on November 8, 1944. At a special meeting of the board, he
submitted his resignation and sold his stock for $52,500 to Wittwer and
Rammer. The following week, with only a passing mention of Kalbskopf's resignation, Wittwer announced Maurer's promotion to treasurer and election to
the Farmers Mutual board of directors. "The important part Mr. Maurer has
played in the development and growth of the company has been so self-evi-
dent since the early days of the company that no further amplification is
needed," Wittwer wrote.

Within Farmers Mutual, little was said of Kalbskopf after his departure. He
became a general agent for Franklin Mutual Life Insurance Company out of
Illinois, reportedly developing a million-dollar business.

Be not the first by whom the new are tried,
nor yet the last to lay the old aside.

—ALEXANDER POPE

FROM SHOE BOXES TO FILING CABINETS

Minnesota Historical Society

With Germany defeated and Japan on the brink of surrender, President Harry S. Truman released more than 7 million men and women from the armed forces in the summer of 1945. Among them were Bob Koch, a motorcycle-riding M.P. in Europe; John (Pete) Miller, a special agent in the Counter Intelligence Corps assigned to the Manhattan Project; Floyd Desch, a B-24 communications officer; Joe Nicolay, a tank commander under Gen. George Patton; John Reed, a navy radar operator in the South Pacific; Joe Chvala, a B-24 pilot hunting Nazi submarines off the coast of Spain; and Bob DeVoe, a radio operator in a B-17 over Europe.

Postwar automobiles like this 1949 Ford captured America's infatuation with speed and power. Wisconsin and other states responded to increasing highway accidents with stronger financial responsibility laws that compelled eight of ten drivers to buy insurance.

These and other young vets—future Farmers Mutual employees like Dale Eikenberry, Charlie Ambrosavage, Sterling Schallert, Robbie Robinson, Jim Pfefferle, Bob Amundson, and Hugh Wallace—returned home to a nation tired of economic depression and war but filled with optimism. They entered colleges and universities under the G.I. Bill, intent on completing their education before embarking on business careers in a land that held consumerism as a moral imperative—the best defense against communism.

"I was taking twenty credits a semester and going around the clock," Koch remembered. "I wanted to finish as soon as I could and beat the tidal wave of veterans who were going to be job hunting."

Koch beat the wave by nearly a year, joining Farmers Mutual as an underwriter in the spring of 1948—on the same day Ambrosavage joined the agency department. It was also the day of the men's annual golf outing. After spending half a day at work, the two rookies found themselves on the rolling hills of Maple Bluff Country Club: "We agreed it was going to be a heck of a company to work for."

It was also a heck of a time to be selling automobile insurance. More than doubling in the four years after the war ended, industrywide sales exceeded $2 billion in 1949. After the war, Detroit worked overtime turning out prewar models to sell at inflated prices to a car-starved country. In 1947, Studebaker unveiled the first "modern" automobile. Low, sleek, and streamlined, it bore little resemblance to its prewar ancestors. The 1948 Cadillac, sporting "fins" on its rear fenders, took automobile style a step farther. Modeled after the P-38 fighter plane, the Cadillac captured America's infatuation with speed and power.

The combination of young vets and powerful new cars was predictably dangerous. Insurance companies responded with premium increases, state governments with stronger financial responsibility laws. In 1946, the Wisconsin legislature passed a bill requiring the driver in an accident to present proof of insurance, put down a security deposit to cover possible damages, or lose the license to drive for sixty days.

People who had driven for years without insurance flocked to agents for coverage to meet the requirements. At Farmers Mutual, earned premiums doubled to $7 million between 1945 and 1947. Although the home office urged the field to accept only those drivers who met strict standards, many agents were more interested in maximum sales—and commissions. Meanwhile, the company's two underwriters found it impossible to keep pace with the steady stream of new business. "The vault," underwriting supervisor Les Ramiker remembered, "was full of unhandled applications."

As with the aftermath of the 1935 judgment law, the surge of new business left Farmers Mutual cash poor because acquisition costs for the flood of new business had to be paid immediately while premiums, placed in reserve, were earned gradually. At the same time, postwar inflation drove up the cost of car repairs and medical care, straining the entire industry. In 500 days between 1945 and 1947, Farmers Mutual lost $500,000. The policyholders' surplus dropped by one-third to $832,000 as premiums soared to a record $6.1 million, leaving Farmers Mutual with a scant 14-cent surplus for every premium dollar—just one-third the recommended ratio.

Insolvency wasn't an immediate threat, but the situation called for drastic action. In the spring of 1947, Irv Maurer scheduled a meeting of the executive staff with state directors. "Gentlemen, our

Birth of an Association

In 1944, the U. S. Supreme Court startled the insurance industry and the forty-eight states with its opinion in the *United States vs. the Southeastern Underwriters Association*. The court ruled that insurance companies operating across state lines participated in interstate commerce, thereby subject to federal regulation. The ruling contradicted more than a century of law giving state governments exclusive domain of insurance regulation.

Apprehensive about dealing with a federal bureaucracy, the insurance industry turned to Congress for help. Congress responded in 1945 with the McCarran-Ferguson Act, delegating regulation to the states, with the admonition that they preserve competition and independence.

The insurance industry quickly organized to help state lawmakers write the necessary legislation. Independent insurers like Farmers Mutual found themselves handicapped by their independence. Fearing that larger stock companies would dominate the process, Herman Wittwer and Irving Maurer traveled to Chicago on June 1, 1945, to represent Farmers Mutual at a meeting of independent insurance organizations.

After four intense hours of discussion, representatives from twenty-nine companies formed the National Association of Independent Insurers (NAII). While Wittwer remained active in the mutual associations, Maurer became Farmers Mutual's ambassador to the NAII and in 1946 was elected to its board of directors. He served as the association's chair in 1967-68, when insurers came under intense public scrutiny due to rapidly increasing premiums and Congress launched a Department of Transportation study of the auto insurance industry.

In 1994-95, American Family Insurance chairman and CEO Dale Mathwich served as chair of the NAII as it celebrated its golden anniversary. By that time, the association had grown to represent nearly 600 companies with more than $220 billion in premiums.

Rolland E. Irish
President of Union Mutual

lifeblood is running out at the rate of one thousand dollars a day," he said. "We've got to do something."

Farmers Mutual responded with the competitive security program, which raised rates 20 percent and lowered commissions to bring them in line with what other companies were charging policyholders and paying agents. Agent training emphasized a return to more selective underwriting. To reinforce the program, Farmers Mutual for the first time linked agents' and district managers' production bonuses to the loss experience on their book of business. The fewer accidents their policyholders had, the larger their bonus checks. The company also linked state directors' bonuses to the profitability of their states.

In Milwaukee, where losses were particularly high, Maurer realized that too many part-time agents, who sold for multiple companies, had little stake in Farmers Mutual's success. So the company severed agreements with half its Milwaukee representatives and consolidated their policies under the remaining agents. Because of the sudden increase in their volume of business, these agents found themselves representing Farmers Mutual exclusively, giving them greater personal interest in the success of the company. The following year, Milwaukee showed an underwriting profit. The competitive security program succeeded—if only temporarily—in slowing premium growth and cutting in half the number of claims per premiums earned.

Entering the Life and Health Markets

The competitive security program solved some immediate problems. But for the long term, Farmers Mutual had to diversify. To compete with large organizations, the company had to reconsider life insurance. In 1940, Kalbskopf made a deal with the National Guardian Life Insurance Company of Madison to sell its line through Farmers Mutual agents in Minnesota. About 100 Farmers Mutual agents actively sold National Guardian policies, putting a sparse $8 million of life insurance in force in five years. The postwar financial crisis ended the relationship, as Farmers Mutual refocused on its auto insurance problems.

Not as cyclical as casualty insurance, life insurance proved consistently profitable and was a way to smooth out the bumps in the casualty market. In 1948, Wittwer and Maurer began searching for a small life insurance company to purchase. At the same time, the Union Mutual Life Insurance Company of

Portland, Maine, wanted to expand into the Midwest. Union Mutual president Rolland Irish heard of Farmers Mutual's interest in selling life insurance and traveled to Madison to meet with Wittwer and Maurer.

For Wittwer, business was a personal matter. He often based decisions as much on his regard for a man as the deal itself. Agreements were a matter of trust and friendship as well as revenue and profit. Such was the case with Union Mutual. As the ninth-oldest life insurance company in the nation, Union Mutual was financially strong and highly respected. But the rapport between Irish, Wittwer, and Maurer cinched the agreement. Irish was a distinguished, well-dressed man, who bore a resemblance to Wittwer in manner and appearance. Formal by nature, he smoked a pipe and introduced himself as Rolland E. Irish. Wittwer was taken by Irish's direct approach, Irish by Wittwer's honest, easy manner. In late 1948, they signed an agreement under which Farmers Mutual became Union Mutual's exclusive midwestern representative for both life and sickness and accident (S&A) insurance. In exchange, the Portland company would teach Farmers Mutual's 2,500 agents how to sell health and life coverage.

Maurer and agency director Gus Kinnamon were pleased with the arrangement. A broader portfolio made it easier to attract and keep high-quality agents. And if Farmers Mutual was ever to be represented by exclusive agents, these new lines were essential.

In the late 1940s, most Farmers Mutual agents were still farmers first and agents second, and virtually all had feet firmly planted in the casualty and fire insurance fields. When he unveiled the agreement with Union Mutual, Maurer estimated that only a hundred of the company's 2,500 agents were prepared to sell health and life insurance. Furthermore, he thought that only one in five could be trained to sell the new lines.

To improve their chance of success, Union Mutual kept it simple. The company provided shortened training and sales material, a condensed rate

In 1948, Farmers Mutual's 2,500 agents began selling Union Mutual life and health insurance. Understood in the agreement was that one day Farmers Mutual would offer its own life and health coverage.

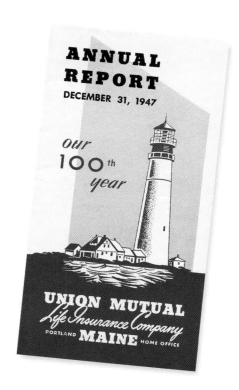

Union Mutual, one of the oldest life insurance companies in the nation, wanted to expand its territory beyond the East Coast.

Maxine Lighthall

Les Schultz

book, and eleven basic policies—eight life and three S&A plans.

Selling began on January 1, 1949, in Wisconsin, Minnesota, and Missouri. Walter Simon, supervisor of Wisconsin District 10, sold the first sickness and accident policy. District supervisor John Giovannini of Kirksville, Missouri, sold the first life policy.

Life department manager Les Schultz and cashier Maxine Lighthall record-ed the apps as they came in, then sent them on to Union Mutual, which han-dled underwriting, issued policies, and sent renewal notices. Lighthall, who ran the windstorm company's clerical operation for eleven years, handled the department with a cool efficiency that enabled Schultz to spend much of his time working with agents in the field. Schultz left Farmers Mutual in early 1952 to join Union Mutual's agency department—and eventually to become the chief executive officer of U.S. Life. Before leaving Farmers Mutual, Schultz recommended that sales personnel manager Bob Koch succeed him.

Fire Insurance—a Hot Line for the 1950s

As one of America's most prosperous decades, the 1950s saw a building boom in which the number of homeowners increased from 23.6 million in 1950 to 32.8 million by 1960. New suburbs with winding streets and cookie-cutter houses sprouted in open fields and farm land. The cocktail party became the cocktail circuit. Young couples gathered at a different house each Friday to drink and talk about work and children over the strain of Eddie Fisher or Harry Belafonte. Just one subject cast a pall over the national optimism. The Cold War with the Soviet Union grew increasingly bitter. In the summer of 1950, North Korea invaded South Korea. Coming to South Korea's defense, the United States and the United Nations undertook a three-year conflict that brought them to the brink of war with the Soviet Union and China.

America's prosperity, however, was undaunted by the deepening Cold War, and the home-building frenzy made fire insurance and extended coverage the hottest lines in the industry. So when Wisconsin and other states passed laws in 1949 and 1950 allowing insurance companies to sell multiple lines, Farmers Mutual rushed in. In deference to the town mutuals that had helped launch Farmers Mutual and still dominated the farm fire insurance market, the company limited its expansion to nonfarm fire insurance.

Typically issued in three- to five-year prepaid policies, fire insurance didn't mesh well with Farmers Mutual's semi-annual approach to auto insurance, forcing the company to establish a separate fire unit. After a year of writing

Wrap It Up

"Policy wallets" were at one time a popular item for insurance agents to present as gifts to customers and prospects. The typical American family carried separate insurance policies for auto, hospital and doctor bills, fire damage, theft, personal liability, and more, giving them a stack of policies to keep on hand.

By the mid-1950s, Americans were tired of carrying half-a-dozen insurance policies—only to find gaps in their coverage after filing a claim. The insurance industry responded with the homeowners policy, rolling fire, theft, and personal liability protection into one package. It was an instant success.

Farmers Mutual joined the homeowners market in June 1958, offering its version of the three most popular policies—homeowners, homeowners with extended coverage, and renters insurance. (A farmowners policy followed in 1962, combining fire, windstorm, extended coverage, theft, and liability.) As it had attempted in 1950 with fire insurance, Farmers Mutual tried to shoe-horn the homeowners policy into its semi-annual approach, replacing prepaid policies with six-month renewals. But financial institutions, worried this provided too many opportunities for coverage to lapse, rejected the plan.

Intense competition for the homeowners coverage caused insurers to commit a multitude of underwriting sins. Policies provided overly broad coverage with low or no deductibles—almost begging for claims to be filed. Minimum coverages all but vanished. Insurance-to-value requirements fell steadily in the face of increasing costs to rebuild or repair. Finally, premiums were ridiculously low—often just a few dollars more than basic fire insurance.

Farmers Mutual—a conservative company by nature—was not above the fray. In 1960, vice president of underwriting Howard Hayes admitted that rates for homeowners insurance were too low. "Do we want homeowners business in spite of the fact that the current rates are probably too low?" Hayes asked in the October 1960 issue of *FM*. "Emphatically—YES!"

Hayes urged agents to be strict in their risk selection, writing the homeowners package policy on only the best risks, while selling fire and extended coverage for all others. "When the time comes for a rate increase our increase can be less than that needed by other companies," Hayes reasoned. "Our rates will be even more competitive."

THIS FARM IS **PROTECTED**
Against Loss by Fire and Wind

FARMERS INSURANCE CO.   FARMERS MUTUALS FAMILY INSURANCE HOME AUTO MADISON, WISCONSIN   MUTUAL OF WISCONSIN

In deference to town mutuals, whose agents helped launch Farmers Mutual Automobile Insurance Company, the company didn't offer fire insurance to farmers until 1957.

fire insurance the conventional way, assistant secretary Alex Opgenorth, underwriting manager Howard Hayes, and chief fire underwriter Don Taylor devised a one-year fire insurance policy with a semi-annual premium. Farmers Mutual was the first and perhaps the only company to experiment with this semi-annual approach to fire insurance. Insurance commissioners, impressed by the innovation, readily approved the plan, but banks and finance companies were not enthusiastic. Fearing semi-annual payments provided too many opportunities to let coverage lapse, many refused to accept the insurance. Farmers Mutual compromised, offering three-year and five-year policies, but with annual payments.

To Build a Better Agent

For more than twenty years, Farmers Mutual grew and prospered with a field force of farmers and tradesmen, gas-station owners and car dealers, bakers and teachers, stitched together by district agents who were themselves farmers and tradesmen selling insurance on the side. Many agents wrote just a few policies a year, keeping records in a shoebox beneath the bed. Training, conducted by the district agents, was informal at best. Many agents' knowledge of insurance didn't extend much beyond the thirty-two-page agent's manual and rate book.

Concerned about the quality and training of insurance agents, the Wisconsin legislature first debated

Among the more than 1,500 agents who completed Farmers Mutual's sales and service training course by the end of 1955 were (standing from left): Loyal Gibbs, Earl Willhite, and James McCloskey; (seated from left): Harland Curry and Harvey Fisher.

a proposal for state testing of agents in 1931. Arguing that testing would discriminate against part-time agents, the state's mutual insurance companies easily defeated the legislation. But in the late 1940s and early 1950s, many states, including Wisconsin, passed laws requiring that agents be licensed.

The passage of multiple-line laws increased the need for well-trained agents. Many companies, wary of spending too much to train agents who also sold for their competitors, resorted to minimum production rules. Beginning in 1951, Farmers Mutual required agents with two or more years' experience to collect at least $2,000 in total casualty and fire premiums annually. New agents had to reach the minimum level in their third year.

If Farmers Mutual expected more from its agents, it also was willing to provide more. In October 1951, the board passed a resolution, drafted by Maurer, aimed at creating "conditions which will encourage the part-time agent to devote continuous time and study to the profession, and which will assist the full-time agents to realize greater development."

In 1951, Farmers Mutual's board of directors started the company down the rocky path toward exclusive agent representation. Clockwise from left: William Aberg, Bernard Gehrmann, August Rammer, Herman Wittwer, Harvey Spriggs, M. A. Koehler, and Irving Maurer.

To create these conditions, the resolution called for an education and research department. Under the direction of Lorin Schoephoerster, the department produced a fifteen-lesson sales and service training course for agents in the field. Within four years, 70 percent of the agents had completed the course. The department wrote educational articles for *FM*, a monthly newsletter for agents, on topics ranging from reading monthly account statements to prospecting for life insurance to insuring television sets. Schoephoerster also produced office aids, such as a prospecting and records management system designed especially for Farmers Mutual agents.

The 1951 resolution included another, more controversial, mandate, requiring district agents to give up personal sales and work full time to recruit, train, and manage local agents. Board members like August Rammer and Harvey Spriggs, who as district agents had some of the company's largest agencies, found this a difficult proposition. Giving up personal sales meant sacrificing a large income. Understanding the need for better training and management of agents, the board nevertheless approved the resolution unanimously.

Although most members of the board and executive staff urged slow implementation, Maurer pushed for immediate action. "Otherwise it'll drag out and never get done," he argued.

When agency director Gus Kinnamon hit the road to work out the details with Farmers Mutual's district agents, he found their reaction predictably negative. Several longtime district agents, particularly in Wisconsin, initially refused to give up their agencies. In the end, most accepted the decision. Some relinquished their districts to remain agents. Others quit or were fired.

State Historical Society of Wisconsin

Stumbling Toward Exclusivity

The number of automobiles on American roadways doubled in the six years following the war, reaching 52 million in 1951. Two of every three families owned a car, and one in ten owned two. A new economy evolved along America's highways. The first Holiday Inn opened in 1951, signaling the advent of the motorlodge. McDonald's served its first burger in 1955. Drive-in movie theaters, restaurants, banks, convenience stores, and churches sprang up. Even drive-up electric-shaving stations enjoyed a brief period of popularity as Americans took to the road.

And there were more roads for Americans to take. An acute housing shortage after the war led to the rapid development of suburbs, all connected to central cities by new highways. With the Interstate Highway Act of 1956, the federal government authorized construction of 41,000 miles of toll-free highways, paid for with a three-cent-per-gallon gasoline tax.

The number of automobiles on American roadways doubled in the six years following World War II, crowding streets and causing accidents.

John Farnsworth   Henry Harvey   Howard Hayes

With more drivers on the road, the rate and severity of accidents increased, leading to another tide of red ink in the insurance industry. Many companies responded by experimenting with their rating systems. Farmers Mutual, however, returned to the fundamentals with Operation Blue Ink, described by Maurer as "more income and less outgo." Developed in 1953 by agency director Gus Kinnamon, underwriting director Howard Hayes, comptroller Henry Harvey, and claims director John Farnsworth, Operation Blue Ink focused on turning underwriting losses in seven of its ten states to underwriting profits through administrative cost-cutting, restrictive underwriting, improved training, and increased sales.

Perceived by many as a short-term, emergency measure, the plan in fact had a long-term goal of "attitude adjustment." The crux of Farmers Mutual's persistent underwriting losses, the committee reasoned, was poor selectivity. Farmers Mutual's unlevel premium approach, with its loaded initial premium and low renewal rate, depended on insuring only preferred drivers, at risk for few accidents. Many agents, however, failed to understand their role in risk selection and focused more on the volume of business rather than the quality. To change the situation, district managers and the directors of the seven red-ink states would have to become more conscious of profit as well as volume.

In the summer of 1953, Farmers Mutual called each of the seven state directors to the home office to discuss the problem and solution and,

Agents who earned the 1952 production bonus don special derbies at the 1953 Midland sales convention in Jefferson City, Missouri. From left: Earl Willhite, Harold Schafer, R. J. Williams, Wilroy Schaffner, George Sallwasser, Leo Huenefeld, Oren Blackwell, and Arthur Bourne.

as Hayes explained in a memo, "to engrave indelibly on their minds that the primary determinant of our success as a company in their states is the ability and willingness of the men in the field to perform their jobs." Chastised, the directors left Madison with a mission—to turn their states around. For many, this meant terminating scores of agents who were inactive, showed high loss ratios, or were unwilling to cooperate with Farmers Mutual in preventing further losses.

Simultaneously, the agency department implemented the metropolitan program. Remembering what happened in Milwaukee when agents dedicated their full time to Farmers Mutual, the program required full-time, exclusive representation in all metropolitan areas by January 1, 1955.

From an underwriting standpoint, Operation Blue Ink was a success. In 1954 and 1955, despite widespread industry losses, Farmers Mutual showed a profit in every state. But the blue ink did not come without taking its toll on the field force.

Implicit in the agency reorganization program was the company's desire to be represented by full-time agents selling exclusively for Farmers Mutual. Except in the metropolitan program, however, the home office never explicitly stated exclusive representation as its goal. Until the fall of 1955, Farmers Mutual described itself as "an agency company," meaning it worked through independent agents who owned the policies they submitted to Farmers Mutual.

Mixed messages from company leaders complicated the situation. Maurer, who disliked the agency system because it divided an agent's loyalty, pushed for exclusive representation. Wittwer preferred the status quo and constantly backpedaled from Maurer's statements on the subject.

State directors and disgruntled district managers further muddied the message. Some managers quickly terminated part-time and multiple-company agents, consolidating their business to support new, full-time agents. Others followed a more temperate approach that delayed exclusive representation but avoided the bad blood brought on by mass terminations. Without a clear message, agents were forced to interpret for themselves Farmers Mutual's intent. Agents representing multiple companies assumed Farmers Mutual was canceling nonexclusive representatives. Part-time agents assumed the company was canceling all part-timers. Those with low sales in one line or another figured their agencies were next on the chopping block. In the process, Farmers

Beginning in 1949, Farmers Mutual agents could offer new life insurance policyholders a "tri-coin savings bank" to help them save enough to pay the annual premium. In some cases, the agent kept the key, ensuring that the owner didn't use his savings for something else.

Irving J. Maurer
At 92, a Legend in His Own Time

Born Ervin J. Maurer on May 11, 1905, he was the fifth of Joseph and Anna Maurer's seven children. His father and mother, German immigrants, had settled in Marshfield, Wisconsin, where they ran a successful business selling ice to the railroads. It was a prosperous time for the Maurers. But when Ervin was five, his father sold the ice business and moved the family to Withee, where he built a broom handle factory. This too proved a success, until fire destroyed the building. Without a penny of insurance, the Maurers could only stand there and watch the factory burn.

Joseph categorized people as either producers or consumers, and he believed strongly in being a producer. He moved his family to Stevens Point and started another ice business. After that failed, he opened a theater with another man who stole money from the business. Financial problems strained the Maurer family, and in 1916 Joseph and Anna separated, and his father moved to Neilsville. Ervin contributed to the family finances by taking a job as a bellhop at the Jacobs House, where his most famous customer was William Jennings Bryan, twice a Democratic candidate for president. He tipped Maurer a 1913 dime. "I was hoping for folding money," Maurer recalled. When his father came down with the flu during the 1918 epidemic, Ervin moved to Neilsville to run the ice business until he recovered.

Books had a tremendous impact on young Maurer. He so thoroughly enjoyed the stories of Washington Irving that he adopted the

President 1959-1968
CEO and Chairman 1968-1977

spelling for his first name. And after reading *The Art of Cross-Examination* for his debate club, he decided to become a lawyer.

Though intent on studying law, Maurer's frugal nature compelled him after graduating from high school to enter Stevens Point Normal School, principally a teachers' college. Here, by taking the teachers' track, Maurer avoided paying tuition.

Shortly thereafter, Maurer accepted an offer from Carl Jacobs, a family friend and the president of Hardware Mutual, to learn the insurance business "from the ground up," as an underwriter. Maurer advanced steadily, learning underwriting and sales management

at Hardware Mutual. Here, too, he met Kathryn Fischer. Intelligent and inquiring, Kathryn developed a strong interest in insurance, and Irving spent much of his free time teaching her everything he learned about the business. They married in 1933 and raised two children.

Maurer joined Farmers Mutual in 1929, hoping to work part time while attending the University of Wisconsin. But the position as underwriting manager was full time, so Maurer rolled up his sleeves and went to work.

Headstrong and well-versed in the insurance business, Maurer was responsible for many early innovations at Farmers Mutual, the credit for which he readily shares with Kathryn. These included the unorthodox, semi-annual renewal plan in 1932, the shift to an exclusive agent system in the 1950s, and the company's venture into the life insurance market. Though often unpopular at the time, these changes ultimately proved essential to the company's success.

As treasurer, president, and finally chairman of Farmers Mutual/American Family, Maurer practiced the art of cross-examination, relentlessly questioning those under him. Employees able to fire back the answers adapted to Maurer's autocratic style. Others simply feared him.

Maurer retired in 1977 but remains extraordinarily vigorous. In 1994, at age eighty-nine, he and his second wife, Nan, bicycled 235 miles across the Loire Valley in France. Jokingly, Maurer says, "Hell is full, and they're rejecting people like me."

FARMERS MUTUALS FM

September, 1953

MADISON 1, WISCONSIN

Vol. 5 No. 9

Need For OPERATION BLUE INK

HOWARD HAYES, Underwriting Manager

For the first time since 1946, the June 30, 1953 operating statement showed a Company loss for the first half-year.

Where?

Normally, experience for the first six months of a year is favorable. Normally, the favorable experience of the first half-year sufficiently sweetens the usually poorer experience of the last half of the year to produce favorable results for the year as a whole.

Naturally, therefore, discovery of red-ink results for the first half of 1953 was cause for probing to determine where the loss came from, why there was a loss and what steps can and must be taken to correct the condition.

Not all parts of the Farmers Mutual body are ill. Wisconsin, North Dakota and South Dakota produced additions to surplus because of favorable experience during the first half of this year. Were it not for the good experience of these three states, the Company's loss would have been much more serious.

Operation in each of the remaining states produced an underwriting loss during the same period. By state, the losses were:

UNDERWRITING LOSS
First 6 Months — 1953

State	
	$ 12,400
Illinois	34,300
Indiana	61,500
Iowa	100,100
Kansas	94,700
Minnesota	132,800
Missouri	84,100
Nebraska	

Because their operations have produced red-ink results for two and one-half years, Iowa, Kansas, Missouri and Nebraska have been under close observation for some time. However, because they suffered a loss during the historically good first half-year, each of the states listed must be considered as being in a critical condition.

Why?

Having located where the loss came from, the next step was diagnosis of the causes of the loss. Although this part of the diagnosis is not completed, obviously the causes of the loss will be found in one or a combination of these general areas:

1. Insufficient Income. Farmers Mutual is dedicated to the lowest renewal rate consistent with sound business practice. The low renewal rate is the spark-plug of our plan of operation. Yet, in some areas, upward adjustments in rates will be necessary — unless solution to the loss problem can be found in some other approach.

2. Excessive Outgo. Farmers Mutual is dedicated to a liberal, but realistic and fair policy in matters of expense. Possibly, however, we will find that the Company has been liberal beyond the point of realism and fairness in some areas.

3. Administration. Men, methods and practices together weave the pattern of any organizations existence. Proper coordination and utilization of these factors produce pleasing, favorable results. Perhaps in this area will be found opportunity for improvement.

What?

In the diagnosis of where the illness exists and the causes for it, each of the State Directors of the affected states has been active.

The State Director will have the responsibility of prescribing cures and in following through to see that the treatment is applied. The State Director is responsible for the health of his state.

The stages of diagnosis, prescription and treatment are designed to turn red-ink to blue-ink results. "OPERATION BLUE INK" already is functioning. By now, most of you in the loss-producing states have heard of "OPERATION BLUE INK" through your State Director. Perhaps, however, you have not appreciated to the fullest degree the imperative nature of the program as one which must succeed.

Perhaps, also, you have not fully appreciated the vital role that each agent plays both in the successful completion of a program such as "OPERATION BLUE INK" and, once the change from red to blue ink has been made, in creating and maintaining conditions that will make such programs unnecessary in the future.

Each Agent a Company

In effect, each agent operates an insurance company. The loss ratio of any State is neither more nor less than the average of all of the loss ratios of all of the agents in the state. Wisconsin, North Dakota and South Dakota produced additions to surplus because the average of the loss ratios of the agents in those states was below the break-even point. Losses resulted in seven states because the average of the loss ratios of the agents in those states was above the break-even point.

In the final analysis, whether or not the seven-state "OPERATION BLUE INK" is successful will be determined by the degree of consistency with which each agent applies the fundamental rules developed by the State Directors as cures for the loss problem.

Operation Blue Ink's objective was to align the agents' incentive with the company's. The implicit goal was to create a field force of agents who represented Farmers Mutual only.

Mutual's field force plunged from 3,258 in 1950 to 1,903 by mid-decade.

Mistrust deepened with a series of lawsuits filed in 1954 by a number of longtime agents and district managers. They argued that the company had violated their "property rights" by sending renewal notices to their policyholders and providing successor agents with policyholder information. The plaintiffs, including Joseph Radtke, former general manager of the windstorm company, argued that their original verbal agreements with Farmers Mutual assured them that agents would own and control the policies. Richard Kalbskopf resurfaced at these trials, testifying that he'd promised the company would follow the American Agency System. Farmers Mutual argued that in a mutual company, policies belong to the members who control where they have their insurance. Farmers Mutual lost every case, paying tens of thousands of dollars in damages.

With agent morale at an all-time low, the executive staff met throughout the summer of 1955 to find a solution to the deteriorating relationship between home office and field force. Discussion focused on the discrepancy between the company's public policy supporting the American Agency System and Operation Blue Ink's implicit goal of exclusive agency. Wittwer continued to raise concerns about the impact of exclusive representation on longtime agents who had relationships with many companies. But underwriting director Howard Hayes produced reports showing that exclusive agents not only sold more than multi-company representatives but also were more selective, creating more income for themselves and the company. With the company facing increasing competition, the exclusive agent seemed vital to its survival. "Should sentiment override judgment if judgment dictates that the salvation of Farmers Mutual lies in exclusive agency?" the executive staff wondered.

In August, the staff completed its deliberations, recommending the board declare exclusive agency representation the official company policy. Wittwer, by this time was in no mood for an argument. After suffering a long illness,

Barbara had died in late July. For years, she'd been his motivation and the source of his strength. But she wasn't there now to see him through this fight.

Maurer, with the help of his wife Kathryn, wrote a memo proposing Farmers Mutual make exclusive agent representation its official policy and begin working toward that goal. Despite Wittwer's reservations, the board approved the recommendation on October 27, 1955. They did, however, urge staff to implement the new policy "with tolerance and understanding," so that agents would not have to "suddenly and arbitrarily" end longtime relationships with other companies.

Pushed by Maurer, the executive staff set January 1, 1958, as the target date for all agents to represent Farmers Mutual exclusively. Because Farmers Mutual didn't sell farm fire coverage, rural agents were exempt from the requirement. However, they were required to place all possible business with Farmers Mutual.

The Minnesota Uprising

The friction between the company and its field force boiled over in December 1955. Disgruntled over being taken off commission and placed on salary, Minnesota state director Len Wolf resigned and joined Market Men's Mutual, a Milwaukee-based insurance company. In itself, Wolf's defection wasn't noteworthy. But he convinced his eleven district managers that they were about to be fired. They too resigned and began recruiting Farmers Mutual agents for Market Men's Mutual. Other competitors had used the turmoil in Farmers Mutual to lure away agents and policyholders. Nothing, however, approached the scope of this mass resignation.

Poor relations with Minnesota insurance commissioner Cyril Sheehan made a bad situation worse. Earlier in the year, Farmers Mutual requested permission to reduce auto rates in Minnesota. But Sheehan—angry about the company's lawsuit forcing him to accept its fire insurance plan—rejected the proposed auto rates as inadequate. As a result, Farmers Mutual had higher auto premiums than its competitors. This combined with the widespread propaganda

On October 27, 1955, the Farmers Mutual board of directors unanimously supported the company's move to a field force of agents representing Farmers Mutual exclusively. But the votes cast by such longtime agents as Harvey Spriggs and August Rammer were not without regrets. Paul Miller, who succeeded Spriggs as district manager, recalled driving past Spriggs' house on the way back from terminating an agent. "Harvey was standing out in his driveway shaking his cane at me," Miller said.

The Minnesota claims office became the hub of activity after Farmers Mutual's Minnesota state director and eleven district managers quit in December 1955.

circulated by Wolf and his men forced many of the company's 327 Minnesota agents to question the wisdom of staying with Farmers Mutual.

After word of the resignations reached Madison, Kinnamon and Koch spent three grueling days and nights working the phones, talking with district managers and agents. Minnesota claims adjusters and resident underwriters joined the effort. Under the direction of Si Sandeen, they immediately drove to their territories to convince agents to stay with the company.

Forty Years of the LCA/All American

"Selling insurance is one of the highest paying hard jobs I know and one of the lowest paying easy jobs," said American Family Insurance chairman Dale Mathwich.

While it's easy to be motivated at district meetings or state conventions, come Monday morning—when its just an agent, the telephone, and a list of prospects—that enthusiasm can wane. Suddenly, it seems more important to catch up on paperwork or clean the desk than make that first call.

"That's one reason this is a good business," said Mathwich, who had thirteen years in the field as an agent and district manager, "because not everyone can do it."

While it's impossible to know who will be a successful agent, two traits commonly found in top salespeople are competitiveness and goal orientation— which keep them at the phone or knocking on doors long after others have called it a day.

From the beginning, Farmers Mutual sponsored contests to foster competition within the field force and give agents goals to achieve. Contests typically ran several weeks, promoting a single line of insurance. To emphasize multiple-line sales, Farmers Mutual introduced the Leading Career Agents Club (LCA) in 1955. To qualify, an agent had to sell at least 100 casualty policies, 120 fire policies, and $100,000 of life, sickness, accident, and hospital insurance, and receive the underwriting incentive bonus. The prize: an all-expenses-paid trip to the Edgewater Beach Hotel in Chicago for the LCA Convention. Arden Wurch, a six-year veteran in Milwaukee, was the first to qualify, fulfilling the requirements by the end of June. All told, fifty-five agents made the trip to Chicago that year.

In 1961, the company opened up the LCA to district managers whose agents met specific goals. On October 31, 1960, Marv Klitzke, a manager in Springfield, Illinois, became the first to qualify.

In recognition of its new name— American Family Insurance—the company in 1964 renamed the annual gathering the All American Convention. Ray Hicks, an agent from Council Bluffs, Iowa, became the first All American, fulfilling the requirements in just three months. The contest emphasized life insurance sales, and only eighty-three agents qualified for the trip to Miami Beach.

Today, one-third of American Family's well-trained, highly motivated force of more than 3,600 agents qualify for the All American Convention.

The art above was taken from FM, *the company's monthly publication for agents.*

The amount of misinformation and the depth of distrust caught the two home office men off guard. Kinnamon responded with a memo to Minnesota agents explaining directly to them—for the first time—the company's policy relating to exclusive agency. At a special executive staff meeting Saturday morning, December 24, Kinnamon and Koch reported what they'd heard from the agents and former district managers. The executive staff agreed that a series of meetings with agents around Minnesota was necessary.

With the early January temperatures well below zero, two home office teams set out for a week of agent meetings in Minnesota. Kinnamon and his team met with agents in the Twin Cities, while Koch and his team toured rural Minnesota.

More than 230 agents turned out to hear what Farmers Mutual had to say. But there was little warmth in the crowded meeting rooms, where angry agents barraged the home office men with questions and accusations based on half-truths and gross exaggerations. Near the end of this taxing week, Alex Opgenorth, a member of Koch's team, phoned home to find that his wife was dead. Suicide. Koch drove his friend to the airport that evening. The next day's drive to Thief River Falls was somber.

After the home office men returned to Madison, the claims adjusters and resident underwriters again hit the road to shore up support among agents.

While some agents questioned their affiliation with Farmers Mutual, others focused on sales. In 1956, 103 agents qualified for the second annual LCA convention at Estes Park, Colorado, the following summer.

In 1942, the average Farmers Mutual agent served thirty policyholders. Ten years later, the average increased to seventy-five. By 1962—less than ten years after the company began its transition to exclusive agency—the average agent served 400 policyholders.

Marvin Klitzke

The First to Sign on the Dotted Line

After Marvin Klitzke returned home from the Korean conflict in 1953, the Reedsburg, Wisconsin, native took a construction job and got married. For insurance, he turned to Frank Feivor, an agent for Farmers Mutual—the company his father used. A few months later, Feivor became a district manager and recruited Klitzke.

In December 1954, Klitzke and his wife Bert moved from their hometown in south central Wisconsin to Seymour, just west of Green Bay. He lost money the first year. But he was breaking even in 1956 when Feivor encouraged him to sign a career agent agreement with Farmers Mutual. Klitzke didn't hesitate and became the first to sign on as a career agent in 1956.

Klitzke remained with the company for the next thirty-nine years, including six as a district manager. But he never slacked off. The month before he retired in mid-1995, Klitzke wrote seventy-five apps and qualified for the All American Convention in San Diego.

"They kept me in the office handling all these claims that came in," said adjuster Milt Olson. "The others traveled all over the state, trying to keep agents, telling them to stay with the company."

In the end, nearly half the Minnesota field force quit, taking with them to Market Men's more than $1 million of the company's $20 million in premiums. "A million dollars in premiums doesn't sound like much today, but in those days it was," Koch said. "But if their commitment to Farmers Mutual wasn't any stronger than that, we figured we were better off without them."

To replace Wolf, the company selected Joe Stephan, who had successfully implemented Operation Blue Ink in Kansas. Perpetually optimistic, Stephan livened up the gloomy St. Paul office with his full-speed-ahead enthusiasm and off-the-cuff one-liners. He approached Minnesota as though he were opening a new state, spending most of his time aggressively recruiting district managers and agents. One of his first recruits was Wally Huebsch, the realtor who sold Stephan and his wife their Twin Cities home.

Huebsch started as a district manager, covering a large area that extended from the Twin Cities' northern suburbs to Duluth. "It was a tough time. Wolf would follow me around and talk to anybody I tried to recruit," Huebsch said. "He'd get the list of people taking the state licensing exam and contact them about joining Market Men's—which went broke a few years later."

John Reed, a young Wisconsin agent, was another recruit, accepting a district manager position in Tracy, Minnesota. "I had thirty-two agents on my list," Reed said. "After finding out who really wanted to sell for Farmers Mutual, I was down to three."

The company bolstered Stephan and his district managers' efforts with nearly $75,000 of advertising and by offering a $2 bonus on new business and a $1 bonus on renewals. But it took years for Farmers Mutual to return its Minnesota sales to the pre-1955 level.

Put it in Writing

With the Minnesota revolt still boiling, Farmers Mutual began work on its first written agent contracts. After consulting with agents, district managers, and state directors across the territory, Alex Opgenorth and Gus Kinnamon developed two contracts. The standard agreement allowed current agents to continue selling for multiple companies. The career agreement—required of all new

agents but optional for existing ones—bound them to exclusive representation. Of the nearly 2,000 agreements signed in 1956, more than 1,700 were standard. Among the fewer than 200 men to sign exclusive full-time career agreements was Dale Mathwich, a former bank manager who signed his agreement on October 3—the company's twenty-ninth anniversary.

The career agreement was far from a one-sided deal. In exchange for representing Farmers Mutual only, career agents had access to company-paid training, advertising assistance, hospital insurance—and advanced compensation. Developed by Koch, budget director Hugh Wallace, and agency secretary Charlie Ambrosavage, the advanced compensation plan offered new agents a monthly subsidy of up to $400 for up to eighteen months, with the requirement that they pay it back over time.

When Koch first approached Maurer about the plan, Maurer's answer was no. "It's a privilege for them to be a part of this company and to represent us," he snapped. "We're not going to pay them for that privilege."

Koch, however, was one of the few people at Farmers Mutual who knew how to stand up to the domineering Maurer. He stuck to his guns, answering every question Maurer fired at him. Koch presented estimates showing that 100 subsidized agents meeting their minimum production levels would produce nearly 35,000 casualty, fire, and S&A applications, plus more than $9 million in life insurance in a year. The company risked little. Successful agents would pay back their advances, most often out of bonus money they

After World War II, agent manuals grew thicker and the need for training mushroomed.

earned. If an agent failed, he and/or his manager would be responsible for 60 percent of the draw, while Farmers Mutual would write off the remainder. Maurer agreed, but for years he referred to the plan as "the dole."

Farmers Mutual also stepped up its training program. In 1957, Floyd Desch, the first sales training supervisor, developed Farmers Mutual's first written sales tracks. Desch and Koch also initiated home office sales schools. They designed the basic sales school as a training ground for successful agents with a year of sales behind them. Intermediate schools were for agents with three to five years' experience. Advanced schools, added later, recognized longtime agents for their years of service and helped improve their ability to sell all the company's lines. Within ten years, 1,700 agents completed basic, intermediate, or advanced sales school.

It wasn't long before Farmers Mutual—and most agents—saw the benefits of exclusive representation. By 1959, 22 percent of the field force represented Farmers Mutual exclusively and sold more than half its new auto, fire, and health policies and 80 percent of its new life insurance coverage.

Filling the Sales Case

Exclusive representation also led to changes in the coverage Farmers Mutual provided. In 1954, the company's slogan was "Everyday insurance needs for farmers, individuals and families." But rural agents increasingly complained that their sales case lacked an important ingredient—farm fire protection. Finally, in 1957, after three years of debate, Farmers Mutual test-marketed farm fire insurance in Wisconsin. Agents wrote 695 farm fire policies that year, totaling $11.9 million in coverage. The company eventually offered farm fire—and later farmowners and liability insurance—in all its states.

Exclusive agency also sped up Farmers Mutual's decision to offer its own life and health insurance policies. Union Mutual knew from the outset that Farmers Mutual eventually wanted to offer its own health and life insurance coverage, but the Portland, Maine-based company believed it wouldn't happen for a decade or more. Exclusive agency changed that. In 1954, the Kansas insurance commissioner

A Farmers Mutual committee selected applicant William Mervar to receive the company's first sickness and accident policy. Mervar purchased from Bob Steffen a "Provider" policy covering himself, his wife, Mae, and their three children. The Mervars represented the "most nearly ideal family," underwriting manager Louis Olson explained. William, a floor covering contractor from Sheboygan, had been a policyholder since 1949 and at the time owned six Farmers Mutual policies.

questioned whether requiring exclusive agents under Farmers Mutual's metropolitan program to represent Union Mutual violated federal law prohibiting boycott, intimidation, and coercion. Though never raised in court, the issue caused concern.

The next year, with companywide exclusive agency in the offing, Wittwer and Maurer raised the subject of independence with Union Mutual president Rolland Irish. Irish understood their desire but urged them to consider the expense, particularly in the area of life insurance.

In Maurer's eyes, Farmers Mutual had the volume to support the move. By the close of 1955, Farmers Mutual agents had sold $45 million worth of life insurance, collecting nearly $1 million in premiums and another $218,000 in S&A (sickness and accident) premiums for Union Mutual. Wittwer was less convinced. Farmers Mutual had sold life and health insurance for only a few years, and he wasn't certain it was ready to manage its own program. Home office relations with the agents were terrible, and the future was far from certain.

Alex Opgenorth, Henry Harvey, Howard Hayes, and Gus Kinnamon—assistant secretary, comptroller, the head of underwriting, and agency director—studied the possibility of offering health and life insurance coverage. In February 1957, estimating that Farmers Mutual agents would sell more than $200 million in new life insurance over the next ten years, the committee recommended terminating the agreement with Union Mutual. They suggested writing S&A first, then life insurance. The Farmers Mutual board unanimously approved the recommendation.

Sickness and accident insurance—and later life insurance—filled out the Farmers Mutual sales case.

That spring, with the nation in a brief but sharp recession, Farmers Mutual announced it would write its own sickness and accident insurance by year's end. Much work had to be done before that could happen. Farmers Mutual had to get licenses in all states, write and print policies, file them with all state insurance commissioners, establish rate schedules and commissions, design and print forms, create training and promotional material, set up machinery to handle the new line, and much more.

Farmers Mutual's first actuary, George Burt, laid much of the foundation for the S&A department. Implementation fell to Louis Olson, underwriting supervisor for Kansas, Missouri, and Nebraska. As the S&A department's first underwriter, Olson handwrote the first two policies, patterned after Union Mutual plans. "The Provider" offered hospital coverage with a six-dollar to twenty-dollar "daily room benefit" and optional surgical coverage. "The Protector" offered income protection through monthly payments in the event of sickness or injury. Breaking with the Union Mutual approach, Farmers Mutual applied its semi-annual plan to S&A. By loading acquisition costs—mainly agent commissions—into the initial premium, the company could offer a lower renewal rate.

S&A sales began November 1, 1957—a month after Farmers Mutual celebrated its thirtieth anniversary—with forty applications arriving the first day. In two months, premiums totaled $100,000. By 1960, annual premiums exceeded $500,000. With the addition of a major medical policy, premiums grew 32 percent the following year, and the number of policies surpassed 6,000. Recognizing the growing importance of this line, the company formed a separate S&A department in 1962, with Fred Luick supervising. Olson continued as underwriter, and John Hicks handled claims.

Life Starts in '58

Not entirely sure when it would be ready to sell its own line of life insurance, Farmers Mutual in March 1957 put up $2 million to form a wholly owned subsidiary for that purpose, with Wittwer as chairman and Maurer as president. Incorporating the new venture as a stock company made it easier to start than a mutual and gave the company a strong financial base—$1 million in capital and $1 million in surplus. Many of the company's senior and middle managers hoped Farmers Mutual would offer stock to agents and employees as many newer life companies had done. But the board—committed to the mutual philosophy—feared that policyholders would frown on an individually owned stock company. "We were so risk-averse that the board wasn't even willing to listen to the idea," recalled company vice president John Reed. "We were very, very careful in those days."

Many assumed the new company would be named Farmers Mutual Life

In 1958, Farmers Mutual incorporated the American Family Life Insurance Company as a wholly owned subsidiary. The double logo indicated the close relationship the two companies shared and the full protection they offered.

Insurance. But Maurer and Koch, among others, felt the name Farmers Mutual didn't sell well in urban areas. Even in Wisconsin, Farmers Mutual was often confused with other agricultural companies. Besides, the name didn't reflect the nature of the new life company.

Although Wittwer wouldn't hear of changing the parent company's name, he didn't fight Maurer on the life company's title. The working name during development was the Family Life Insurance Company, but a small Seattle firm had that title. Maurer considered "family" an essential part of the name, and he had plans to expand nationwide. In a June 1957 memo he mused, "Perhaps we should merely incorporate a geographical prefix and call the company American Family Life Insurance Company (AFLIC)."

Later that summer, sales promotions manager Charlie Ambrosavage went to Capitol Square in Madison and, with a list of possible names in hand, asked passersby which was the best for a life insurance company. American Family won. "That was the extent of our market research," Koch remembered with a laugh.

Koch was the obvious choice to manage the new company. He'd headed the life department in the early 1950s before being promoted to sales person-nel manager, a position he held through the turbulent transition to exclusive agency. He'd impressed Wittwer and Maurer by handling the situation in a friendly, easy manner that earned him the trust and respect of a wary field force and a frazzled home office.

Just thirty-three years old, Koch assumed the new position on January 1, 1958. Maurer, in typical full-speed-ahead style, set July 1 as the launch date for the American Family Life Insurance Company—leaving Koch just six months to set up the operation. "That was absolutely the busiest, the most frantic time I've ever had with the company," Koch remembered. "Still, it was fun, because we were creating something from scratch."

Not entirely from scratch. Farmers Mutual had nine years of sales training under Union Mutual, during which time it sold $75 million of life insurance. But the company had no real home-office experience in managing a life insurance operation. Jim Dallman, previously director of the life department, stayed on as life services manager, but after the transition Maxine Lighthall joined Union Mutual as its Madison office manager. Union Mutual agreed to train its new competitor's employees. Other companies helped as well. Maurer

Bob Koch

In the 1950s, every aspect of American free enterprise was viewed as a blow for freedom in the fight against Communism. In President Dwight D. Eisenhower's eyes, life insurance was a foot sol-dier in the war. "One of the clearest evidences of the faith of our people in the free institutions and the future of America is the fact that 90 million of our citizens own life insur-ance policies. Their ownership of life insurance is more than a $304 bil-lion bulwark of family protection. It is the kind of thrift which provides productive capital. This capital, invested in farms, factories, homes, transportation, utilities, and other resources, helps to give this nation the economic power needed to but-tress freedom in the world."

Jim Dallman

Even cartoons in FM *carried a message.*

spent several days in Bloomington, Illinois, learning how State Farm struc-
tured its life insurance operation. Koch and Kinnamon contacted still others—
Travelers, Northwestern Mutual, and Franklin Mutual Life among them—for
insights on how to run a successful life insurance company. And American
United Life Insurance Company of Indianapolis, the reinsurance company
Koch selected, also provided extensive training.

Koch's outgoing personality and enthusiasm for the new company helped
him draw much-needed support from across the Farmers Mutual organization.
Desch worked overtime writing training manuals. Comptroller Hugh Wallace
designed a punch-card system to process the policies. The printing and supply
departments scrambled to get promotional and sales materials to the agents.
And when help was needed to collate the agent packets, the entire company
stuffed folders.

Because of the short time available to set up the new company, Koch and
Maurer kept its structure simple and economical. Koch kept administrative
expenses down by adopting Farmers Mutual's semi-annual approach rather
than the costly monthly billing system common among life insurance carriers.
Noting that four basic policies accounted for 90 percent of sales under Union
Mutual, Koch started with just those policies—Whole Life (paid-up at 85),
Executive Life (paid-up at 90), 4-Way Security (20 pay life), and the Insured
Savings Plan (endowment at age 65). By adopting these basic policies along
with Union Mutual's premium and dividend schedules, Koch lopped months
off the development stage and enabled agents to begin with familiar products.
Not until 1960 did the company have its own forms, rates, and schedules.

"We are committed to the proposition that the simpler we keep our plans
and our sales presentations, the more we enhance your opportunity to build
your agency through life insurance sales," Koch told agents.

Identifying the company's market was important. Family income increased
15 percent during the prosperous Eisenhower years. As their lifestyles
improved, parents of the burgeoning baby-boom considered the protection
offered by life insurance a necessity. But many of the "life only" companies
continued to focus on upper-income families who made more than $10,000
or $15,000 a year. Koch believed the key to American Family's success was
serving 200,000 middle-income families—the same ones who had their car,
health, and property insurance with Farmers Mutual.

A Million-dollar Day

The hottest American product in the summer of 1958 was Wham-O's Hula-hoop, selling for $1.98. Within six months, 30 million people were gyrating—most unsuccessfully—to keep the plastic hoop moving around their waists. In the midst of this craze, the American Family Life Insurance Company opened for business. Agents in Wisconsin, Indiana, and the Dakotas began selling American Family policies in June. They turned in their applications before the end of the month so they'd be in the home office by July 1, when the company's charter became effective. As Koch walked toward the office that morning, he hoped American Family Life would have a fraction of Wham-O's success. American Family set the goal high—$1 million the first day. When the numbers were finally tallied, the result was an astounding $1.6 million of life insurance sold—$1.29 million from Wisconsin alone. It was the biggest opening day any life insurance company had ever posted.

By the end of the month, American Family Life Insurance had $3.5 million of life insurance in force covering 780 people. Dennis Streif, an agent in New Glarus, Wisconsin, had the busiest first day, selling $54,700 of life insurance. Joe Sanks of Stevens Point, Wisconsin, had the biggest month, writing $155,000 of life coverage.

American Family Life's first-day sales set the bar high for the six states the company would enter in the following twelve months. Before each opening day, state directors and district managers pointed to Wisconsin's $1.29 million figure. "Are we going to let

June 1950 was Farmers Mutual's first million-dollar month. Casualty premiums alone totaled $1,022,802. Just twelve years earlier, the company had celebrated its first million-dollar year.

Missouri agents more than doubled the opening-day life insurance sales record set by Wisconsin. Pictured are (standing from left): W. G. Lauer, state director Jim Caskey, J. C. Rudloff, Lyle Cummings, Joe Williams, Paul Moosmann, Noel Warren, Russ Seibert, and Bob Mudd; (seated from left): Bob Littrell, Dave Impey, Dick Lowry, Vern Bridwell, and Walt Rottmann.

Milton Mantz (left), an agent in Sussex, Wisconsin, receives the first AFLIC trophy from vice president Bob Koch in January 1960.

Wisconsin beat us?" the state director would shout. "No!" was the resounding response.

As the company's home state, Wisconsin boasted the most agents, the longest experience, and the greatest market penetration, making it almost impossible to beat. But on June 1, 1959, American Family entered Missouri. Known as J. E. to district managers and agents alike, state director Jim Caskey had built a strong, fiercely loyal field force, making the state second only to Wisconsin in production. But J. E., by god, was tired of being second. He leaned hard on his men before the June 1 kickoff, and they weren't about to let him down. When the numbers were tallied, they'd sold a whopping $2.66 million of life insurance. Jack Mainprize, a Kansas City agent, led the field, writing $140,000 of life insurance.

Koch understood the motivational power of recognition and constantly sought new ways to reward the field force for its achievements. To keep agents focused on life insurance year round, he expanded on some district managers' programs to develop the American Family Life Insurance Club in 1959. To qualify, an agent needed to write $250,000 of life insurance in a calendar year. Milton Mantz, an agent in Sussex, Wisconsin, was the first to qualify, exceeding the goal by August 31. While 110 agents qualified for the Leading Career Agents (LCA) convention that year, only eleven made the American Family Life Insurance Club.

Just twelve days after American Family Life Company's phenomenal opening, Bernard Gehrmann died following a heart attack, creating an opening on both the Farmers Mutual and the American Family Life boards. Alex Opgenorth, already secretary on the AFLIC board, filled Gehrmann's seat on the Farmers Mutual board. At Maurer's urging, the life company directors promoted Koch to vice president and named him to succeed Gehrmann on the board. The title didn't change Koch's role. He stayed in the trenches, doing everything from training agents to hauling boxes. In contrast to Maurer, who was unpopular among agents because of the changes he made, Koch spent a great deal of time in the field. Agents responded with a loyalty to the life company that rivaled the fierce allegiance of early agents to Farmers Mutual.

Chapter Four

Long range planning does not deal with future decisions
but with the future of present decisions.

—PETER DRUCKER

TOO MANY PEOPLE, TOO LITTLE SPACE

At some point in their first few days at Farmers Mutual, new employees took the stairs to the second floor to see Herman Wittwer. The prospect of meeting the founder made most a little nervous; having to first pass Edna Shaeffer, Wittwer's executive secretary since 1930, didn't ease their apprehension. Shaeffer was stern and proper, with a husky voice used sparingly. Her straight hair was cropped above the shoulders, her wardrobe dominated by sensible navy blue dresses. Even more frugal than Wittwer, Shaeffer shared with a friend a season ticket to Badger football games. She went to the first half, her friend to the second.

Farmers' Mutual Auto. Ins Co Madison, Wis Sept. 30, 1

An exacting woman, she expected others to do precisely what she asked. If she requested two sheets of paper from the supply department, she meant *two*. Should more be delivered, she'd send back the remainder.

Once inside Wittwer's office, new employees found a pleasant, unassuming man who seemed genuinely interested in who they were and why they'd joined Farmers Mutual. Wittwer took special pleasure in telling them how the company started and emphasized that service was the key to its success.

The home office's commitment to service helped Farmers Mutual and its 2,500 agents do more than $7.5 million of business in 1947, twice its 1945 volume. But providing excellent service became increasingly difficult. The number of employees tripled to more than 200 between 1944 and 1947, forcing some to work in the halls.

An addition behind the Boyd mansion doubled the office space and bought

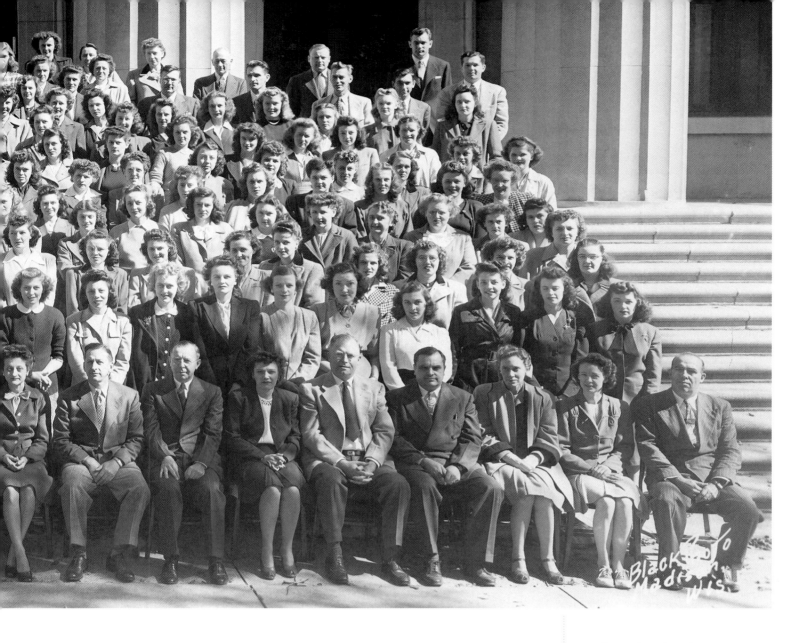

The number of employees at Farmers Mutual tripled between 1944 and 1947. More than 200 employees posed for this 1946 photo.

Farmers Mutual a few more years on Wisconsin Avenue. Although air conditioning was becoming common by 1947, the brick annex didn't include such a luxury. During heat waves, Farmers Mutual ran water from a hose onto the roof to cool the building. Parking was another problem. With no company lot, employees left their cars on the street, where parking was restricted to one hour. Someone always kept an eye out for police officers marking tires. Then everyone poured out of the building and jockeyed their cars around to avoid tickets.

Despite the addition, Farmers Mutual quickly outgrew the Boyd property and by 1950 made plans to move. Economic development divided Madison into two halves separated by the State Capitol. West Madison comprised predominantly white-collar businesses, while east Madison was blue collar. True to Farmers Mutual's roots, Wittwer insisted the company remain in east

An architect (right) from the Chicago firm Childs and Smith shows Bob Kelliher (center) and Harold Frank blueprints for Farmers Mutual's new home office. Above, an artist's sketch provides a glimpse of how the $1.36 million headquarters would appear when completed.

Madison. Later that year, Bob Kelliher, director of office operations, chose an old gravel pit just east of the city limits as the site for the new headquarters.

The nation was in a building boom, and on several occasions material shortages delayed construction at 3099 East Washington Avenue. The cornerstone of the $1.36 million building wasn't laid until August 6, 1951, and Farmers Mutual, which already had sold its current home, had to move by January 1. When employees came in over the Christmas weekend to help move into the unfinished building, they found plywood covering the lobby windows and wires dangling from the uncovered ceiling. For weeks, the 350 employees worked to the rhythm of hammers and saws.

The low-slung building had a classic 1950s appeal that captured the personality of Farmers Mutual. *FM,* the company publication for agents, described it as "conservative and strong, yet modern and efficient without being ornate." Indiana limestone and large thermopane windows gave the building a bright, clean look. As visitors drove up the curved blacktop to the front entrance, they saw a two-story building. But employees who parked in the rear found a third story cut into the hill. Among the building's many modern features were heated pipes set beneath the sidewalk to keep the pavement clear during

Wisconsin's snowy winters, acoustic ceiling tiles, and "non-skid" plastic floors.

Though the new home more than doubled Farmers Mutual's office space, it brought employees closer together by bringing them into the same building. With no restaurants nearby, the home office had its own cafeteria with a staff of eight serving breakfast and lunch. Now, instead of a quick lunch and window shopping downtown, employees ate together, talking and playing cards afterward. A shuffleboard court in the back provided additional entertainment.

Regular bus service went only as far as Schenk's Corners—more than a mile shy of the company's new home. To help Farmers Mutual employees get to and from work, a special bus picked them up at Capitol Square every morning, returning again at 4:15 in the afternoon. This was the beginning of the company's seven-hour-and-forty-minute work day.

In the fall of 1952, Farmers Mutual held an open house. To promote the event, the company purchased a special four-page section in the *Capital Times*. Nearly 5,000 people toured the new building September 20 and 21, and all three local radio stations covered the open house. Two weeks later, during the district managers' convention at the home office, Farmers Mutual celebrated its twenty-fifth anniversary with a giant anniversary–birthday cake replicating the new building. With annual premiums approaching $20 million—twenty times larger than Wittwer dared dream in the spring of 1927—the founder was amazed at his company's success. "We finally have a building we'll never outgrow," he confidently told the district managers.

On August 6, 1951, the Farmers Mutual board of directors hosted a small cornerstone laying ceremony for the company's new headquarters. From left: Herman Wittwer, August Rammer, Irving Maurer, Bernard Gehrmann, Harvey Spriggs, and William Aberg.

Cafeteria chef Paul Goede helped the company celebrate its twenty-fifth anniversary with a birthday-cake replica of the new home office.

In a few years, company quarters were again cramped, walls were knocked out to create more room, managers were forced to share private offices, and the need to decentralize operations became as much an issue of limited space as sound management.

Decentralizing People and Processes

Processing insurance "apps" and claims has always been a labor-intensive job. This was particularly true before the advent of computers, when nearly a third of all Farmers Mutual staff time was spent checking and rechecking facts and

"Red Scare" Taints Mutual Companies

Following World War II, the United States entered a long and bitter Cold War with the Soviet Union. Concerned about espionage, President Harry S. Truman established a temporary Commission on Employee Loyalty in 1946, leading to loyalty boards investigating all federal employees. In January 1950, Sen. Joseph McCarthy, a Republican from Wisconsin, announced that he had the names of 205 Communists working for the State Department, bringing the "Red Scare" to new heights of hysteria. For a thousand days, McCarthy led a campaign of innuendo and incrimination—even charging Gens. George C. Marshall and Dwight D. Eisenhower with aiding the Soviets.

The hysteria spilled over into all facets of life in the United States. Mutual insurance companies, with their

Sen. Joseph McCarthy allowed nothing or no one to be above suspicion. A group of for-profit insurance companies even accused mutual insurance companies of supporting the Communist conspiracy.

American roots stretching back 200 years to Benjamin Franklin, found themselves the unlikely target of anti-Communist propaganda. A handful of for-profit insurance companies formed the National Tax Equity Association, to lobby Congress about rewriting the 1942 federal tax law that exempted small mutual companies from paying federal income tax. To promote its cause, the association launched a smear campaign, suggesting that mutual companies somehow advanced the cause of Communism and Socialism in the United States. Farmers Mutual,

State Historical Society of Wisconsin

which in 1950 paid more than $100,000 in federal taxes, joined other mutuals—large and small—in defending the rights of mutual companies and their members. The mutuals successfully fought changes to the tax code until 1962, when Congress imposed a 52 percent tax on underwriting profits and investment income.

figures that others had typed or manually calculated. Meanwhile, eight employees spent their entire day pulling files and replacing them.

As Farmers Mutual grew, it began to look for ways to improve these processes. In the 1930s and 1940s, the assembly line epitomized efficiency, and service industries looked to manufacturing for ways to improve productivity. In 1941, Kelliher, with the help of a management consultant, organized each department into three regional sections—Wisconsin, Minnesota, and Other. Paperwork passed through the assembly line from department to department in geographic batches—but everyone worked from a single central filing system.

In 1947, Kelliher, Alex Opgenorth, and Howard Hayes took regionalization a step further. Their research showed it was most efficient for single units to serve from 65,000 to 100,000 policies each. On this basis, they organized three geographical service units, each with its own filing system, to handle the flow of paperwork from beginning to end. Wisconsin, under Kelliher, had seventy-six employees; Minnesota, under Hayes, had thirty employees; and Missouri and Other States, under Bill Hoppe, had a staff of thirty-seven. This reorganization shortened lines of communication within the home office and laid the groundwork for further decentralization of the company.

With this strategy in mind, Farmers Mutual designed its new home office to service up to 400,000 policies and planned to build regional offices as the number of policies in an area reached 100,000. To this end, Farmers Mutual established the Northwest Division, comprised of Minnesota, North Dakota, and South Dakota, in early 1951. Two years later, the company announced its

Established in 1951, the Northwest Division of the home office served nearly 100,000 policyholders in Minnesota, North Dakota, and South Dakota.

Farmers Mutual split the Other States Division into the Central and Southwest divisions in 1954. The Central Division included Illinois, Indiana, Iowa, and Kansas, with about 60,000 policies. Southwest, which included Missouri and Nebraska, served roughly 90,000 policyholders.

John "Pete" Miller

A New Generation for a Changing American Family

Pete Miller had already accepted a job selling life insurance for another Madison company in the summer of 1945 when he walked into the Wittwer & Webster Agency to pay his mother's auto insurance premium. After hearing the young man had a law degree, Lod Webster took Miller upstairs to see Alex Opgenorth, Farmers Mutual's claims director. After spending an hour with Opgenorth, Miller agreed to join the company as a claims attorney in northeastern Wisconsin.

The next day, Miller was in the office studying the policies and claim forms. Two days later, he was on a bus to Fond du Lac, Wisconsin, to work with claims attorney Bob Putman. Ten days after that, Putman moved to the home office, and Miller took over.

Born in Marinette in northeastern Wisconsin, on August 10, 1917, John was the youngest of five children. Named after his father, John acquired his nickname from the housekeeper, who insisted on calling him Peter. "I was in high school before I realized my given name was John," Miller once said.

After receiving his law degree from the University of Wisconsin Law School in 1941, Miller served a brief stint with a Chicago-based trust company before joining the army's Counter Intelligence Corps. Assigned to the Manhattan Project, he spent the war in the Southwest, closely watching suspected security risks and foreign agents while scientists developed the atomic bomb.

Miller helped put himself through school by playing poker and pool, and both remained pastimes as he traveled northeastern Wisconsin, adjusting claims and negotiating

President 1968-1977
President and Chairman 1972-1977
Chairman and CEO 1977-1982

John Miller [signature]

settlements for Farmers Mutual. "We used to play cards after a day on the road," recalled Jim Mintz, underwriting director, auto and health lines. "He could follow his cards—and I think my cards—and talk constantly about something else. I could never beat him because I couldn't concentrate like he could."

When the personnel manager's position opened up in 1951, Miller—set on someday heading the claims department—ignored the posting until Herman Wittwer asked him to apply. Miller won the job and returned to Madison to head the personnel department, which consisted of himself and Helen Esser.

A favorite of both Wittwer and Irv Maurer,

Miller chaired the decentralization committee in 1955, shaping the company's regional structure. He also organized the operations department, merging the personnel, methods, and materials divisions into a single unit.

The board of directors named Miller the company's first functional vice president in 1958. He became president of American Standard Insurance Company in 1961 and executive vice president of Farmers Mutual the following year.

Upon Wittwer's death in 1968, Miller advanced to the presidency, four years later he was named chief executive officer of the American Family Insurance Group. When Maurer retired in 1977, Miller became chairman of the board.

As an executive, Miller's hands-off style flattered and frustrated those around him. He believed the men and women working for American Family were capable people who needed little supervision. While the executive staff enjoyed the confidence Miller put in them, at times they wanted more direction.

Miller's keen intellect and personable though somewhat introverted manner made him highly regarded within the industry. While chairman and CEO of American Family, he served on the boards of both the National Association of Independent Insurers and the Health Insurance Association of America in addition to various other positions in industry organizations.

Miller stepped down as chairman of American Family in 1982 but continued to serve on the board of directors and the finance committee until 1987. Fully retired, he now lives in Madison.

Dale Eikenberry   Al Gruenisen   Bill Kleinheinz   Les Ramiker

intent to build a regional office in the Minneapolis/St. Paul area.

Several factors, however, forced Farmers Mutual to table those plans. Years of underwriting losses and the onset of Operation Blue Ink demanded the company's immediate attention, as did controversy surrounding Farmers Mutual's transition to exclusive agent representation.

But senior management remained committed to decentralization, and despite having their hands full with mass dissension in the field force, persistent underwriting losses, and intense competition, the harried executive staff continued planning for decentralization. In 1955, at Maurer's urging, the board got behind the effort, appointing personnel director Pete Miller to chair a decentralization committee comprised of Hayes, Kelliher, Kinnamon, and John Farnsworth. Working with a consultant who helped State Farm and Nationwide decentralize their operations, the committee spent nearly two years developing a regionalized management structure for Farmers Mutual.

The first step, in February 1957, was to organize an operations division by merging the personnel, methods, and materials divisions, improving decision-making and implementation. This new division, under Miller, became the "line," implementing policies and procedures developed by the executive staff. Previously, the executive staff—the comptroller and the directors of the agency, claims, personnel, and underwriting divisions—had been responsible for doing the work they planned and programmed, blurring the lines between staff (policy making) and line (implementing) operations.

Later that year, Farmers Mutual decentralized the operation division into four regions, each with a regional manager reporting to Miller. Regional managers oversaw distinct staffs that included personnel, agency, claims, underwriting, sales, and services. The Central Region, under sales promotions manager Bill Kleinheinz, included Illinois, Indiana, and Iowa. The Northwest Region,

An Eagleville, Missouri, agent named V. J. McWhinney earned fifty dollars by suggesting the headquarters in St. Joseph be named the Midland regional office. "It describes the location now, and also later if more states should be added, since St. Joseph is near the center of the United States," McWhinney explained.

Groundbreaking for Farmers Mutual's regional office captured the attention of the St. Joseph, Missouri, media. Ten radio and television broadcasts carried the groundbreaking story, and the St. Joseph Gazette carried this photo in its November 15, 1957, issue. Those with shovels are (from left to right): state directors Darwin Liljegren, Kansas, and J.E. Caskey, Missouri; St. Joseph agent Walter West; contractor Andrew Glaze; St. Joseph district manager J. C. Rudloff; and Nebraska state director A. J. Egan.

headed by underwriting manager Les Ramiker, included Minnesota and North and South Dakota. The Midland Region, under Dale Eikenberry, manager of the Kansas City claims office, comprised Kansas, Missouri, and Nebraska. Wisconsin became its own region under Al Gruenisen, the Milwaukee branch claims manager.

Meet Me in St. Joseph

Though largely autonomous, the four regions remained headquartered in the home office. But with Farmers Mutual now serving more than half a million policyholders, employees were again working in the halls, increasing the need for at least one regional office.

With Minnesota devastated by the mass resignation of agents and managers, the decentralization committee bypassed the Northwest Region, choosing instead the rapidly growing Midland Region. The committee selected St. Joseph, a thriving, industrial community in northwestern Missouri, as the site for the first regional headquarters. Centrally located in the Midland Region, St. Joseph offered a strong labor market, good schools, and excellent transportation. Because Farmers Mutual already had a claims office in town, St. Joseph city officials wanted the regional office in their community and sold the company five acres of land overlooking the Moila Golf Course for five dollars. On November 14, 1956, Farmers Mutual broke ground at 3131 Frederick Avenue.

Although twenty home office staff members would move to the new regional center, with other employees transferring from claims offices in Kansas City and St. Louis, most of the more than 100 employees would come from St. Joseph. On October 6, 1957, seven women—the first clerical supervisors for the Midland regional office—boarded a train bound for Madison. "It was an overnight train ride," Phyllis Benitz, Midland clerical supervisor, later recalled. "We didn't know each other, any of us, but we formed some great friendships."

Don Breitenbach and Virginia Wiggen met them at the Madison train depot the next morning for a tour of Farmers Mutual. "We were quite a spectacle. Everybody wanted to see

The arrival of the RAMAC 305 caught employees' attention in 1959. Pictured with the computer are (from left) Evelyn Peterson, Maybelle Seery, Lucy Ashwill, Marian Longfield, and Jennnie Lewis.

Modern Computing—the Old-Fashioned Way

As late as 1958, Farmers Mutual employees spent nearly a third of their time checking and rechecking facts and figures that others had typed and manually calculated. This labor intensity forced the company—and other insurers—to hire additional staff as business grew.

But on August 3, 1959, Farmers Mutual helped lead the insurance industry into the Information Age, becoming one of the first insurers to use an IBM computer. Installed initially in the Wisconsin Region, RAMAC (Random Access Method of Accounting and Control) was a room-size mass of wires, tubes, keyboards, card punches, flashing lights, and whirling "magnetic memory disks."

Director of systems and procedures Bob Kelliher, who had ushered the first generation of International Business Machines into Farmers Mutual in 1942, was responsible for leasing the computer at an estimated annual cost of $250,000. Data resources administrator

George Riege and his assistant Bill Henry handled the system design and programming—which involved hardwiring the boards.

RAMAC was intended to improve the efficiency of processing applications and renewal notices. The computer could handle a week's worth of apps and 1,000 renewal notices in two-and-one-half hours, compared to forty hours of manual work. There were, of course, glitches—a misplaced decimal point resulted in one policyholder receiving a premium notice for $3,452, rather than $34.52—and Riege and his staff frequently endured ninety-hour work weeks.

Farmers Mutual found useful the vast amount of data stored on the memory disks, which resembled records in a jukebox. Each disk held five to 10 million characters, making it far

easier to store and manipulate data than with the old punch cards. "Faster information processing was available," Riege recalled in a 1977 interview, "provided a tube didn't blow, the information-seeking arm didn't touch a disk and clear the whole darn track, and none of the records just somehow disappeared."

Just about the time Farmers Mutual got most of the bugs worked out of RAMAC—and Riege and his staff were catching up on their sleep—IBM unveiled the 1400 series, which used magnetic tape to store information.

Seven St. Joseph, Missouri, women step off the train in Madison, where they'll spend a cold Wisconsin winter training to be clerical supervisors in the Midland regional office. Pictured with Virginia Wiggen (right foreground) of the home office's Midland unit are: (from left to right) Rita Bender, Phyllis Benitz, Carole Harvey, Darlene Hahn, Patricia York, Mary Coil, and Esther Gasper.

who these people were from Midland," Benitz recalled. "They thought we had terrible southern accents. But they were very nice."

The company rented two apartments for the trainees, who stayed in Madison until May—with a single trip home for Christmas. Over the course of the winter, more than forty St. Joseph women joined them for training before returning to work at the new regional center.

In May 1958, a skeleton crew left for St. Joseph to get the office ready for operation. Heavy rains greeted them and soaked the torn-up ground around the new $700,000 building. The road, the parking lot, and trucks filled with office equipment were mired in muck. The sidewalks had not yet been laid, and temporary wooden sidewalks helped employees get into the building, an island in a sea of mud. This was the first of several floods at the new site.

Setting up a brand new office for more than 100 people and organizing the files for 150,000 policies was an arduous task. Not until mid-August was the St. Joseph facility ready to begin serving 400 agents and 26 district managers in Missouri, Kansas, and Nebraska.

Centrally located in the Midland Region, St. Joseph made an ideal site for the regional office.

Nebraska

Omaha •

Lincoln •

St. Joseph
⊙
• Kansas City

Topeka •

Kansas

St. Louis •

Missouri

Wichita •

Changes at the Top

In the late 1950s, Maurer initiated several steps to bring Farmers Mutual's organizational structure up to date. Although Harvey Spriggs was named Resident vice president in 1953, Farmers Mutual did not have functional vice presidents (division directors constituted senior management). In 1958, however, the board approved the creation of vice presidential positions when "time, circumstances, and affected personnel performances warrant." They then named Pete Miller vice president of operations—making him heir apparent to the presidency. Shortly thereafter, the board named Hayes, Kinnamon, and Amory Moore vice presidents of underwriting, agency, and claims.

Active in the National Association of Independent Insurers and other industry groups where his peers were presidents and chairmen, Maurer had always disliked his title of treasurer. In 1959, he convinced the directors to modernize Farmers Mutual's board structure. Wittwer, who'd carried the title secretary, became chairman of the board, Rammer vice chair, and Maurer president. Alex Opgenorth became secretary, and comptroller Henry Harvey joined the board as treasurer.

In 1960, the Farmers Mutual Automobile Insurance Company dissolved its management agreement with Farmers Mutual Managers, Inc., buying the company for $10,000. The managers, Irving Maurer (left), Herman Wittwer (center), and August Rammer, each received ten-year deferred compensation packages that began after they retired from Farmers Mutual.

To improve its responsiveness, the board created an executive committee—including Wittwer, Maurer, Opgenorth, and Bill Aberg—empowered to act on its behalf between quarterly meetings.

Maurer also disliked Farmers Mutual Managers, the management company he once fought to join. The main reason for his disdain was that regulators in some states distrusted mutual insurance companies with management contracts and refused to issue them licenses. Although Farmers Mutual Managers had waived tens of thousands of dollars in fees almost every year since its

Death of a Legend

All organizations have their legends, stories told again and again until people who weren't there claim to remember the moment distinctly, and events that never happened become gospel truth. One such tale in the history of American Family Insurance surrounds the death of August Rammer, the company's president from 1927 to 1960. As the story goes, when the board met after Augie's death, a great debate ensued as to what tribute should be placed in the minutes. Finally, Harvey Spriggs, the sheep farmer from Racine with a wit dry as wool, leaned forward on his cane and said, "How about this: The first of September was the last of August."

The story could not be true. August Rammer passed away October 14, 1960, nearly a year after Harvey Spriggs's death. And so it goes.

inception, this prejudice remained—limiting Maurer's plans for a national company. "We were all dressed up with nowhere to go," he commented.

From the outset, Farmers Mutual Managers hired the employees and paid all the operating expenses, for which it received a percentage of the premiums. Over the years, Maurer convinced Wittwer and Rammer to shift increasing responsibility from Farmers Mutual Managers to the Farmers Mutual Automobile Insurance Company. At the same time, the management company reduced the percentage of premium income it received—from 42 percent in the 1940s to 17.5 percent in 1956.

Finally, in 1960, Maurer succeeded in severing the management agreement altogether. He proposed ten-year deferred compensation packages for the managers—Wittwer, Rammer, and himself—providing Wittwer and Rammer with the income security they wanted while freeing the insurance company of its management contract. Under the agreement, Farmers Mutual bought out the management company for $10,000 plus the deferred compensation. Farmers Mutual changed the management company's name to Webb, Inc. after the avenue that ran behind the office. Webb, Inc. lay dormant until the late-1960s, when it was resurrected as American Family Financial Services, Inc.

The passing of time also changed the composition of Farmers Mutual's leadership. On July 12, 1958, while sitting on his front porch, Bernard Gehrmann, the old Progressive, died of a heart attack at age seventy-eight. A year later, Harvey Spriggs—at ninety he still pinched "the girls" and told off-color jokes when he visited the office—died, as did August Rammer in the fall of 1960.

The board eulogized all three men at length, noting their contributions not only to Farmers Mutual but also to farmers in general and the community at large. Their passing marked the beginning of a new era for Farmers Mutual. With new leaders like Miller stepping in, the company began making moves toward becoming an industry leader able to meet all the insurance needs of American families.

ADVERTISING THE AMERICAN FAMILY

Dale Mathwich turned up the radio of his '56 Ford and sang along with Hank Williams as he drove into New London. Mathwich wasn't like other young men. He liked country-western more than the new rock 'n' roll, and at twenty-two, had already been a bank manager and part-time insurance agent. Now, in October 1956, he was moving to the small Wisconsin community to become one of Farmers Mutual's first "career agents."

The previous Farmers Mutual agent in New London was a farmer who sold insurance on the side. He had about 150 pol-icyholders—mostly friends, relatives, neighbors—among the town's 5,000 residents. Like most Farmers Mutual agents, the farmer hadn't advertised. So, apart from the 150 accounts he was taking over, Mathwich essentially was starting from scratch.

Raised a Lutheran, Mathwich made the largest Lutheran church his first stop in New London. After introducing himself, Mathwich asked the minister whether he knew anyone who rented rooms. The pastor referred him to Molly Pribbenow, a widow whose bungalow had a bedroom on the first floor and two small, empty rooms upstairs. Pribbenow rented him both second-story rooms—one for a bedroom, the other for an office—and agreed to let him use her phone for business. "I'd answer the phone, 'Farmers Mutual Insurance, Dale Mathwich,' and it might be the next door neighbor calling to see if Molly wanted to have tea," Mathwich recalled.

Mathwich's district manager, Frank Feivor, was a strong proponent of agent advertising. Under Feivor's guidance, Mathwich bought two four-foot-by-eight-foot signs from the company, then he convinced two people living at either end of town to allow him to put up his signs. That afternoon, he dug the post holes himself and hung the signs so that everyone entering New London knew he was the Farmers Mutual agent. To this, Mathwich added an advertisement in the local newspaper and a daily regimen of mailing ten prospecting letters, which he followed up two days later with ten phone calls. He put an ad in the phone book, a sign on his car, and used every Farmers Mutual promotional aid at his disposal. But building his business was still a matter of knocking on doors in the small town where everyone was a native and newcomers were not readily accepted. When he came home at night, tired and sometimes discouraged, Molly Pribbenow invited him to watch television with her—maybe *I Love Lucy* or Groucho Marx's *You Bet Your Life*. He'd relax for an hour or so in front of the old black-and-white set before turning in for the night.

Mathwich's experience wasn't unusual. Not until 1949 did the home office provide ad slicks for agents to place in local newspapers—at their own expense—and more recently radio copy. Trouble was, nineteen of twenty Farmers Mutual agents still worked part time and didn't consider advertising worth the expense. As a result, many Wisconsin residents hadn't heard of the thirty-year-old company—or they confused it with other farm organizations.

A firm believer in the value of hard work and advertising, Farmers Mutual agent Dale Mathwich put up a pair of four-foot-by-eight-foot road signs himself, one on each end of New London, Wisconsin. Every day, he mailed ten prospecting letters, which he followed up two days later with a phone call.

Advertising Averse

From the outset, Farmers Mutual, preferring promotional items and old-fashioned prospecting, did little traditional advertising. The company's 1927 financial statement shows no separate line-item for advertising. Policyholders at the annual meeting in January 1928 approved the design of a radiator emblem for advertising purposes. That year, Farmers Mutual spent a whopping $665.17 on advertising, much of it on radiator emblems for its 4,500 policyholders. The following year, the advertising budget nose-dived to $53.

A few pioneering agents placed ads in local newspapers. Written by men not well versed in the laws applying to insurance advertising, these ads occasionally drew complaints to the commissioner of insurance about misleading statements or inaccurate claims. To avoid fines and even the revocation of its license, Farmers Mutual insisted that all advertising bearing the company name be cleared through the home office.

In the early 1930s, Lod Webster, agency director for a brief period, convinced Wittwer and Kalbskopf to sponsor a morning news show on WIBA, a Madison radio station. A WIBA employee with no advertising experience wrote the copy, featuring the catch phrase, "Insurance that really insures." When underwriting manager Irving Maurer complained about the quality of the radio spots, Wittwer gave him the job. For an extra twenty-five dollars a month, Maurer wrote daily radio spots—often resembling dissertations more than commercials.

In addition to the WIBA radio spots, Farmers Mutual ran ads in the *Wisconsin Agriculturist*, the state's largest farm publication, and conducted a

This metal radiator emblem (top) and penny postcard (center) stand among Farmers Mutual's earliest advertising efforts. The 1940s-era coaster (bottom) advertises Gerald Woelffer as the man to see about low-cost auto insurance in Baraboo, Wisconsin.

In 1949, Farmers Mutual began offering its 3,200 agents ready-made advertising mats to place—at their own expense—in local newspapers. But with 90 percent of the agents selling part time, few found the cost of advertising worth the investment. Others found that pooling their money made advertising more affordable. The earliest record of this "cooperative" approach to advertising is found in the June 1952 issue of *FM*. The newsletter reported that district supervisor Spencer Burke worked with sixteen agents in the Eau Claire, Wisconsin, area to share the cost of advertising in the *Eau Claire Telegram*.

Bill Kleinheinz

After complaining about the quality of Farmers Mutual radio spots on WIBA—Madison, underwriting manager Irving Maurer took on the task of writing the company's radio commercials.

few direct-mail campaigns. In 1938, the company introduced *Farmers Mutual News*, becoming one of the first insurance companies to send promotional material along with renewal notices.

After the war, competition in the rapidly growing auto insurance market convinced Wittwer and Maurer to step up promotions and develop closer ties with the field force. Looking for talent within the home office, they tapped underwriter Bill Kleinheinz. Ineligible for the military because of a bad knee, Kleinheinz joined Farmers Mutual after graduating from the University of Wisconsin in 1943. The war created a shortage of reporters, and Kleinheinz moonlighted as a sports writer, covering high school games for the *Wisconsin State Journal*. That was enough experience to qualify him as Farmers Mutual's first advertising supervisor.

Kleinheinz's position fell under the agency department and its new director, Gus Kinnamon. Starting his career with General Motors' insurance division, Kinnamon joined Farmers Mutual's claims division in 1941. He transferred to agency a couple years later and advanced to director in 1947. The division handled advertising and promotions, managed the appointment and termination of local and district agents, administered nearly 3,000 agent accounts, and produced weekly production reports. Lacking sales experience, Kinnamon occasionally seemed out of place in his role. But friendly and agreeable, he

related well to the agents and gave those who worked in the division a free hand. If a program worked, Kinnamon made sure the person who initiated it received the credit; if it failed Kinnamon willingly took the blame. It was a style that worked well, given the talent that flourished in the division over the next quarter century.

Kleinheinz was one such talent. To bring the agency force closer together, in 1949 he introduced *FM*, a monthly agents' publication providing information about the field force, the home office, and the industry. He also encouraged agents, most of whom worked out of their homes, to promote themselves—and Farmers Mutual—more aggressively, primarily through the production of camera-ready advertising mats and spot radio announcements for agents to use at their own expense. Some agents found that county fair booths drummed up business, and in 1952 Kleinheinz constructed four Farmers Mutual display boards for agents to reserve for county fairs.

Kleinheinz also accelerated Farmers Mutual's use of specialty gifts beyond key chains and key cases. In 1947, he introduced the Farmers Mutual calendar blotter. In three years, agents ordered more than 600,000 desk blotters at 22 cents a piece. In 1950, Kleinheinz introduced the "ad-tip" pencil at 3 cents each, and two years later ball-points, two for a quarter. He put the company emblem on ice scrapers, policy wallets, rulers, letter openers, calendars, clocks, thermometers, savings banks—and tape from the Topflight Tape Company. Each roll contained 1,300 company emblems and agent imprints. Initially, only the Farmers Mutual name appeared on many of these items. But as modern manufacturing techniques brought production costs down, Kleinheinz made it company policy to list the agent and company name whenever possible—and to share the cost.

One of the most successful and enduring promotional items was the *Rand McNally Road Atlas*. Beginning in 1948, agents could purchase the atlas, which retailed for $1.25, for 35 cents apiece. In 1953, Farmers Mutual had its own atlas cover printed in orange and black. Two years later, Kleinheinz commissioned a Native American artist in northern Wisconsin to paint a northern woods scene for the cover. For the next 10 years, motorists associated Farmers

Kenosha County agents Ed Tobias (right) and Dick Nachreiner (center), and district manager Paul Miller drum up business with a booth at the Kenosha County Fair, circa 1960.

Bob Salisbury

Mutual with the beautiful four-color rendition of a deer and her fawn by a wooded lake.

Kleinheinz's job grew with the company, and in 1956 a consultant working with Farmers Mutual on its decentralization plan recommended dividing his position into three jobs—advertising, sales promotion, and public relations. Kleinheinz assumed the public relations role, including publications, and hired Fran Hanson as *FM* editor.

Bob Salisbury, another underwriter, filled the advertising post. Salisbury had worked in Washington, D.C., for the top-secret National Security Agency during the Korean conflict, joining Farmers Mutual in 1953. As advertising supervisor, he directed the production and distribution of direct-mail letters, newspaper ads, circulars, and other sales aids available to agents.

Agency department secretary Charlie Ambrosavage became Farmers Mutual's sales promotions manager. An Air Force veteran who served in Africa and Italy during World War II, Ambrosavage joined the company in 1948. He'd worked closely with Kleinheinz on sales promotion material, and he served as *FM* editor for several years. As agency secretary, Ambrosavage took on special projects related to Farmers Mutual's transition to exclusive agency. Among them, the advance compensation plan, the agent-company agreements, and the agents' hospitalization plan.

Advertising Partners

Traditionally managed by conservative men who'd come up through the legal or underwriting ranks, most insurance companies were averse to advertising. "Insurance executives are bottom-line people," Salisbury explained. "It's hard for them to see the role that advertising plays in the sale of insurance."

Beginning in 1959, Farmers Mutual shared 50 percent of the cost of highway signs with its exclusive agents.

Under the leadership of Wittwer and Maurer, Farmers Mutual was among the most conservative of advertisers. With earned premiums exceeding $17 million in 1954, Farmers Mutual was the eighth largest mutual automobile insurance company in the nation. But its advertising budget amounted to a mere $65,000.

Maurer, possibly more than Wittwer, believed in the value of advertising—but considered it the agents' job. "We are the wholesaler. The agents are the retailers," he pronounced. "It is the retailer's responsibility to advertise."

But with most agents representing multiple companies, few agents placed a high priority on Farmers Mutual advertising, dampening attempts to build a company image. The conversion to exclusive agency made the situation worse for the short term. In 1950, the company had more than 3,200 agents. Within eight years, that figure fell to 1,647, cutting in half the number of agents who might place a Farmers Mutual ad in local newspapers.

To boost customer awareness and provide additional benefits to full-time career agents, Ambrosavage and Salisbury developed a cooperative advertising program meant to share with qualified agents the cost of advertising. Beginning in June 1959, the home office paid 50 percent of the cost of highway signs and 25 percent of the cost of newspaper, radio, and television advertising.

The following year, Ambrosavage presented Kinnamon with a detailed study comparing Farmers Mutual's advertising budget and growth trends to those of its main competitors—State Farm and Allstate. Both companies were much larger than Farmers Mutual and naturally had larger advertising budgets. But from 1954 to 1958 State Farm's advertising expenditures totaled 1.01 percent of premiums and Allstate's 1.47 percent, compared with just .49 percent for Farmers Mutual. In the same period, State Farm and Allstate each grew more than 80 percent, Farmers Mutual just 4.8 percent.

Improved printing processes enabled agents to personalize Farmers Mutual safety flares, matchbooks, and other promotional items by adding their own name and address.

Stunned by the numbers, Wittwer and Maurer quickly approved Ambrosavage's proposal for a $100,000 advertising campaign—more than the company had spent the previous year on all its promotions.

Serving the Everyday Needs of American Families

Throughout the 1950s, company leaders began to realize Farmers Mutual's name no longer reflected the company itself. By 1960, city dwellers outnumbered farmers two to one among the company's 600,000 policyholders. Recognizing that Farmers Mutual had grown far beyond auto insurance, the company adopted the slogan, "Protection for the everyday insurance needs of the individual and the family." The life insurance subsidiary also adopted the name American Family Life, creating some awkwardness in advertising and a fuzzy image in the eyes of the public.

In December 1959, Amory Moore, vice president of claims, drafted a memo recommending that the company change its name to American Family Mutual Insurance Company. Maurer presented Moore's recommendation to the board in February. Wittwer and Aberg spoke against it, arguing that the company was at heart a farm organization.

"When you look at who we serve today," Maurer argued, "American Family is the more appropriate name." Maurer's reasoning was sound, but Wittwer still controlled the board. Without a consensus on the name change, the directors decided a change was premature. Grudgingly, however, Wittwer allowed the staff to research a new name—beginning with the field force which, after all, directly represented the company. The following month, the agency department surveyed the field.

Of 900 responses, 532 agents and 61 district managers favored changing the name, while 291 agents and just 7 district managers opposed it. "Even in Wisconsin, where we were strongest, the agents were for the name change," Ambrosavage recalled.

The next question was how the public would react. A research firm conducted opinion polls in Wisconsin, Missouri, Nebraska, and Minnesota to determine how well Farmers Mutual was known and how people felt about the name American Family Insurance. The polls showed that although

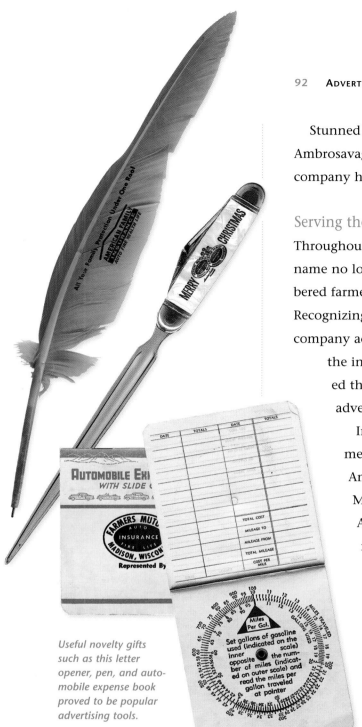

Useful novelty gifts such as this letter opener, pen, and automobile expense book proved to be popular advertising tools.

Farmers Mutual was widely known in Wisconsin, people in other states weren't as familiar with it, often confusing Farmers Mutual with other agricultural organizations. "The images the people had of a company called Farmers Mutual ranged from a strong national company to a bunch of farmers passing the hat to pay claims," the researchers reported. Respondents, however, liked the name American Family Insurance, preferring it over such names as Allstate, Nationwide, Prudential, and State Farm.

Wittwer eventually dropped his opposition, and the issue again came before the board on August 11, 1961. After some debate, Maurer, Jim Caskey, Pete Miller, Alex Opgenorth, and Walter Renk voted to rename the company American Family Mutual Insurance Company. Wittwer abstained, saying he did not oppose the change but preferred not to support it. Aberg remained adamant, voting against the new name. Policyholders approved the name change on March 6, 1962. But formal adoption would wait until the next policyholders' meeting in March of the following year.

Changing the organization's name was a Herculean task dominated by details. One of the most critical was a new logo. To test the effectiveness of the company's present logo, Salisbury scrambled the letters and took it to Madison's Capitol Square. Three out of four people couldn't name the company or what it sold. Ambrosavage conducted the same experiment in four Wisconsin communities within an hour's drive of Madison. Only one in five recognized it. Clearly, changing the logo had little down side.

Farmers Mutual invited advertising agencies, design firms, artists, and others to submit ideas for a new logo. In the meantime, Ambrosavage and Salisbury asked Naegle Outdoor Advertising Company, which handled Farmers Mutual's signs, to design a large sign for the home office to acquaint people with the American Family name. Many employees complained that such a sign would be undignified. But with 20,000 cars passing daily, it was an easy, low-cost way to familiarize Madisonians—and thousands of others traveling to the Capitol—with the new company name.

Naegle presented a basic red-white-and-blue logo. A simple roofline symbolized home and protection, with the company name beneath it. "This would be a great logo," Ambrosavage said after considering it for several minutes. "Absolutely."

"It says it all," Salisbury agreed.

An American Icon

"The trademark we suggest is a shape symbolizing the home. The home suggests security. The off-center design attracts attention and suggests the modern comfort of a contemporary home, rather than the static, symmetrical cold feeling of an institution.

The roofline with its sharp, red angles and diagonal lines is an exciting key to the design, suggesting a protective barrier to the elements of the outside world. We were careful not to make it too heavy as to be crushing, nor too light as to be flimsy.

The word insurance is rightfully at the base of the design, as a foundation of the home. The colors red, white, and blue point up the word American.

We strove for simplicity; to say as much as possible in a few lines. When a design gets complicated, the reader's eyes skip over the minor elements and remembrance quotient drops."

—The Naegle Outdoor
   Advertising Company

Maurer was less impressed. He approved the sign only as a provisional logo. "I think any official stamp of approval on a company emblem might better come from board action, and had better await more inspirational research," he wrote in a later memo. The board, however, loved the design and approved it as the company's logo before construction of the home-office sign began.

Naegle bolted on the last panel of the giant red-white-and-blue sign on October 3, 1962—the company's 35th anniversary. Construction cost $11,000, but Naegle didn't charge American Family for the logo design. The 70-foot-long, 20-foot-high sign was the largest in the city. Easily visible in the day and brightly lit at night, the American Family logo became a friend to airplane pilots, who used it as a reference when landing on the airport's north-south runway. Full-page ads in the *Capital Times* and the *Wisconsin State Journal* heightened the sign's impact. "It really put us on the map," Salisbury recalled later.

An Old Friend with a New Name

Changing the company's name presented a once-in-a-lifetime promotional opportunity. To broaden the public's interest in the name change and present the image of a successful, regional organization, Ambrosavage and Salisbury proposed advertising in regional editions of a few leading national magazines. Working with a Madison advertising agency, Shumway and Carman, they created the "Take a closer

look" campaign emphasizing Farmers Mutual/American Family's protection for the entire family. The campaign opened in February 1962 with a full-page ad in *The Saturday Evening Post*, followed by ads in *LOOK* and *LIFE* magazines in March and April. Each ad cost more than $8,000, but combined, the three publications reached 52 percent of the households in the ten-state sales territory.

To tie local agents to the national ads, the home office provided duplicate ads for placement in local papers as well as reprints for direct mailings. Also that month, the company sponsored a special cooperative advertising campaign, sharing 50 percent of the cost of agent advertising with a seventy-five-dollar limit.

On March 5, 1963, policyholders voted to adopt the new name, making it official. Within a year of the change, American Family had built strong and widespread name recognition through its overall advertising campaign combined with agent co-op advertising. Ambrosavage and Salisbury were concerned that those gains would be lost, however, if agents suddenly reduced their advertising. "It takes a long time to build advertising awareness," Salisbury explained. "But when you stop advertising, awareness drops precipitously, and you have to start all over again. It's a steady drop of rain that soaks through the soil."

Ambrosavage had this philosophy firmly in mind as he put together his 1964 budget. He struggled with the problem of how to keep agents advertising, finally settling on an approach he called "Push All Lines" (PAL). Since 1959, the company had shared 25 percent of the cost of agent advertising, up to a certain amount—increasing to 50 percent for special promotions. Under the PAL program, Ambrosavage proposed four special three-month promotions a year, each

focusing on the company's different lines—fire insurance in winter, auto in spring, sickness and accident in summer, and life in the fall.

After looking over the proposal—and its increased costs—Kinnamon peered up at Ambrosavage. "Charlie, if you do this, we'll have a fifty-fifty program all year."

"Well, yeah," Ambrosavage began, expecting rejection. But Kinnamon, trusting Ambrosavage's instincts, let it go at that.

Pushing an idea such as PAL through the home office was only half the job. The agents also had to be sold, since the responsibility for local advertising remained in their hands. In the fall of 1964, Ambrosavage and Salisbury took to the road, introducing the PAL program at a series of special workshops. Mild-mannered, with a receding hairline and heavy glasses, Ambrosavage seemed an unlikely promoter. But in front of a group he became an off-the-wall evangelist with a penchant for jokes and double entendres that made the agents howl. To get the agents involved, he followed every other statement with an enthusiastic "Right?" Quickly he became known as "Mr. Right."

"You notice the signs on the walls with the phrase Push All Lines?" he asked agents in one meeting after another in late 1964. "That's what we always want to do—Push All Lines. Right?"

"Right!" the agents echoed.

"Well, we came up with a program to do this, and what do you think we're going to call this program?"

"Push All Lines!"

"You're right—the Push All Lines program. And what's the objective of this program?"

"To push all lines," the revved-up agents yelled.

"You're right again—to push all lines. The whole idea is brilliantly conceived—Right?"

"Right!" the agents roared.

The agents loved Ambrosavage, and they loved his PAL. Besides increasing agent advertising, it provided a theme around which to organize quarterly meetings and gave the company a yearly opportunity to update agents on changes in each of the major lines and provide them with new or updated promotional material.

Turn on the Tube

Television was introduced in the mid-1940s, and Americans were quick to tune in. In 1947, there were 10,000 television sets sprinkled across the United States—offering just a few hours of programming each day. A decade later, American families spent an average of six hours a day in front of 40 million black-and-whites, making it a powerful vehicle for advertising. But it wasn't until the spring of 1963 that two North Dakota agents—Maurice Allshouse and John Soli, both under district manager Wayne Wadeson—led American Family onto the airwaves. The two pooled their co-op advertising money for American Family's "vacation special" campaign to sponsor five evenings of a local 10:20 p.m. newscast.

The idea clicked with Salisbury and Ambrosavage, who promoted it to district managers across the ten states. Most were skeptical, but with the home office increasing its share of agent advertising to 50 percent, more managers and agents found their way onto television. In January 1964, a second North Dakota manager, Henry McKay, convinced his ten agents to pitch in five dollars a month to sponsor the evening sports report once a week.

In April, *The All American*, the agent newsletter, reported that district managers Al Henning in North Dakota, Joe Dittmer and Walt Rottmann in Missouri, Fran Thomson and Frank Feivor in Wisconsin, and Dale Mathwich in Illinois were developing TV advertising programs.

Pioneers in TV Advertising

District managers Frank Feivor and Fran Thomson were among the first American Family managers to pool their agents' co-op advertising money to advertise on television. In the fall of 1964, the two districts sponsored the "Team of the Week" segment on the Green Bay sportscast. Each week, a committee of sports experts chose the best team that week from among the ninety high school football teams in the viewing area. On the Wednesday night broadcast, an American Family agent presented the winning coach and captain with a football autographed by the Green Bay Packers. "Agents are finding that they are 'TV stars' and enjoy being recognized wherever they go," *The All American* reported.

Following up on the success of a collective radio advertising program, district manager Wally Huebsch and state director Joe Stephan convinced agents in Minneapolis and St. Paul to sponsor three one-minute commercials every week on the popular Mel Jass *Evening Movie*. Jass, a colorful television personality, "talked" the American Family commercials directly to his 72,000 viewers, giving the ads a warm, friendly appeal.

East Wisconsin Agents at Sales Promotion Workshop

In the winter of 1964-65, Charlie Ambrosavage (above right) and Bob Salisbury introduced the cooperative television advertising program at a series of special meetings with American Family's 1,700 agents.

Advertising manager Bob Salisbury and promotions director Charlie Ambrosavage were always careful to point out that advertising—whether it was on television or in some other medium—didn't sell insurance. But name recognition and the public's awareness of the company helped open the door. When agents questioned the value of advertising, Salisbury replied, "Tell you what. You go out next week and start prospecting for the Salisbury Insurance Company. See how many appointments you get."

As they set up their programs, these and other district managers naturally looked to Madison for the commercials. But Salisbury didn't have any yet. With the help of Shumway and Carman, he quickly developed advertising slides and copy for local announcers. These ran a week or two before district managers called to ask for new ones. In December 1964, Shumway and Carman produced a series of commercials at Madison's WKOW-TV to promote AmPlan, American Family's new monthly payment plan.

Each of the television stations sent their bills to Salisbury. After paying them, he divvied up the charges between the company and the agents, charging each agent's share to his account. But as more agents advertised on television, this decentralized approach proved unwieldy. It also exposed poor advertising choices by some agents and managers. "One guy was buying time on *Romper Room*!" Ambrosavage recalled. "Why? Because he could afford it."

By the autumn of 1964, Salisbury and Ambrosavage knew they needed a different approach. Minnesota state director Joe Stephan, excited by Wally Huebsch's success at pooling his agents' money for radio advertising, convinced five district managers and sixty agents in the Minneapolis/St. Paul area to join a cooperative radio advertising program—and he was looking into television. With that in mind, Salisbury and Ambrosavage considered a company-wide television advertising program.

About that time, the Mathisson Advertising Agency, a highly regarded

Milwaukee firm that handled the Miller Brewing Company's promotions, approached Salisbury about American Family's print advertising. Salisbury and Ambrosavage told Mathisson they were more interested in television. After explaining that senior management would be wary of an expensive program run by the home office and that the district managers, many of whom enjoyed the prestige of working with local television stations, might resist, Ambrosavage asked the ad agency to make a proposal. "I can't pay you for any work up front," he said. "But if the program goes through, you'll be our agency."

Mathisson accepted the challenge and put together a presentation for the executive staff. American Family, through Mathisson, would produce the commercials and contract with television stations across the ten states. The preferred time slot was the local, late evening news—when people were in the mood to be informed. If that wasn't available, time slots immediately after the news or during the popular *Tonight Show* were the second and third choices. To make the plan affordable, the company needed at least 700 agents chipping in twenty-five dollars a month, with American Family matching the agents' contributions.

American Family's executive staff agreed to support the program—provided Ambrosavage and Salisbury convinced enough agents to participate. That would be difficult. In 1964, American Family had 1,700 field representatives. But full-time career agents—those most likely to participate—numbered fewer than 500.

So in the fall of 1964 and the winter of 1965, Salisbury and Ambrosavage again hit the road to sell the agents on a cooperative TV advertising program. And again Charlie "Mr. Right" Ambrosavage carried the ball. "Greetings. It's a pleasure to have you see me again—right?" he began. "Bob Salisbury and I make a great team—right? You and I make a great team—right? You and your managers make a great team—right? You and regional VP Dale Eikenberry make a great team—right? You and Herman Wittwer make a great team— right? Working together—pooling our talents and resources—that's the secret to our success—right?"

As Salisbury had predicted, some district managers resented the home office takeover. Some agents didn't like the proposed time-slots. But by the time the two men returned to Madison, nearly 800 agents had signed on to the TV advertising program, providing—with the company's contribution—nearly

Bob Salisbury (left) and Charlie Ambrosavage take a last-minute look at the script for a new television commercial.

Harvey Pierce, then a district manager in Windom, Minnesota, supported co-op advertising. But with eighteen independent agents still serving multiple companies, he dreaded the meeting about co-op television advertising. After Ambrosavage and Salisbury ended their pitch, the room fell silent. "Then Millard Ehlers, an agent from Marshall—sort of a veteran spokesman—started to laugh," Pierce recalled. "He said, 'Just wait till policyholders see my face out there! This is wonderful!' Boom—it was sold."

half a million dollars for television advertising.

That summer, Ambrosavage and Salisbury began looking for someone to write a jingle to go along with their radio and television commercials. Pouring over directories and making phone calls, they came upon David Carroll, a respected Chicago orchestra leader who wrote jingles on the side. He went on to become musical director for *The Smothers Brothers*, the top-rated Sunday evening television show in the late 1960s.

Pulling the line "All your family's protection under one roof" from one of Salisbury's brochures, Carroll wrote a fifty-second tune, complete with two stanzas and an instrumental bridge. A few weeks later, Ambrosavage and Salisbury returned to Chicago to hear the jingle for the first time. "He'd come up with this march," Ambrosavage recalled. "I tell you, it was an inspiring experience to listen to that."

The first recordings were made using Carroll's fourteen-piece orchestra and a male quartet. They recorded the song thirty-seven times before Carroll felt it was just right. Copyrighted July 9, 1965, the jingle made its debut later that month at the All American Convention in New York City. The jingle was an instant success with the field force. Not only could agents order a taped version for radio spots and a color-film version for TV ads, they could also receive, without charge, a 33-rpm record with the three commercial versions on one side and three instrumental versions on the other. "This high fidelity recording is for you to enjoy at home," Salisbury wrote in a memo to the agents.

In March 1966, after nearly a year of preparation, American Family's first cooperative television ads aired on thirty-six stations, reaching more than 2 million homes. The series of five commercials featured "Charlie," an American Family agent, talking with typical families about their insurance needs and coverage.

A-mer-i-can Fam-ly In-sur-ance

Bob Salisbury hams it up while shooting a Dixieland version of the American Family jingle.

Never shown on camera, Charlie could have been any agent. The company capitalized on this effect by providing agents with lapel buttons bearing the name Charlie. "I have been wearing my Charlie button, and people have noticed it and remarked about it," one agent told *The All American* that spring.

The quality of the commercials and the regularity of their appearance during popular programs gave American Family unprecedented visibility. By 1974, 1,500 agents enrolled, and the advertising and promotions budget skyrocketed to $1.8 million.

"With agents agreeing to pay half the cost of advertising, we were able to out-advertise our competitors from that moment on," Salisbury said. At the same time, the company kept its total advertising budget—as measured against premium volume—at 1 percent.

A series of five commercials featured Charlie, an American Family agent who never appeared on camera, talking with his customers. To capitalize on this effect, many agents wore "Charlie" buttons, linking themselves with the popular TV commercials.

Leaving the House

Before the mid-1960s, Farmers Mutual/American Family urged agents to work out of their homes. Not only did a home office reduce an agent's overhead, it helped avoid walk-in business from unwanted risks. But as the company and the agents worked together to increase their visibility, a handful of agents emerged from their homes to rent office space in shopping centers and downtown districts.

It's uncertain who established American Family's first store-front office. Wisconsin East state director Paul Miller put two agents in a Kenosha office in 1964. About the same time, two Missouri agents, Harland Curry and Jim McCloskey, opened an office on Natural Bridge Street in St. Louis.

But Wally Huebsch, a district manager in St. Paul, commonly receives credit for popularizing agent offices. In 1964, Huebsch leased space in the basement of St. Paul's Apache Plaza Shopping Center, across the hall from the rest rooms. "It was the cheapest space available," he said.

Initially angered by Huebsch's disregard for company policy, state director Joe Stephan visited the office and was convinced of its benefits. Soon Huebsch had agent offices in two more shopping malls. "It wasn't long," he said, "before we were leading the company in sales."

After visiting St. Paul, sales research director Bill Kleinheinz proposed a program under which American Family leased both office space and equipment and shared the cost—roughly $3,000 in 1965—with the agents. Reluctantly, agency director Gus Kinnamon agreed.

Combined with the cooperative television advertising program, cooperative agent offices gave American Family a polished, professional image that helped recruit and retain high-caliber agents.

By the middle of 1966, the company had twenty-five co-op offices sprinkled across its eleven-state territory. Four short years later, nearly half the company's 1,000 full-time career agents worked out of co-op offices. Today, just a handful of American Family's 3,600 agents prefer staying at home.

The Old Soft Sell

A year on television did more to put American Family in the public's mind than thirty-five years of radiator emblems and novelty items. In 1967, Salisbury scrambled the letters of the American Family logo and stood on a street corner in Milwaukee asking people to name the company. More than 80 percent could—a four-fold improvement over the company's previous emblem. "They even started singing our jingle," Salisbury said.

Name recognition translated into dollars and cents. After stagnating for several years, the number of American Family policies increased to 726,899 in 1966, up from 688,440 the year before. Full-time agents jumped from 509 to 590 in the same period. "We grew more in numbers of policyholders, upgraded our manpower, developed more premium volume, and earned a larger profit than during any other year in the past decade," Maurer reported to policyholders in January 1967.

Those trends continued as American Family grew in both size and market share. "Success has many authors, and there were many factors contributing to the growth of American Family," Salisbury reflected. "But advertising played one of the principal roles."

The Piano

Since the mid-1960s, American Family has produced some of television's most memorable commercials. American Family's 1977 award-winning *Piano* spot was one such commercial. This delicate, soft-edged commercial allows the viewer to perceive more of the advertisement's meaning with each viewing.

Piano opens with a little girl struggling to play Brahms's "Waltz 15 in A Flat." The playing grows perceptibly more accomplished as the camera pans family photos on the wall and the narrator talks about how a father spends most of his life paying for life insurance. "It isn't something he can see or put his arms around," the gentle voice says. "It's really just a good feeling he gets knowing that her future is secure." The commercial ends with a young woman playing Brahms beautifully and the announcer saying, "American Family Insurance says, 'You don't buy life insurance for you. You buy it for her.'"

Many viewers not paying close attention, did not until the second or third viewing notice that the father appears only in the earliest pictures, leaving just the mother and daughter in later shots. The subtle message is that the father's life insurance paid for his daughter's piano lessons and her upbringing.

Chapter Six

*Problems are opportunities
in work clothes.*

—HENRY J. KAISER

RIDING THE INSURANCE CYCLE

With the end of gas rationing—
and its convenient gauge of
miles driven—most insurers in the late 1940s
abandoned the mileage factor in setting premiums and returned to the prewar classification
system. Underwriters, stereotyped as seeing only
black and white, found themselves swimming in
gray. Limited to a few broad categories, they
were forced to lump unrelated risk groups
together. Women under age twenty-five were
grouped with their parents. People who drove long distances for
work shared a higher rate class with young, unmarried men. As a

After World War II, Farmers Mutual's underwriting department struggled to fit too many drivers into too few categories.

On Labor Day 1951, the millionth American soldier to die in 176 years of war fell in Korea. The millionth traffic fatality on American roadways occurred a few months later—after only half a century of driving.

result, rates were too low for some drivers and excessively high for others.

To compensate for the inadequacy of the system and stop persistent underwriting losses, many insurers in the early 1950s turned to merit/demerit plans that increased premiums for people involved in accidents while lowering rates for accident-free drivers. But Howard Hayes, who joined Farmers Mutual in 1937 and served as its underwriting manager since 1944, opposed merit rating, arguing that it penalized the careful driver who nevertheless had an accident. Instead, Farmers Mutual emphasized strict underwriting rules. The company refused to insure males under age twenty-five, for example, though it often lost longtime members when their children reached driving age. Strict underwriting enabled the company in 1955 to turn its first underwriting profit in years. But its market share fell as other insurers refined their classification systems, enabling them to offer lower rates to preferred classes.

Working at tables piled high with punch cards containing detailed information on Farmers Mutual's half a million policyholders, Hayes, assistant controller Don Breitenbach, and underwriter Jim Pfefferle shuffled and reshuffled the data, trying to find a new scenario. The outcome: the selective merit plan, which reintroduced the mileage factor, charged higher rates to people who drove to work or long distances for business, and reduced rates for "family pleasure and convenience" drivers. The plan also imposed higher rates on drivers under age twenty-five. Young, unmarried men with their own cars paid the highest rate—and Farmers Mutual insured them only if their parents had been policyholders for eighteen months or more.

Many insurers eventually adopted the selective merit plan's basic principles, but Farmers Mutual initially suffered under it. The comparatively low rates for young drivers attracted a flood of young men, accounting for one-third of the company's new apps. Premiums for the to-and-from-work class were too high, driving away business. And rate reductions for pleasure-car drivers failed to attract new low-risk motorists.

To improve its pricing, Farmers Mutual hired its first actuary, former South Dakota state insurance commissioner George Burt, in 1956. But the trouble lay not only in the rates but in the classes. Farmers Mutual fine-tuned its new rating system and in 1960 introduced the safe young driver program, a merit/demerit plan for unmarried men under age twenty-five. The company also dropped the to-and-from-work class because it unfairly penalized small-town residents. Instead, it applied the higher rate to those driving 30 or more miles per week to work. The new system also charged a higher rate to those who drove more than 7,500 miles a year. Two years later, Farmers Mutual became the first insurer to offer a preferred rate to drivers beginning at age thirty rather than the industry standard of twenty-five, and it increased rates on drivers over seventy.

To help agents use the new system correctly and improve their risk selection, the company started a resident underwriting program. Previously, all underwriters worked in the home office, visiting their districts once a year to get to know the agents and teach them how to classify applicants. Moving to St. Paul in April 1962, Fran Brewster became the first resident underwriter. Brewster soon had counterparts in Indianapolis, Topeka, Omaha, and Milwaukee.

Between 1960 and 1970, 37 million new drivers climbed behind the wheel, among them 15 million drivers between the ages of eighteen and twenty-nine—the group with the worst record for fatal accidents.

As underwriting losses mounted, many insurance companies, including Farmers Mutual, refused to cover young drivers like these.

Success and the Standard Risk

For more than thirty years, Farmers Mutual prided itself on being a class mutual, keeping rates low by restricting membership to preferred risks, leaving less discerning companies to cover the standard classes. This approach, however, made it difficult for agents representing Farmers Mutual exclusively to make a decent living. Other companies, however, prospered by insuring all types of drivers. One such company was Dairyland Insurance, founded by

Damage appraiser Walt Froelich inspects a dented fender at one of American Family's drive-in claims centers.

Adjusters Put a Face on the Company

"The adjuster is the connecting link between the insurer and the insured," claims training director Frank Horner told an audience of American Family adjusters in 1974. "The adjuster is the personification of the insurance policy created by the underwriter and sold by the agent."

To a family who's just lost their home to a tornado or someone who's had an auto accident, the adjuster—the person who surveys the damage, takes the statements, and often times writes the check—*is* the company. Their quick, courteous, professional service provides the best word-of-mouth advertising.

In the early days, claims adjusters worked from the home office, traveling their territories during the week, returning to Madison on Friday for paperwork and reports. To serve far-flung regions, the company hired local attorneys.

In the early 1940s, Urban Schmitz became Farmers Mutual's first resident claims adjuster. Working out of his home, Schmitz investigated and settled claims in St. Paul. Within a few years, Farmers Mutual had branch claims offices with resident underwriters in Kansas City, St. Louis, and Milwaukee.

Because adjusters must understand insurance law, most of these adjusters were attorneys. During the first half of the century, three-fourths of Farmers Mutual's claims adjusters held law degrees. But in America's postwar economy, attorneys were in high demand. By the end of the 1950s, less than half of the adjusters were lawyers. Ten years later, there were fewer than one in ten with law degrees.

The transition coincided with the evolution of package policies, which required adjusters to have a broader knowledge of insurance law and repair costs. Farmers Mutual improved its training program beyond a simple,

half-day, on-the-job experience. Sterling Schallert wrote the first claims technical manual in the late 1950s. Shortly thereafter, new adjusters attended training at Val Technical Institute in Blairsville, Pennsylvania, to learn about the parts of an automobile, how to read the manuals, and to make repair estimates.

Quick, friendly service became increasingly important. In the late 1950s, insurers experimented with drive-in claims centers. John Farnsworth, vice president of claims, wrote off the concept as a passing fad. But in 1968, American Family opened its first drive-in claims center in Milwaukee. With free estimates and on-the-spot payments, drive-in centers epitomized the quick, friendly, professional service people wanted from their insurance company. Today, American Family has forty-nine drive-in centers serving claimants across thirteen states.

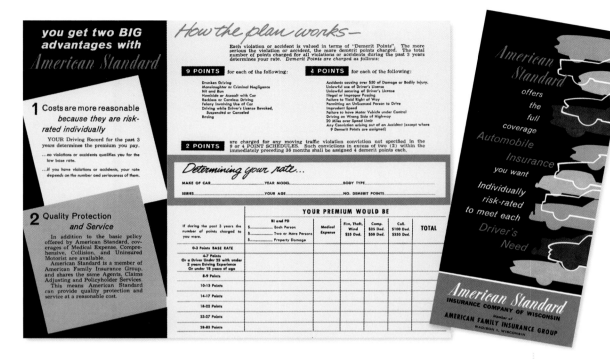

Using a merit-system to set premiums, American Standard insured drivers who didn't qualify for coverage with Farmers Mutual. The more points a driver had, the higher the premium. Moving traffic violations earned two points, "improper" passing four points, and violations such as drunken driving, racing, or assault with a car earned nine points.

Don Anderson and Stu Struck, a former college friend of Al Gruenisen. After visiting with Struck, Gruenisen, then American Family's Wisconsin regional vice president, toyed with the notion of insuring standard risks. Aggressive and outspoken, Gruenisen often found little support for his ideas among the executive staff. But on this issue, he found a powerful ally—treasurer Hugh Wallace. Together, the two men developed an underwriting-for-profit plan that would allow Farmers Mutual to insure standard risks by charging higher premiums. Articulate and staunchly conservative, Wallace enjoyed broad respect throughout the organization. Nevertheless, the proposal received a cool reception from the executive staff.

But public outrage over the growing number of drivers unable to buy insurance had many insurance executives worried about state—and possibly federal—action. After much soul searching, the Farmers Mutual board in early 1961 approved the formation of a subsidiary to insure drivers who did not qualify for Farmers Mutual. Although the Farmers Mutual board had put up $2 million to be the lone stockholder in the American Family Life Insurance Company, it invested only $400,000—half what was needed—to launch the American Standard Insurance Company (ASIC). The board insisted its affiliated windstorm and life companies provide the balance. Summing up the board's attitude, Alex Opgenorth said, "Farmers Mutual can't shoulder this loss alone."

By 1958, a small, oddly shaped car from Germany, the Volkswagen Beetle, had captured 5 percent of the American market. Within a decade, the Beetle and other economy cars accounted for nearly 30 percent of the cars on the road. Reasoning that these smaller cars were more maneuverable, weighed less, and required less room to park, Farmers Mutual and other insurers in 1960 offered a compact-car discount. But when fatality rates in compact cars proved twice that of larger automobiles, insurers quickly repealed the discounts.

With a green light from all three boards, Hayes, Kinnamon, Gruenisen and vice president of operations Pete Miller developed plans for ASIC. Slowly, others in the company began to see merit in ASIC. Careful underwriting could weed out the worst risks, and quarterly—rather than semi-annual—renewals would enable the company to raise rates or cancel policies promptly. More important to some, American Standard could improve Farmers Mutual sales and underwriting profit. Rather than cancel policies and send drivers to competing companies, Farmers Mutual could transfer its marginal risks to American Standard. After a period of safe driving, they could return to Farmers Mutual. Similarly, young drivers could be insured through American Standard until they qualified for Farmers Mutual. This would improve agent incomes, making it easier to recruit and retain an exclusive field force.

With Miller as president, Gruenisen executive vice president, and a staff of five, American Standard opened its doors in Wisconsin on September 30, 1961. There was no fanfare, no photographs, no breathless anticipation. Agents were not to prospect for ASIC but only submit applications for those who applied to Farmers Mutual but did not qualify.

The opportunity to sell to a wider range of people excited many exclusive agents. Those who sold themselves and their policyholders on Farmers

The Shape of Things to Come

Innovation is a hallmark of Farmers Mutual/American Family, where people constantly reexamine what others take for granted. In 1958, Bob Kelliher, director of systems and procedures, brought this sense of innovation to desk level. In the midst of yet another space crunch, Kelliher took a fresh look at the standard sixty-inch metal desk. The typewriter always seemed to be in the way—particularly for policy typists, who had to spread their work around the bulky machine.

Kelliher, with the help of staff members George Riege and Frank Kuemmel, designed a 55-inch desk with a wing for the typewriter. The "L" shape increased the desk's work space while reducing its overall length. The "RK 55" (for Robert Kelliher as well as Riege and Kuemmel) also boasted a lower desktop and a built-in wastebasket. The desk won first place in the 1958 National Office Management Association's annual

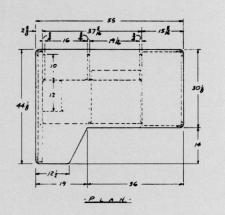

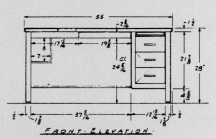

Schematics of the RK 55 desk designed by Robert Kelliher in 1958.

awards and was written up in the *New York Times*. Custom-built for Farmers Mutual, the RK 55 remained popular among clerical staff into the 1970s.

Mutual's strict standards, however, kept the new company at arm's length. Meanwhile, non-exclusive agents, most of whom placed standard risk drivers with other companies, were happy to insure more of their cus-

tomers with Farmers Mutual. In the first two weeks, ASIC issued 418 policies. With expansion into Iowa and Minnesota, sales reached 2,400 by the end of December and 10,000—with $1.3 million in premiums—in the first year.

Marketing manager Joe Chvala aimed American Standard's advertising at three growing markets—the young, the elderly, and military personnel. Premiums doubled the second year, and the company turned in an underwriting profit of $107,000. By 1966, American Standard collected $8.5 million in premiums on 40,000 policies. Such rapid growth—with its corresponding increase in acquisition costs—stretched the young company's surplus just as it was about to receive its first A. M. Best rating. Without additional capital, American Standard would rate a "C+." American Family Life and American Family Mutual stepped in with a $1.5 million contribution to surplus, earning ASIC a "BBBB" financial rating and an "A+" policyholders rating.

Joe Chvala

From Sea to Shining Sea?

In 1960, with the nation in a deep recession and the company suffering its fourth straight year of underwriting loss, the American Family Mutual board of directors approved the gradual acquisition of licenses in additional states—provided staff requested no funds for expansion until the Midland Region became profitable and there was adequate manpower available. At the annual meeting the following year, Maurer told policyholders of the company's expansion plans. "To sustain the momentum we now have, we should plan to expand into thirty-eight additional states in the next ten years," Maurer said.

But it was more a dream than a possibility. "He sort of dropped that on us to get us thinking beyond what we were doing at that time," Koch said.

When Irving Maurer announced plans to make Farmers Mutual a national company, the regional insurance carrier served just ten midwestern states.

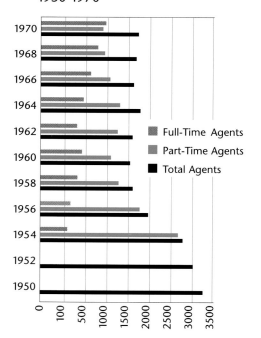

American Family Field Force
1950-1970

Planning for expansion forced Farmers Mutual to evaluate its existing regional structure. Wallace and Kinnamon estimated that a region required 150,000 policies to support its management structure. With just 66,000 casualty and fire policies, the Central Region lagged far behind projections, pushing per-policy expenses 40 percent above the other regions. On October 1, 1961, Farmers Mutual disbanded the Central Region. Illinois and Indiana became part of the Wisconsin Region, and Iowa joined Minnesota and the Dakotas in the Northwest Region. Regional vice president Bill Kleinheinz returned to the agency division as sales research director.

The major question of how to enter a state economically using the company's field structure remained unanswered. Wallace and Kinnamon estimated the break-even point to be $4 million in annual premiums—50,000 to 75,000 policies. Using a top-down development plan beginning with a state director and four district managers, the company would suffer ten years of losses before the new state would start to turn a profit. The executive staff opted for a bottom-up approach. Research indicated that about 2,000 policyholders moved out of the ten-state service area every year. To keep some of them as members and establish a base in new states, the company allowed independent agents outside the ten states to service American Family policyholders beginning in 1962. The company would augment the natural growth of the fastest-growing areas with direct-mail marketing. Once a state had a few hundred policyholders, American Family would send in agents and district managers and eventually a state director.

But first, the company had to expand and strengthen its field force. To begin this work, the executive staff asked sales training supervisor Joe Nicolay to design an innovative district manager development program. Most companies promoted successful agents to managers. But experience showed a good salesperson didn't always make a good manager. Consequently, companies regularly lost talented agents who failed in management.

Nicolay's management development program provided agents with extensive training before they committed to becoming managers. To ease anxiety, the program—emphasizing that no one outranks the salesperson—treated the move to district manager as a job shift rather than a promotion. Any agent-turned-manager who decided the job wasn't working out could take over the next available agency. "You didn't go down to being an agent, you simply returned to being an agent," Nicolay explained. "Some of the best agents in the company are former managers."

In March 1961, the first twelve agents in the management development program attended a four-day training school at the home office. Afterward, each agent completed twenty-four hands-on management projects, such as recruiting an agent. Upon finishing these projects, an agent was eligible for—though not guaranteed—a district manager position. To further ease the transition, the company developed an advanced compensation plan and group health insurance plan for district managers.

Related to the need for more district managers was the need for additional agents. Decimated by the agency reorganization program, the company's field force—once more than 3,200 agents strong—fell to just over 1,500 by 1961. To improve recruiting, Miller centralized the function in 1962, appointing Nicolay director of sales manpower development. "You're the manpower czar. You don't report to anybody but me," Miller, the company's only executive vice president,

Pat Peirce operates a film reviewer and cleaner that automatically stops when it detects a bad sprocket hole or splice, allowing her to fix the film.

Promoting Safety Through Movies

Prodded by the insurance industry, President Dwight D. Eisenhower in 1954 created the President's Action Committee on Highway Safety to address the rising highway death toll. The committee declared December 15, 1954, "Safe Driving Day" and turned to insurance companies for promotion. The insurance industry picked up the "S-D Day" banner and waved it enthusiastically before an uninterested public.

In 1956, as part of its continuing safety campaign, Farmers Mutual purchased and made available to agents eight 16-mm films prepared by the president's committee. Safety films became a popular tool to set the stage for talks on safety at drivers' education classes, PTA, lodge, or service club meetings. By 1973, American Family's film library, handled by archives clerk Pat Peirce and library assistant Rosie Peterson, had more than 400 prints viewed by nearly half a million people each year. Ten years later, the annual audience for American family's safety films approached 1.5 million, most of them driver's education students. Today, American Family's safety film library includes 1,200 copies, representing 75 titles. Loaned to community groups and schools throughout its service area, these films reach more than 700,000 people each year. Beginning in 1997, American Family's library included CD-ROM titles for loan to schools and community groups.

To keep the young American Family Life Insurance Company in the agents' minds during the frenzied activity of the 1960s, vice president Bob Koch sponsored creative contests such as the 1962 Space Age Campaign. Here, sales training instructor Don Mahoney (right) presents Koch with $180,000 worth of apps from Illinois.

told the former tank commander. "You go over the regional vice presidents and state directors and right to the district managers if you have to. You can cut through all levels and all lines."

Nicolay identified several barriers to recruiting and retaining full-time agents. American Family responded by removing the requirement that district managers repay a portion of a failed agent's advance. The company replaced the underwriting bonus, which dampened growth, with a bonus plan that rewarded selective underwriting *and* growth. And management revised agent contracts to eliminate separation benefits that inadvertently encouraged agents to leave the company, introducing instead an extended earnings program that rewarded long-tenured agents.

A forceful leader, Nicolay had a bearing that demanded respect. In the field, his decisive, no-nonsense style resembled that of George Patton, the general he served under in World War II. Demanding and resolute, Nicolay leaned hard on the district managers to recruit, imposing quotas and expecting results. His efforts paid off. Although the total number of agents increased only slightly during the three-year experiment with centralized recruiting, the number of full-time agents more than doubled to nearly 600. In 1965, when Al Gruenisen became secretary and general counsel, Miller promoted Nicolay to Wisconsin regional vice president.

Go West

By the mid-1960s, American Family held licenses in most states west of the Mississippi, planning was complete, underwriting profits had returned, and a new name was in place. The company was ready to go west. First stop—Denver. Growing at the rate of 2,500 people a month, the mile-high capital of

Colorado was home to 1.1 million people in 1966.

Minnesota state director Joe Stephan and Twin Cities district manager Wally Huebsch volunteered to lay the groundwork in Denver while keeping their Minnesota jobs. The home office agreed. In the spring of 1966, they rented space in Denver's new Villa Italia shopping complex, a 72-acre mall that boasted one-third the retail space of all downtown Denver. In June, Huebsch recruited two of his best agents, Frank Jones and Don Baker, to be the first Denver district managers. Oliver Dirks, an agent in Canton, South Dakota, moved to Denver in July as the first agent. The quick work enabled American Family to begin Colorado sales on August 1, 1966—two months ahead of schedule. For the next couple of years, Huebsch regularly flew to Denver to help recruit and train. But progress was slow. "It was a lot tougher on those guys than we thought it would be," Huebsch said. "It was lonesome. Nobody knew American Family. Nobody cared to. There was no claims staff, no underwriters, no support."

Wally Huebsch

Joe Stephan

But they forged ahead.

By the time Don Mahoney, former Nebraska state director and sales training instructor, became the first Colorado state director in 1968, American Family had five district managers and forty-two agents in the state. A year later, Colorado sales surpassed Iowa and South Dakota. Development costs, however, remained high, and in 1970 the executive staff tabled plans for further expansion, preferring to concentrate on filling gaps in the company's existing markets. "We simply hadn't established a profitable manner of opening up new states," Maurer said.

New Colorado state director Don Mahoney stands on the balcony of the Capitol in Denver.

Norb Vanden Heuvel (far left), Hugh Wallace, Howard Padley from the contractor Orville Madsen & Son, Irving Maurer, and Bob Kelliher review plans for the 1966 construction of a 60,000-square-foot east wing. Less than ten years later, plans were underway for the 77,000-square-foot west wing.

Monthly Payments and Long-Term Loans

In the 1960s, Americans became enamored with credit cards and monthly payment plans that helped them buy now what they could afford later. By the time Wallace recommended that American Family develop its own monthly payment plan, several insurance companies had similar programs. Working with Koch and Miller, Wallace developed the American Monthly Payment Plan (AmPlan) to make it easier for middle-class families to budget for insurance payments. The plan encouraged people to place all their insurance with American Family and roll all of their premiums into a single monthly bill.

To manage AmPlan, Wallace hired senior underwriter Gene Wilpolt, who had learned monthly billing procedures during a five-year stint in the management program at Montgomery Ward. With a five-person staff, AmPlan began operation January 1, 1965. In three weeks, it had 330 accounts. By year's end, AmPlan had 5,700 accounts representing more than 12,000 policies. Except for its monthly billings, AmPlan was not computerized. "We hand-posted every charge, credit, and payment," Wilpolt said, "and manually balanced accounts at the end of the month." Within four years, AmPlan was turning a profit.

As the nation began to take prosperity for granted, debt lost its tarnish, and interest payments became tax deductions. Consumer credit companies opened offices in strip malls across the country, and automakers launched their own finance companies. This new competition forced banks to become aggressive lenders. Many paid finder's fees to insurance agents referring car-buyers to them for loans. Fearing that banks and automakers might one day also sell insurance, insurance companies decided to beat them to the punch by opening their own finance firms. Seeing the trend, Wallace, Gruenisen, and Robbie Robinson, among others, urged American Family to enter the finance market. American Family and American Standard together insured more than 800,000 automobiles, with notes against roughly two-thirds of them. Financing just 500 of those cars would equal $1 million in loans.

In 1969, American Family resuscitated Webb, Inc., the old management company, to provide auto loans to American Family policyholders. Maurer chaired the new company, named American Family Financial Services (AFFS), and Miller became president. Unable to find an experienced loan manager in the American Family Group, Miller looked outside and found Frank Luedtke, a former manager for Transamerica Finance Corporation. With fifteen years' experience in the consumer loan business, he had the expertise to get AFFS off to a fast start. By June 1969, Luedtke and his assistant, Dean McCarthy, another former Transamerican, had AFFS up and running.

A stocky, boisterous man, Luedtke didn't fit easily in the conservative home office. But he understood that the key to Financial Services' success lay in the field, and he forged relationships with strong district managers like Paul Moosmann in Washington, Missouri, and Joe Sanks in Janesville, Wisconsin. In four months, AFFS had $1 million in loans, and within a year, $2.5 million. By its fifth anniversary, the company had eight branch offices, 12,000 accounts, and more than $23 million in loans.

Frank Luedtke

Dean McCarthy

Government Steps In

In the 1950s, state legislatures continued to debate the virtue of compulsory auto insurance, which the insurance industry resisted vehemently. As an alternative, the industry proposed uninsured motorist coverage, which broadened medical coverage and provided death and disability payments to insured motorists involved in accidents with uninsured drivers. Many at Farmers Mutual raged against the new—and costly—direction. "This is immoral,"

Farmers Mutual was among the leaders in offering uninsured motorist protection in 1957.

Network news cameras roll as Irving Maurer, chair of the National Association of Independent Insurers, speaks at the NAII's 1968 annual convention in New York City.

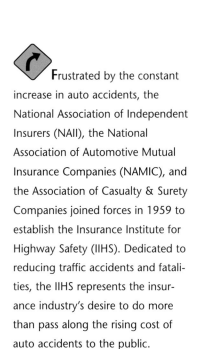

Frustrated by the constant increase in auto accidents, the National Association of Independent Insurers (NAII), the National Association of Automotive Mutual Insurance Companies (NAMIC), and the Association of Casualty & Surety Companies joined forces in 1959 to establish the Insurance Institute for Highway Safety (IIHS). Dedicated to reducing traffic accidents and fatalities, the IIHS represents the insurance industry's desire to do more than pass along the rising cost of auto accidents to the public.

With a $1 million annual budget to fight a national epidemic, the IIHS limited its initial efforts to three states—Wisconsin, Arizona, and Florida. In Wisconsin, the IIHS priorities included legislation to adopt uniform accident reporting, expansion of drivers education, and more effective driver improvement programs.

vice chairman Bill Aberg decried when the executive staff recommended board approval of such coverage. Despite objections, Farmers Mutual became a leader in offering this protection in 1957.

Eight years later, Ralph Nader's book *Unsafe at Any Speed: The Designed-in Danger of the American Automobile* ignited a national debate on auto safety. Congress responded with the Highway Safety Act, which mandated improved auto and highway design. Insurance carriers, long conscious of the need for car and driver safety, weighed in through the Insurance Institute for Highway Safety and the National Association of Independent Insurers (NAII) auto repair committee chaired by Gruenisen, American Family's secretary. As inflation battered Americans in the late 1960s, critics chastised insurance companies for "exorbitant" rate hikes. By 1967, regulators in twenty-four states were investigating the insurance industry. At the same time, three congressional committees and the U.S. Department of Transportation conducted inquiries into allegations of price fixing through the national rating bureaus, the future of state-federal regulation, whether investment income should be considered when setting rates, and the advantages of no-fault insurance. As chairman of the NAII in 1967-68, Maurer led independent insurers through this difficult period. In testimony before congressional panels and through an aggressive public relations campaign, the NAII and its members successfully defended an industry caught in the inflationary spiral of skyrocketing medical and repair costs and the ever-increasing number of accidents.

On the no-fault issue, Gruenisen served on—and eventually chaired—the NAII's no-fault committee, which developed a modified no-fault plan that became a model for many states. The plan ensured instant payment of a person's medical bills regardless of fault while preserving the right to sue for additional damages. By the mid-1970s, fifteen states enacted similar legislation, and Congress abandoned national no-fault legislation.

Gruenisen's work with legislative issues convinced him that American Family needed a full-time public relations person. In 1974, he, Miller, and Kinnamon constituted a PR committee. The following year, Gruenisen hired Kathryn Gibson as part of the corporate legal staff to handle public relations and employee communications.

'I Lost a Good Friend Yesterday'

On March 30, 1968, Herman Wittwer suffered a stroke at his home in Fort Lauderdale, Florida. All that week, anxious letters and telegrams traveled between Fort Lauderdale and Madison. Doctors initially listed Wittwer in fair condition. But his health declined, and the following Sunday—April 6, 1968—Herman Wittwer died at age seventy-nine.

Wittwer had retired five years earlier but remained chairman of the board and maintained his office at American Family. He and his second wife, Dorothy (Stearns Mayer), spent much of the winter in Florida. When in Madison, however, Herman always stopped by the office, his lively walk and cheerful "good morning" brightening executive row. After reading the mail, he chatted with whoever came through the door. Rarely was that person Irv Maurer. In fact, the two men didn't speak for the last two years of Wittwer's life.

One of Wittwer's regular visitors when he was in the office was longtime custodian Ray Sather. For years, Sather joined Wittwer for a cigar and conversation about the Wisconsin Badgers. The day following Wittwer's burial in Madison's Roselawn Cemetery, Sather sat in Wisconsin regional vice president Joe Nicolay's office pensively smoking a cigarette. "I lost a good friend yesterday," Sather said. It was a loss shared by many.

After Wittwer's death, Maurer advanced to chairman and CEO.

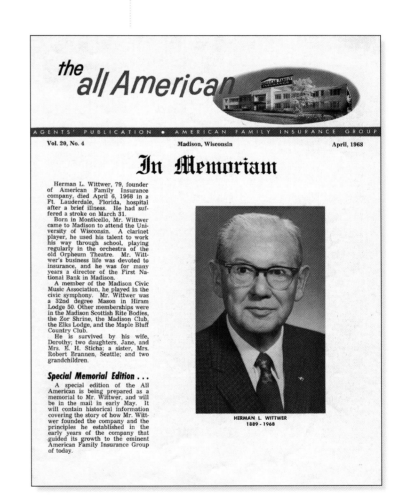

Koch became president of American Family Life, and Miller of American Family Mutual (the parent company), American Standard, and American Family General (the windstorm company). Koch and Miller worked well together, by and large avoiding conflicts. At the board level, Koch succeeded Wittwer on the mutual board, and Wallace succeeded Wittwer on the life board.

Planning for Profit

Hobbled by ineffective underwriting tools, intense competition, and tight rate regulation, insurers experienced ten years of underwriting losses between 1955 and 1965. During this decade-long down cycle, American Family accumulated $4.4 million in underwriting losses. Inflation added insult to underwriting injury. By the mid-1960s, many insurers tacitly accepted underwriting losses—provided they were offset by investment income.

At Farmers Mutual, treasurer Hugh Wallace and money center specialist Ruth Kutz managed the group's $36.8 million portfolio through a Chicago brokerage firm. Following the conservative course set by Wittwer, Wallace and Kutz invested $34 million in double- and triple-A bonds, $2.5 million in stocks, and the remainder in mortgage loans. In 1960, the company hired thirty-year investment veteran Fred Morton as its first vice president of investments. Though a conservative financial manager, Morton increased investments in lower-rated, higher-return "A" bonds and common stocks to take advantage of the strong economy.

By creating this new position, Farmers Mutual acknowledged the growing importance of investment income. But it did not accept underwriting losses as a way of life. The executive staff vowed to set adequate rates to show an underwriting profit. While insurance carriers following the American Agency System struggled with the situation, Maurer felt confident that his company's time had come. The group's capacity ratio—the measure of premium revenue (risk assumed) against surplus (ability to handle risk)—stood strong at $1.79-to-$1. The group had a lean operation, seasoned leaders, and a growing force of well-trained, exclusive agents. His confidence was justified. Blue ink returned in 1965 and—with few exceptions—remained for nearly a decade. In 1967, American Family had its first of many "best years ever." Total applications exceeded 200,000, group premiums reached $69 million, and single-year life insurance sales surpassed $100 million.

In 1969, American Family treasurer Hugh Wallace, budget director Brent Johnson, and controller Don Breitenbach introduced contributions accounting to American Family—and the industry. The system recognized fixed and variable expenses—concepts previously not applied to the insurance business. Contributions accounting enabled American Family to more accurately measure the cost of sales and service for individual segments of its business. The new system also helped management estimate when a new line or territory would begin to turn a profit.

Fred Morton

W. Robert Koch
Working Up Through the Ranks

Bored with his homeroom class at Madison's Central High, Bob Koch stared absently out the window towards the old Boyd mansion, where more than 100 people worked for Farmers Mutual, and wondered what the people there were doing. Thirty-five years later, Koch often told the story, chuckling before he added, "Now, as president, I look out at everyone working and wonder what in the world they're all doing."

Born on March 25, 1925, to a fourth-generation Madison family, Koch and his older sister came of age during World War II. His parents, like many others, lost everything in the Great Depression. At age six, he moved with his family into a relative's second-floor apartment on West Washington Avenue. Koch lived there until 1943, when he graduated from high school and joined the military. He served as an M.P. for Gen. George Patton's Third Army as it rolled north across Europe.

After the war, Koch enrolled in the University of Wisconsin and returned to his high school job at the Chocolate Shop, then Madison's most popular restaurant. There he received his first lessons in management. The owners, a couple named Daniels, didn't hire waiters; they hired dishwashers who worked their way up to the wait staff. "Train people from the ground up," Koch summarized. "And give them incentives. The more responsibility you give someone the better they'll respond." Koch responded well to the approach, eventually managing the restaurant in the Daniels' absence.

President 1977-1982
CEO and Chair 1982-1989

W. Robert Koch.

After the Daniels sold the popular eatery, Koch learned the value of selling a quality product. The new owners didn't believe in working on Sunday, and receipts dropped 40 percent. To cut costs, they purchased lower-quality food. Within three years, the restaurant closed its doors.

Koch graduated from the university in June 1948, immediately receiving a job offer from the Vicks Corporation. While the thought of moving to New York City greatly appealed to him, he decided for family reasons to remain in Madison a year before joining Vicks. In the meantime, he took an underwriting job at Farmers Mutual.

For Koch, one year stretched into forty-one. He advanced quickly to senior underwriter and in December 1951 was named head of the life department. Eighteen months later, he moved to the agency department as sales personnel manager. Here he helped develop the company's exclusive agency plan, including the advanced compensation plan. In 1957, he initiated home office sales schools.

That autumn, Koch was selected to head Farmers Mutual's new life insurance venture—American Family Life Insurance Company (AFLIC). His enthusiasm created a sense of excitement and team spirit that helped AFLIC become one of the nation's fastest growing life insurance companies.

Koch became vice president of AFLIC in 1959 and president in 1968. Following the 1977 retirement of Irving Maurer, he became president of the American Family Insurance Group and five years later chairman and CEO. During his tenure with the company, Farmers Mutual/American Family rose from one of the twenty largest insurers in Wisconsin in 1948 to one of the twenty largest property-casualty companies in the nation when he stepped down as chairman in 1989. He remained on the board until March 31, 1995.

Always active in community affairs, Koch maintains an office at the Madison Area Chamber of Commerce and continues to be one of the community's strongest supporters.

On January 1, 1970, American Family Mutual Insurance Company merged with American Family General—the windstorm company—forming the general lines division that handled windstorm, farm fire, and farmowners insurance.

Jim Pfefferle

But challenges remained. By the time President Richard M. Nixon took the oath of office in January 1969, annual inflation was 6.2 percent. The new president immediately cut federal spending and tightened the nation's money supply, pushing interest rates to the highest level in a century. Unemployment jumped from 3.5 percent to 6.2 percent by January 1970. Stock and bond prices plummeted, adding momentum to a downward spiral that led to the nation's steepest economic decline since the Great Depression.

The recession wreaked havoc on the insurance industry. Inflation made estimating future replacement and repair costs difficult. The problem was even more acute in health lines, where unforeseen medical advances drove up the cost of diagnosis and treatment. Traditional actuarial formulas proved inadequate, forcing Jim Pfefferle and the actuarial staff to rely on their judgment and intuition more than ever.

As insurance companies raised premiums in the face of rising costs, they struggled to maintain a balance between premiums and surplus. Normally, investment income bolstered surplus. But with stock and bond markets declining, investment losses reduced industry surpluses as premium revenues shot up. The result was an industrywide capacity crunch. To keep premium-to-surplus ratios in balance, many companies limited—or even prohibited—the sale of new policies. The restrictions angered agents, who found their incomes restrained just as the cost of living was going through the roof.

American Family, however, filled an enviable position at the turn of the decade. Under its pricing-for-profit approach, the group's policy count grew from 716,000 in 1964 to 995,000 in 1969, and policyholders' surplus jumped from $20 million to $31 million. As a result, American Family Mutual and American Standard maintained a capacity ratio of $2.18-to-$1. Taking advantage of its strength, the company stepped up promotions for auto insurance in 1970. This included a direct-mail campaign to the public for the first time since the company's early years. Nearly 500 agents signed up for the program, allowing the company to send letters promoting American Family's two-car discount to 1 million non-policyholders.

Sales increased 20 percent in 1970. New applications reached an all-time high of 288,507, pushing the all-lines policy count to 1.1 million. American Family improved its position in the market, and cemented relations with its 1,800 agents. The following year—hoping to solidify its connection with more

than a quarter million new policyholders—
American Family focused on homeowners,
health, and life insurance sales. "Throughout
1971," Miller said, "we plan to stress our all-your-
family-protection-under-one-roof concept."
Direct-mail campaigns helped agents drum up
new business in the company's other lines.
Applications that year hit 323,818, led by
a 43.5 percent increase in health lines.

   "When we merely follow competition," Maurer told the executive staff,
"we lose our individuality… Then we
are engineering ourselves to mediocrity,
and we become just another insurance
company." But by realistically defining
objectives and developing plans to
meet those objectives, Maurer
explained, "we are acting like a leading insurance company."

   Through the mid-1970s, inflation,
driven by the Arab oil embargo, a
slumping stock market, and cata-
strophic storms, hammered property and casualty insurers.
In 1974, the American Family Group suffered a $9 million operating loss, forc-
ing the company to dip into surplus. Miller called it "a year most fire and
casualty insurers would like to forget."

*In 1974, twenty-one severe
storms, including a hailstorm in
St. Louis (top photo) and a tornado in Oshkosh, Wisconsin,
resulted in $6.2 million in
claims paid by American Family.
Storm losses contributed to a
disastrous year for the group,
forcing management to draw
$9 million from policyholders'
surplus.*

United We Stand

When Bob Koch became president of American Family Life Insurance
Company in 1968, the ten-year-old organization had $500 million of life
insurance in force. Annual premiums exceeded $6 million, surplus neared $4
million, and assets totaled almost $22 million—a sturdy springboard for con-
tinued growth. To succeed himself as vice president of AFLIC, Koch chose
John Reed, sales personnel director. Reed started with the company in 1954 as
an agent in Mauston, Wisconsin, and earned his stripes as a district manager

In 1971, American Family Life Insurance Company introduced the AFLIC Life Diamond Club, presenting diamond rings to agents who sold more than $1 million of life insurance in a single year. That year, AFLIC president Bob Koch presented rings to Chuck Webster, Joe Tisserand, and Don Payne.

American Family Life president Bob Koch (left), leading life insurance district manager Joe Tisserand (center), and vice president John Reed unveil a new award for districts selling more than $5 million of life insurance in 1974.

in Tracy, Minnesota, after the Minnesota uprising. Traveling together to promote life insurance sales to the field force, Koch enjoyed and respected Reed. As he became more involved with the American Family Group, Koch readily entrusted the management of AFLIC to Reed. "I knew he was there if I needed him," Reed said. "But as long as things were going well, he was hands off."

Over the years, the field force gained more confidence in selling life insurance. In 1966, Chuck Webster of the home office agency became the first American Family agent to sell more than $1 million of life insurance in a year. In 1971, Joe Tisserand, another Madison agent, broke the $2 million mark.

The following year, Tisserand, a natural teacher and coach, became a district manager in Madison. Combining advanced life insurance training with a highly competitive attitude, he led his team to the top life spot in 1973—a position they held for the next twelve years. "I was a firm believer that training builds confidence and confidence equals sales," Tisserand, now vice president of AFLIC, said. "We were more aggressive in life insurance."

Aggressiveness became essential to success in the life insurance market in the 1970s. Before that, life insurance was a gentleman's game dominated by conservative, established companies. In the 1970s, conglomerates bought many of those companies as cash-flow vehicles, ratcheting up the competitive level. AFLIC flourished in this atmosphere, reaching $1 billion of in-force life insurance in 1972, $2 billion in 1976, and $3 billion in 1978.

American Family's health lines had a slower start but evolved into a major contributor to the group's overall success in the 1970s and 1980s. Considered an accommodation line in the early 1960s, health insurance initially received little attention from senior management. But with health care costs rising at twice the rate of inflation, middle-class Americans wondered how they could continue to pay for health care. Convinced of the growing demand for quality health insurance, product training supervisor Robbie Robinson led American Family's effort to make health insurance a major line. In 1968, health lines had its first 2,000-app month. The following year, at

Robinson's urging, American Family became one of the first insurers to sell a comprehensive health care plan that featured a $10,000 or $20,000 benefit cap. Sales climbed, and in 1971 the company started a ten-person night shift to service health lines. Still, the department lacked a director.

In the early 1970s—as Congress debated a national health care program and American Family considered disbanding the health lines department—vice president of marketing Floyd Desch appointed Jim Klokner as health lines director. Klokner found his experience as the first resident underwriter in Milwaukee useful in his new job. "They had the same problems that Milwaukee had in auto lines—lack of profit, sporadic production, lack of training, and low morale," he said.

Under Klokner's direction, American Family found its niche in the competitive health insurance market. Most people in urban America received health coverage through group plans offered by their employers. Klokner focused on rural areas, where group coverage was scarce, making the company's individual health policies popular. He also developed a group health plan aimed at small businesses. Agents like Silver Everhart in Lindsborg, Kansas, found huge markets in small towns. By 1976, health lines—still predominantly a manual operation—handled more than 80,000 policies and $23 million in premiums.

Jim Klokner

New Lines for a New Era

In the mid-1960s, the executive staff began to consider the mass marketing of auto insurance after the RAND Corporation approached American Family about starting a group auto plan. Citing the success of group health and life insurance, mass marketing advocates envisioned a time when people would obtain car insurance—and possibly other personal lines—through their employers. Proponents claimed this approach could shave 15 percent off per-policy administrative costs. But after more than a year of discussions with RAND, American Family backed away from the scheme, realizing that it was not prepared for such an undertaking.

By 1970, mass marketers had captured 3.5 percent of the auto insurance market. The most successful companies also offered group health and life insurance, raising concerns that an all-in-one package might become a reality. With this in mind, Miller decided American Family should develop its own mass marketing program as a defensive action. In the spring of 1970, he

Floyd Desch (seated, center) heads the newly established marketing division in 1971. Seated (from left) are Charlie Ambrosavage, Desch, and Bill Kleinheinz. Standing (from left) are Fran Hanson, Robbie Robinson, Tom Frost, Bob Salisbury, Dick Harmeling, Flynn Roskam, and Dick Adler.

named Floyd Desch to the newly created position of vice president of marketing. With actuary Lyle Sorenson and sales research director Bill Kleinheinz, Desch began work on a mass merchandising plan for auto insurance. A year later, when Gus Kinnamon retired as vice president of agency, Miller folded the agency division into marketing.

To take over the mass merchandising project, Desch appointed Colorado state director Don Mahoney in 1972. Because American Family remained committed to offering products through its field force, Mahoney developed a plan that relied on agents to prospect and make initial contacts; district managers, state directors, or mass-marketing specialists to close the sale; and agents to service the policies. American Family's venture into mass marketing began in July 1974 with two pilot projects. Slowly Mahoney added eight more groups. "This wasn't something we intended to do unless we had to," Mahoney said. "We wanted to be very cautious, go slow." The cautious approach paid off. The mass-marketing fad fizzled by the end of 1976, and American Family, with just $59,000 in premiums, easily shelved its program, converting group plans to individual policies.

Commercial insurance proved a more successful venture. In the 1970s, several states subjected farmers to workers' compensation laws. To fill their need for low-cost workers' compensation insurance, Miller and Joe Chvala, vice president of American Standard, opened a commercial lines division. They selected John Scharer, American Standard operations manager, to direct the new department. Initially Scharer focused on workers'

Lights, Camera, Action

In 1973, Milwaukee resident underwriter Bob Hinz moved to Madison to coordinate American Family's health lines training. Hinz put his photography and video background to work, producing slide, video, and audio training programs. A couple of years later, sales training director Dick Harmeling created the audiovisual (AV) department in the marketing division and hired Hinz to staff and manage the new unit. Hinz provided basic slide shows and video programs, using a razor blade to splice the reel-to-reel audio and videotape.

Steve Tingley joined Hinz as AV coordinator in 1975. The following year, American Family purchased its first color video system and produced *Insight.* The home-grown training video starring twenty-two employees was American Family's first video using dramatization as a training tool. Other projects that year included a farm lines training video, a video to acquaint people with their new computers, and a

monthly audio newsletter for district managers called *Marketing Notes.*

In 1981, the media production center came under the umbrella of human resources' new corporate training and development department. Focused on slide, audio, and video productions, the AV unit didn't have a computer until 1985. But by 1987, Hinz and his staff were producing computer graphics and working with interactive video. Seven years later, the media center unveiled an interactive multimedia kiosk in the lobby of the national headquarters and in 1995 produced its first interactive CD-ROM.

Hinz retired in 1992 and newly hired public relations director Rick Fetherston assumed responsibility for the media center. A year later, he promoted Tingley to supervisor and later media manager. Today, Tingley and his staff of highly trained producers, digital imaging technicians, multimedia developers, and graphic illustrators work with state-of-the-art equipment, including a digital video editing system that moves and edits video and audio clips with the

Media production center manager Steve Tingley works with state-of-the-art equipment in American Family's editing suite.

click of a computer "mouse."

Working under the direction of the marketing division's sales promotion department, the media center handles staging and video production for the All American Convention, the annual sales management conference, the life diamond leaders' conference, and twenty-two state spring conventions. The center began the agent portrait program in 1990 and maintains a digital library of the company's 3,600 agents. The unit establishes guidelines, researches, and purchases all corporate AV equipment, and is responsible for the safety video library. In addition, the media center is involved in developing American Family's "Intranet" and the company's home page on the world-wide web.

Out of the Kitchen and into the Field

Women attended the home office sales school for the first time in August 1975. These pioneering women were (from left) Sheri Fries, Claudia Allison, and Virginia Larimer.

Concerned about the growing conflict in Europe, the United States in 1940 began preparing for war. An advisory commission to the Council of National Defense geared up industrial production as the Selective Service inducted men and women into the armed forces. Between 1940 and 1945, 15 million American men and women joined the military, and millions more were pressed into service at factories and shipyards. During this period, women found opportunity as agents for Farmers Mutual. In 1940, Olga Purdie, a widow with two young children, became one of Farmers Mutual's first employees in the Minnesota claims office. To earn extra money, Purdie sold insurance in the evenings and on weekends from 1940 to 1946.

After the war, Purdie and the other women who sold for Farmers Mutual abandoned the field to the men. Over the next three decades, few women picked up a Farmers Mutual sales kit. In 1970, Margot Hornsey, an agent in Alton, Illinois, became the first woman to qualify for the All American Convention.

Shortly thereafter, American Family implemented an affirmative action program to boost the number of women and minorities in its field force. By the mid-1970s, twenty-five women pounded the pavement for American Family.

In August 1975, Claudia Allison from Aurora, Colorado, Sheri Fries from Denver, and Virginia Larimer from Oelwein, Iowa, became the first women to attend sales school. And in 1978, Gloria Hannon of Emporia, Kansas, was the first woman to enter the distinguished Life Diamond Club by selling more than $1 million of life insurance.

By the mid-1980s, there were nearly 200 women among the company's 2,400 agents. Today, 574 women tote a sales case for American Family Insurance, comprising nearly one-sixth of the company's sales force.

compensation and commercial liability plans for small- and medium-sized businesses. But after a conference in Milwaukee introduced him to the concept of a business owner's package policy that combined the most popular coverages in a single, convenient plan, Scharer and his staff changed emphasis.

American Family's commercial lines opened in Wisconsin on July 1, 1975, with a broad array of plans, including a business owner's package policy (BOPP). By the end of the year, commercial lines had 1,669 accounts, and the following year more than 10,000. Steady growth followed, and by 1980 commercial lines had 32,000 policies. By its tenth anniversary, the division—renamed business lines—had more than 180 employees servicing 54,000 policies totaling more than $23 million in premiums.

John Scharer directed the new commercial lines department in 1975.

New Leadership for a New Half Century

On March 1, 1972, Irving Maurer, at age sixty-seven, retired from his day-to-day duties at American Family. Like Wittwer before him, Maurer retained the title of chairman of the board and continued to attend executive staff meetings. But he handed control and the title chief executive officer to Pete Miller. For Maurer, who derived his greatest satisfaction from work, retirement was a difficult step. As he had done throughout his career, Maurer turned to his wife, Kathryn, for support. "If I find that less work doesn't suit me, I can depend on my wife to see that I change my attitudes, beliefs, and behavior," Maurer joked, quoting one of his old adages.

At the 1972 policyholders' meeting in March, Miller paid tribute to Maurer as the "surviving member of the first generation of management." He cited Maurer's creative ideas, competitive drive, and perseverance as a basis for American Family's success. The National Association of Independent Insurers also praised Maurer, who had served on the association's board of governors since 1946. Citing his leadership, wisdom, and loyalty, the association thanked Maurer for his

Agent Arden Wurch (left) with his 1927 Pontiac and charter member Anthony Jacobs were among the most popular guests at American Family's fiftieth anniversary celebration in Madison.

Memorabilia from American Family's fiftieth anniversary includes this gold pin.

"invaluable contributions to the NAII and to the independent insurance cause."

On May 11, 1977—his seventy-second birthday—Maurer stepped down as board chair and retired with Kathryn to their winter home in Florida. The board elected Robert Bock, dean of the School of Business at the University of Wisconsin-Madison, to fill Maurer's seat, and Miller stepped in as board chair and CEO. The board eliminated the separate presidency for American Family Life, and Koch became president and chief operating officer of the group companies.

A few months later, American Family celebrated its fiftieth birthday with open houses at the home office, its two regional offices, and numerous branch offices and agencies across the eleven-state area. For American Family, it was a year of unprecedented growth. Despite declining stock markets and twelve major storms, the group ended 1977 with a record 2.3 million policies, revenues amounting to nearly $450 million, and assets approaching $600 million. The group processed a record 690,000 new business applications submitted by 2,360 agents—a far cry from 1927, when Farmers Mutual closed its books with 236 agents, 486 policyholders, and $8,100 in premiums. "But two things haven't changed," Miller emphasized. "Our policyholders are still most preferential to us, and our goal is still to provide them with the best insurance at the lowest possible cost."

Chapter Seven

*Too many organizations are being driven
and too few are being led.*

—LAWRENCE G. BRANDON

MORE THAN
A SURVIVOR

*While the economic roller coaster of the 1980s
took its toll on the insurance industry,
American Family was building and growing.*

The nation's economic malaise worsened in the late 1970s. Driven by a renewed energy shortage, inflation shot up to 9.6 percent in 1978. Unemployment hovered around 8 percent, and the stock market tumbled. American Family complied with President Jimmy Carter's requests for voluntary wage and price controls, holding premium increases in all lines except health to a two-year limit of 19 percent and cost-of-living salary adjustments to an annual 7 percent.

This economic medicine came on the heels of two strong growth years for the American Family Group. To improve its balance between premiums and surplus, the company altered its prices and sales promotions to slow growth in its auto business just as other carriers fired the first tentative volleys in what became another long and devastating price war. American Family's fine-tuning pushed annual life insurance sales over $1 billion for the first time and led to a 96 percent increase in American Family Financial Services' loan volume—aided by its innovative home equity loan. As a result, new business premiums grew 11 percent to $91 million in 1978, and total policies increased 10 percent to 2.5 million.

Inflation troubled more than just President Carter. Large insurance companies, tired of annual double-digit increases in health care costs, began challenging medical bills. Many insurers agreed to pay only a set amount for some

procedures. This often left the policyholder—unaware in advance of what the physician charges and insurer pays—responsible for the unpaid portion of the bill. "We wouldn't do that," said Jim Klokner, then American Family's health lines director. "We fought for an actual reduction of the bill."

American Family's field commander in this fight was Pat (Snell) Jackson, a former claims adjuster with the San Diego (California) County Medical Society. American Family hired Jackson as a senior health adjuster in 1976 to review medical fees and negotiate reductions. "Jawboning"—the practice of negotiating lower fees—wasn't new to American Family, whose adjusters were experienced with parts-and-labor manuals and evaluation guides for auto and property claims. But telling doctors and hospitals that their charges were too high was a new battlefield. Jackson developed guidelines to help adjusters recognize more than forty common overcharges then taught them how to negotiate lower fees.

Health services director Pat (Snell) Jackson (seated), claims coordinator Sandie Nimocks, and senior health claims adjuster Fred Frenczak review a health claim for overcharges.

As health line sales grew and claims costs spiraled, American Family needed a more focused approach to jawboning. In 1980, the company established a medical services department under Jackson to investigate questionable health claims. During the first three months, Jackson saved policyholders $155,000 in overcharges. By adding two people to the staff, medical services was able to review 700 claims a month, cutting $467,000 of overcharges in 1980—well beyond its $250,000 goal. Originally limited to evaluating charges submitted under American Family's health care policies, the medical services department—with a staff of

Fire set by an arsonist left only the skeleton of this policyholder's home in 1995. Expert analysis by American Family's special investigations unit helped identify the cause of the fire, which was set by a man ultimately convicted of murder.

seven—began reviewing medical bills from all lines and the company's own employee benefits program. In 1983, annual savings amounted to $1.3 million.

Arson represented another burning issue for insurers in the late 1970s. The fastest growing crime in the nation, arson-for-profit cost insurance companies—and their policyholders—$1.6 billion a year, with total costs to the nation reaching $15 billion. Ralph Arnold, American Family's vice president of claims, responded with an arson loss-control program to help claims staff recognize and report possible arson cases. Two years later, American Family became one of the first insurance carriers in the nation to form its own special investigations unit (SIU) under Stan Davenport, retired captain of detectives for the City of Madison. By the close of 1979, after less than a year in operation, Davenport supervised investigators in Madison, Minneapolis, Kansas City, and St. Louis, saving the company $40,000. Among Davenport's first investigators was Bill Lundy, a fire marshal, former Madison police detective, and investigator with the Wisconsin Department of Justice. "As a fire marshal, I constantly fought with insurance companies to give me information," Lundy said. "Here was an insurance company that was actually going to do something about it. I thought it was a great idea."

When Davenport died in 1982, Lundy took over the unit. The new manager's staff included twelve investigators and two field supervisors and saved the company $2.75 million annually in fraudulent-claims costs. Working from

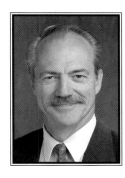

Bill Lundy

In 1982, Bill Lundy, American Family's special investigations unit manager, helped found the International Association of Special Investigations Units to promote information sharing and education among insurance company investigators. In 1996, the association had 3,500 members representing more than 400 companies.

their homes, investigators handle five to six cases each month, covering all forms of insurance fraud, including inflated claims, suspicious workers' compensation cases, false stolen-property claims, and "choreographed" auto accidents. The goal is not to deny legitimate claims. "Our company has a very strong ethic. We're going to pay the claims we should pay," Lundy said. "But it's our responsibility to policyholders to keep their rates down by making sure we don't pay fraudulent claims."

Regional Development—Moving Up and Out

To increase sales, American Family needed to bulk up its field force. Prodded by regional vice presidents (RVPs) Al Gruenisen and Joe Nicolay in Wisconsin, Les Ramiker in Northwest, and Dale Eikenberry in Midland, state directors hit the recruiting trail in the 1960s and 1970s. Drawing on the pool of managers created by the management development program, state directors opened more than 50 new districts between 1964 and 1977, raising the total to 128. The success of American Family's cooperative advertising program—particularly television advertising—and the co-op office program created a more professional image that helped attract new agents. As a result, the field force grew from 1,755 in 1964 to 2,360 in 1977. With more agents, better training, and improved products, American Family's policy count shot up from 680,000 in 1964 to 2.3 million at the end of 1977.

Largely considered a success, the regional structure—after dissolving the Central Region in 1961—remained unchanged, and the RVPs were left alone to focus on growth. In 1974, Ramiker, who had built the Northwest Region to nearly half a million policyholders in Minnesota, Iowa, and the Dakotas, was named senior vice president of underwriting. To succeed Ramiker, Pete Miller selected Kansas state director Clayton Nelson. Rather than move to Madison, where the Northwest operating unit resided, Nelson went to Minneapolis and ran the region from the regional claims office. A year later, he proposed building a $2 million headquarters in suburban Eden Prairie.

To prepare for the 300-mile move, Northwest regional service manager Dick Haas relocated the Northwest operating unit to the old A&P building across the street. For several months, the unit functioned as though it was hundreds of miles from Madison, conducting business with the home office by mail and phone. In the spring of 1978, nearly forty employees moved to the Twin Cities.

The Insurance Information Institute estimates that fraudulent claims account for 10 percent of the cost of all claims paid, adding $120 billion to people's premiums in 1996. "Those who defraud insurance companies aren't getting away with anything," said Bill Lundy, manager of American Family's special investigations unit. "They're just making insurance more expensive for themselves and everyone else."

In July, Haas and company loaded 500,000 policies onto trucks and drove them to the new three-story, 60,000-square-foot regional office. "We unloaded them and were ready to work Monday morning," Haas said.

But the computer system wasn't ready. The week-long computer failure created a backlog of work that took months to get through. "We had paper piled up everywhere," Nelson recalled. "Some people quit in the middle of the afternoon because they couldn't take it anymore." Low wages added to the frustration. American Family based wage scales on the Madison market, which paid less than the Twin Cities. A retention program focusing on benefits and the office environment improved the situation, but nearly two years passed before the regional office gained its footing.

A strong field manager, Nelson didn't let the building project distract him from his primary mission—increasing sales. In 1977, he split the region's anchor state into two operating territories, Minnesota North and Minnesota South. State director Noel Warren took over Minnesota South and helped Nelson convince Harvey Pierce to lead Minnesota North. Pierce, a district manager in southwestern Minnesota since 1966, was happy in Windom and had turned down several promotions. But Nelson wouldn't take no for an answer. "We're going to need leaders, and I think you have the ability to be one of them," he told Pierce. "I'll help you as much as I can."

Reluctantly, Pierce accepted the promotion and, after twelve years in Windom, moved his family to Minneapolis. "It was one of the most difficult moves we ever made," he said.

Further south, Eikenberry's Midland Region also was expanding. By 1977, Eikenberry had more than 700 agents serving 732,000 policyholders in

With more than half a million policies in the Northwest Region, American Family built a regional office in Eden Prairie, Minnesota, a Minneapolis suburb, in 1977.

Harvey Pierce

Clayton Nelson

Missouri, Kansas, Nebraska, and Colorado. Regional staff numbered nearly 600, with more than 400 employees working in the St. Joseph, Missouri, regional headquarters. To make room for continued expansion, American Family in 1979 constructed a three-story, 100,000-square-foot building across from Missouri Western College.

In Nicolay's Wisconsin Region, Illinois was the rising star. Under state director Dale Mathwich, the number of American Family districts grew from seven to thirteen, agents quadrupled to 164, new business applications increased fivefold to 50,000, and annual premiums jumped from $2.7 million to $34.9 million—a portion of that growth coming from Mathwich's pioneering efforts in the suburban Chicago market. In 1979, Mathwich convinced Nicolay and marketing vice president Floyd Desch to divide Illinois into two sales states—Illinois North and Illinois Central. Mathwich directed Illinois North from his Rockford office, and Bill Ihnow opened the Illinois Central office in Peoria. Six months after the split, Desch brought Mathwich to Madison as marketing director.

In 1980, Wisconsin became the last region to move out of the home office building, leaving the home office to the corporate staff. No need for a dress rehearsal on this move. The $7 million, 145,000-square-foot regional headquarters settled at the intersection of Highway 30 and Stoughton Road, just a mile east of home base. Wisconsin services manager Phil Strand

More than 400 people worked for American Family in the St. Joseph, Missouri, area when the company replaced the 1958 regional headquarters with this 100,000-square-foot office in 1979. Regional services manager Derril Jones oversaw the move.

Bill Ihnow (middle) and Dale Mathwich (right) split the state of Illinois. Midland regional vice president Joe Nicolay looks on.

The Wisconsin Region moved into this new 145,000-square-foot building in 1980.

coordinated the relocation of nearly 500 employees. Besides the Wisconsin regional operation and the computer system, the regional office housed the AmPlan division, the Madison branch of American Family Financial Services, and the Madison-area claims office.

Cash-Flow Suicide

Attracted by double-digit interest rates and skyrocketing land values, the insurance industry's periodic flirtation with cash-flow underwriting blossomed into a torrid romance in the 1980s. Inflation—which fueled the high interest rates—intensified the industry's down-cycle by driving up claims costs. "I'd gladly trade the investment increase for a decrease in inflation," American Family president Bob Koch said in 1981.

The nation's economic engines obliged Koch the following year, when a sharp recession drove down inflation—and the real estate market—and pushed unemployment over 10 percent. Cash-conscious consumers flattened insurance industry revenues by raising their deductibles, reducing their liability limits, and dropping some coverages altogether.

An explosion of liability suits—sparked by a series of highly publicized product-liability cases in the late 1970s—compounded the industry's troubles. A U.S. Supreme Court decision allowing attorneys to advertise fueled the tort frenzy as lawyers took to the airwaves and newspapers, appealing to people injured not just by faulty products but in everyday mishaps. Multimillion-dollar judgments convinced still more people to file law suits. By the middle of the 1980s, a glut of civil suits jammed the nation's court system, with one private suit for every fifteen Americans. Insurers picked up most of the tab. In 1978, the amount of money insurance companies spent to defend their policyholders accounted for 9.6 percent of all claims losses. Ten years later, defense costs were nearly 15 percent of losses. Unprepared for the trial

Stick to Your Business

The 1980s became synonymous with such expansionist business practices as leveraged buyouts, hostile takeovers, mergers, and acquisitions. The insurance industry was not immune. Attracted by the high cash flow, conglomerates purchased many insurance companies. Other insurers merged to survive or compete. And it seems they all were interested in providing financial services beyond insurance to attract and retain customers.

American Family prepared itself for the aggressive decade by establishing AmFam, Inc. in 1981. The wholly owned subsidiary was intended to give the American Family Group greater flexibility in acquiring or engaging in other businesses. The conservative corporate upbringing that Pete Miller, Bob Koch, and Dale Mathwich enjoyed tempered AmFam's willingness to enter new ventures. Although the company researched several options, it resisted the urge to expand into areas in which it had no experience. "It's important for a company to stay focused," Mathwich explained. "Stick to what you do best. Companies often get into trouble when they enter areas they don't know anything about."

CAT People: Meeting Catastrophes Face to Face

Ambulances weaved their way through the streets as Farmers Mutual adjusters Robert Caplinger and Bob Lamb surveyed the remains of Udall, Kansas. Earlier that morning, May 25, 1955, a tornado destroyed all but one house, killing 77, and hospitalizing 200 of the town's 566 residents. With no disaster plan, Caplinger and Lamb put everything else on hold and hunkered down for a string of 18-hour days. With the help of agent Bill Near, district manager Bob Fullinwider, and a few outside adjusters, this makeshift catastrophe team processed claims totaling $60,000.

A dramatically different scene unfolded thirty years later when grapefruit-size hail tattered North Kansas City and suburban Gladstone on May 30, 1985. Processing the 8,830 claims, resulting in a record $9.3 million in damages, still required long days. But the forty-four American Family employees, five district managers, and ninety agents in the Kansas City area weren't left to their own devices. The Midland Region had a regional "CAT plan" that transferred adjusters from across the company to work on the Kansas City "CAT team," allowing local offices to keep up with day-to-day work.

Rising catastrophic losses compelled American Family to devise a centralized CAT response program. In December 1986, the company's disaster response planning committee asked property claims director Marv Mundt to implement a CAT program for 1988. A longtime veteran of American Family's claims division, Mundt preferred to act rather than wait. With just three months before the start of the 1987 storm season, Mundt went to work. By April, he'd organized 60 of the company's 300 property adjusters into seven CAT teams with members from all regions.

When a CAT response is initiated, team leaders arrive first to find temporary headquarters, usually in a vacant store front. Once the office is set up, the rest of the team arrives. A storm administrator commands each team, assisted by auto, property, and support team leaders. The size and composition of a team varies on the size of the storm and number of losses.

American Family's catastrophe response has evolved over the past ten years. Cooperation and coordination have expanded beyond the claims division. While office administration supplies CAT teams with material and equipment, advertising steps in to inform policyholders about how to receive claims service. Public relations coordinates media relations efforts. The teamwork means many policyholders receive checks on the spot.

"You can sell a lot of policies or lose a lot of policies, depending on the service you give after a storm," said Mundt. "We get people out there immediately."

In 1997, an American Family catastrophe team responded to record flooding along the Minnesota-North Dakota border. Joe Nedbal (left) of Schaumburg, Illinois, and Andy Boone of Lincoln, Nebraska, inspect a car damaged by the floodwaters.

Catastrophic storms battered the nation in 1984, contributing to a record $3.5 billion operating loss for the insurance industry.

lawyers' aggressive attitude, many insurance companies failed to establish adequate reserves for liability cases, eventually leading to capacity and solvency problems.

Pushed by lawsuits, cash-flow underwriting, and catastrophic storms, the industry's combined ratio—the measure of claims and operating costs against premiums—increased for seven consecutive years. By 1985, for every dollar of premium insurers collected, they paid out $1.18 in claims and expenses. The result was a record $5.5 billion operating loss in 1985. Scores of carriers declared bankruptcy—forty in 1985 alone. Survivors retrenched. Companies sharply increased premiums, restricted new business, abandoned entire regions, eliminated agencies, and laid off employees—drawing more venom from an already hostile public.

Caution and Creativity

With nearly $1 billion in assets at the beginning of the decade, the American Family Group was among a handful of insurance companies that rode out the stormy insurance cycle by resisting the lure of cash-flow underwriting. Rather than cut rates to attract business, American Family implemented modest price increases where possible and trimmed back promotional efforts. Total policies in force grew slowly but steadily from 3.05 million in 1981 to 3.4 million in 1985. "We laid low during the price-war days," Koch said.

To compensate for its less competitive prices, American Family's actuarial division under Jim Pfefferle refined the auto rating system with an accident surcharge plan and ZIP-code-based rating. American Family Life also developed several innovative products, including the L-95 life insurance policy for nonsmokers. Introduced in 1981, the L-95 won instant favor, accounting for 22 percent of AFLIC's 400,000 policies in force by 1984. American Family's universal life policy—with its flexible premium and higher dividend—met with equal enthusiasm in October 1984. After just eight months, AFLIC had more than $1 billion of universal life insurance in force.

In 1982, American Family Mutual introduced the Gold Star Homeowners policy, bundling several of the most popular coverages together. The company followed this with a combined farm/ranch package and coverage for older homes. American Family Financial Services entered the auto leasing market in 1984, and health lines introduced a Medicare supplemental insurance policy in 1985.

Under Floyd Desch and Dale Mathwich, marketing responded with equal creativity. As director of marketing, Mathwich initiated an aggressive step to keep sales up and agent incomes strong. American Family agents received a flat commission—ten dollars for full auto coverage—generated by an initiation fee collected with the first premium. As a percent of premium, the flat fee made sense before hyperinflation. But by 1980, American Family commissions were woefully out of date—particularly in urban areas where expenses had increased dramatically. Mathwich and planning and development director Robbie Robinson proposed replacing the flat fee with a 10 percent commission on new and renewal business. Commissions in some cases tripled, motivating agents to keep selling during this difficult period. To protect rural agents—who in many cases would see their commissions decrease under the 10 percent plan—Mathwich set a seven-dollar minimum commission, equal to the average rural agent commission under the previous plan.

Directing American Family's profitable health lines operation in the early 1980s were (from left) claims director Bob Scott, health lines director Bob Powers, services manager Bonnie Rostad, and underwriting director Marty Brewer.

Despite its $4 million price tag, Desch and Koch approved the revision. The result: a 5.1 percent surge in policies in force in 1981. "All of a sudden, our agents were making some real money selling automobile insurance," Mathwich said. The improved commissions helped agents maintain their income during the competitively difficult years of the early 1980s. In the latter half of the decade, the commission structure contributed significantly to the company's growth.

Also in 1981, the marketing division revised American Family's district manager (DM) agreements. Strong in the 1970s, suburban growth was expected to continue unabated in the 1980s. Because American Family's district managers had exclusive rights to designated counties, many of the fastest growing suburban markets were underserved by American Family agents. Working with Minnesota North state director Harvey Pierce, Wisconsin South state director Jim Johnson, and marketing administration director Bill Kleinheinz, Mathwich revised the DM agreements. By eliminating exclusive territories for newly appointed managers, the company could place multiple DMs in large suburban counties. To unlock counties controlled by veteran managers, the committee developed a program to compensate them for turning over some of their agents to new district managers. This helped new DMs get started and encouraged veteran managers to recruit new agents. As a result, the number of districts grew to 159 by 1987.

In 1983, after a rash of district managers appointed their relatives to take over large agencies, Mathwich implemented a rule barring district managers from appointing relatives as agents. DMs, however, could appoint relatives of other managers.

The marketing division offered additional support to metropolitan agents through an in-house advertising agency. At Mathwich's urging, advertising manager Bob Salisbury hired Annette

Business lines contributed to American Family's success with the 1987 introduction of the heartland package to insure older buildings.

Succeeding Charlie Ambrosavage as director of sales promotions in January 1983, Dick Adler combines crazy antics with a keen understanding of what motivates agents.

Knapstein in September 1983 to help metropolitan agents use their co-op advertising dollars more efficiently. "Agents in major metropolitan areas couldn't make their co-op money go as far," Knapstein explained. "And with many agents or groups of agents advertising, they weren't presenting a unified image of the company." Starting in Milwaukee, Knapstein worked with metro-area agents to buy advertising. Not only did this unified approach give the agents additional buying power, but the 15 percent commission Knapstein earned as an advertising agency went back to the field force. By 1985, nearly 800 agents had enrolled in the metro advertising program.

To finally give rural agents a full line of products, Mathwich and Robinson worked with farm/ranch (then called general lines) director Darrell Riley to expand the farmowners policy. The company had introduced farm fire insurance in Wisconsin in 1957 but had expanded the line to only three additional states by 1982. Mathwich, Robinson, and Riley brought the popular farmowners policy to all eleven states by March 1984.

American Family further enhanced the careers of agents and district managers in the late 1970s and early 1980s with disability insurance, errors and omissions coverage, a lifetime extended earnings program, and increased limits on its group hospital and life policies.

Jerry Rekowski

All Your Protection Under One Roof

Insurance can get weird. Take, for example, the college athlete who insures himself against career-ending injuries, or the Elks Club that promises to give an automobile to anyone who sinks a hole in one during their fundraiser, or the horse owner who insures a prizewinning thoroughbred. There are carriers that cover these and other extraordinary risks, but finding them can be difficult. In 1985, to help American Family live up to its motto "All your protection under one roof," the marketing department launched American Family Brokerage, Inc. (AFBI). Conceived by vice president of marketing Dale Mathwich, AFBI serves agents and policyholders by finding insurers to cover hard-to-place risks.

To develop and manage AFBI, Mathwich chose Jerry Rekowski. A ten-year veteran with American Family, Rekowski had spent the previous five years as the Midland Region's business lines underwriting manager. Rekowski hammered out the details of AFBI's operation and was the new company's lone staff member when it opened for business in March 1985. Within a year, Rekowski had seven employees serving 2,600 policies, representing a quarter of a million dollars in premiums. Although AFBI serves American Family policyholders only, annual premiums soared to $11 million in just ten years.

The brokerage company also serves as a testing ground for the American Family Group. "We generate loss results that someone else is insuring, then make a decision about whether it is wise to go into that market," Rekowski explained. Based on its brokerage experience, American Family decided not to insure small planes but to cover jet skis and similar personal watercraft. "Through the brokerage company, we gained some knowledge of that market, the demographics, the loss results, what the premiums should be," Rekowski said, "then we stepped in."

American Family's underwriting division under Jim Klokner pitched in with an old stand-by—a field underwriting program—that had a new twist. Instead of the "shotgun approach" that previous field underwriting programs had aimed at the entire field force, the agent profit program (APP) targeted the 40 percent of agents whose business produced losses for the company. Designed by underwriter John Bornick, APP did more than train agents to be selective. Through APP, the underwriting division taught agents and their office staff to recognize opportunities to sell additional coverages, increasing premiums and profits.

As part of the agent profit program, underwriter Tom Spilde (left) reviews the files of agent Ed Grzenia (right), while district manager Joe Tisserand looks on.

The Midland Region field-tested APP in 1982, which suited incoming regional vice president Harvey Pierce. He preached profit—not for profit's sake but for the financial strength it rendered, enabling the company to hold premiums down and stay in business. "We stressed a philosophy with the agents: For every dollar you make, you need to make the company a dollar," Pierce said. APP went companywide in 1983. American Family bolstered the program with direct-mail campaigns that offered to increase selected policyholders' health, auto, and homeowners coverage. The combined effort reduced underwriting losses while adding millions of dollars in premium income—benefiting policyholders, the company, and the field force.

Tightening the corporate belt also contributed to American Family's survival during this difficult period. An old-fashioned "checkbook awareness" policy made staff more conscious of the cost of everything from travel to paper clips. Employees understood the importance of being good stewards of policyholders' money. Thanks to their efforts, American Family's expense ratio (operating expenses in relation to premium revenue) dropped from 35.7 percent in 1982 to 30 percent in 1985, saving millions of dollars. None of these savings came from layoffs; in fact, the number of full-time employees grew by 500 to 4,731.

In 1982, Pete Miller celebrated his sixty-fifth birthday and stepped down as chairman and CEO (remaining on the board as an outside director until age

In 1984, American Family paid just $77,000 into state-operated guaranty funds to cover claims against insolvent insurance companies. As the industry's price war took its toll, however, guaranty-fund assessments skyrocketed. American Family paid $2.5 million into the funds in 1985, $3 million in 1986, and $4.2 million in 1987.

Computerization contributed to cost-control efforts in the early 1980s. Here, Mary Moravec (right) and Diane Noyes enter information into CLASS, the new comprehensive life application servicing system.

In 1956, John Sreenan traveled to Chicago for the first Leading Career Agents Convention. He earned his way to every LCA/All American Convention after that. At the Toronto All American Convention in 1981, Sreenan became American Family's first twenty-five year Hall of Fame member.

seventy). Like Herman Wittwer, Miller often chose to stay in the background, letting others do their jobs. This style contributed to a smooth transition following his retirement. "Pete believed in delegation," Koch said. "Many times, with tough decisions, I would walk in to Pete's office and say, 'Here's the situation, and this is what I would recommend.' He would always say, 'Go ahead. I know you'll do a good job.'"

That confidence prevailed as Miller turned over the $1.2 billion organization to Koch on August 1, 1982. The NAII shared Miller's confidence in Koch, electing him to serve out Miller's term on its board of directors. To succeed him as president and chief operating officer (COO) of the American Family Group, Koch chose Floyd Desch, vice president of marketing. "Floyd had all the elements I was looking for. He had a strong marketing background. He was ethical, dedicated, loyal, and highly intelligent," Koch said. "He was a real gentleman."

Enough's Enough

Vision and planning were among Koch's managerial attributes. But Koch, like everyone around him, found less and less time for these essential activities. Senior managers spent more time putting out fires. This left little energy for strategic thinking, leading to burnout and uncertainty throughout the organization. To address the situation, Koch named underwriting director Lou Olson as vice president of corporate research in 1980. As head of research, Olson chaired the strategic planning team, which included Miller as chairman, Koch as president, and the vice presidents of office administration, management information systems, investments, marketing, and finance. Olson developed the blueprint for the corporate research division and moved forward on developing a five-year strategic plan. He died, however, in April 1982 and was succeeded by underwriting director Alan Hunter.

In 1983, Hunter's strategic planning committee presented a five-year plan that laid out six objectives: (1) improve productivity 5 percent each year, (2) reduce the expense ratio 0.5 percent each year, (3) hold losses due to catastrophic storms to no more than 12 percent of all claims, (4) increase the number of policies in force 5 percent each year, (5) achieve a return on net worth of 15 percent or the industry average, and (6) maintain a combined loss-and-expense ratio of 100 percent or less.

Following the plan, American Family parted ways with the industry in 1983, aggressively raising premiums where necessary, controlling expenses, and adhering to profit-minded underwriting policies. The company's determined attitude led to a dramatic turnaround a full year before the industry began similar steps toward recovery. In 1983, American Family cut its underwriting loss to $24 million, half the $50 million loss in 1982. Investment income helped the company add $70 million to surplus. The company's combined loss-expense ratio stood at 102 percent, compared to the industry's 111 percent. The following year, catastrophic storms staggered the industry, forcing many companies to draw on their surplus. But a record $17 million profit from AFLIC combined with investment income and profits from health lines and financial services offset auto and homeowners losses and enabled American Family to add $24 million to surplus.

In 1985, "cash-flow" companies, some with capacity ratios exceeding $3-to-$1, increased premiums, dumped business, jettisoned agencies, and laid off employees. Once again, American Family found itself at a competitive advantage. New business applications surged to a record 858,000—a 26 percent increase over 1984. With a capacity ratio of $1.96-to-$1, American Family was ready for the growth spurt. "We are one of the survivors of a period of

Alan Hunter

Sales trainer Ralph Kaye (left) presents Floyd Desch with a collection of ties given to the American Family president by agents attending an October 1983 advanced sales seminar.

In 1984, cash-flow insurance companies attempted to recover losses through large premium increases. The trend hit the liability market particularly hard, where insurers tightened underwriting rules and increased rates from 500 percent to 2,000 percent. Suddenly, many bars and restaurants, day-care centers and school districts were unable to afford liability coverage—or even find a company willing to provide it. This opened the door for American Family's business coverage, which was the company's fastest growing line in many states the following year.

cash-flow suicide," president Desch told the executive staff in March 1985.

Desch, however, did not survive to enjoy the success he helped engineer. Diagnosed with cancer just a few months earlier, he died on April 12, 1985. "Floyd Desch was a man who possessed the highest ethical standards in all his dealings. He was a gracious man, and throughout his life his first concern was for others," Koch said of his friend in a memo to all employees. "We have lost a good friend, and we at American Family will miss him." Days later, home-office staff and field men and women from across American Family's eleven states crowded into Bethel Lutheran Church, built on the site of the old Boyd mansion, to pay their respects to one of American Family's finest leaders.

A smooth transition followed Desch's death, thanks to a reorganization plan that he, Koch, and vice president of human resources Norb Vanden Heuvel had developed. The plan created four executive vice president (EVP) positions reporting to the president. Previously, half the vice presidents reported to the president and half to the chairman. The new structure enabled the chairman to spend more time as American Family's representative to the community and industry—roles for which the knowledgeable and affable Koch was well suited.

Weeks before Desch died, Koch announced the appointment of the EVPs: Bert Hutchison, corporate legal; Jim Klokner, operations; Dale Mathwich, administration; and Clayton Nelson, marketing. Though the appointments didn't become official until June 1985, the new EVPs stepped in immediately to pick up the slack. But it took awhile for these four strong-willed men to settle into their new positions.

At the board of directors' request, Koch assumed the additional

American Family's remarkable turnaround prompted The Capital Times *to proclaim the company a "bright star" in the troubled insurance industry.*

Floyd R. Desch
A Gentleman at the Head of the American Family Table

I n the summer of 1954, Floyd Desch, his wife, and three young children left Grinnell, Iowa, for their new home in Spencer and a new job as district manager with the Farmers Mutual Automobile Insurance Company. The move was hard. Desch had worked in the treasurer's office of Grinnell College, and the extra money he made as a part-time agent for Farmers Mutual, helped him and his family enjoy a good life. Ellie, his wife, loved the idyllic college town east of Des Moines, and two of his children were in grade school. But the prospect of management appealed to Desch, and after some soul searching he accepted the district manager's position.

Born in Des Moines, on September 17, 1921, Desch grew up in the heart of America's farm belt during the Great Depression. After graduating from high school in 1939, he spent two years working for the Central Life Insurance Company in Des Moines. In 1942, he left home for Burbank, California, and a job at Lockheed Aircraft. Shortly thereafter, Desch joined the air force. His three-year stint included two years as a B-24 group communications officer over Italy.

After the war, the young vet married Eleanor Brustman and entered the prestigious Grinnell College. Three years and two children later, Desch graduated with honors and took a job as assistant to the treasurer and later as cashier. Friendly yet respectful, Desch found success as a part-time agent. As a district manager, his willingness to listen and eagerness to help quickly earned him the respect

President 1982-1985

and loyalty of his agents—and the attention of agency director Gus Kinnamon. He brought Desch to Madison as sales training manager in 1956 to establish Farmers Mutual's home-office sales schools and write the company's first sales tracks.

In 1958, Desch returned to the field as the Nebraska state director. A year later, he succeeded E.A. Bergemann in the enviable position of Wisconsin West state director. American Family president Pete Miller appointed Desch to the new post of marketing vice president in 1970. A year later, when Kinnamon retired, the agency function became part of Desch's marketing division. As

marketing vice president, Desch pushed the company to hire more women and minorities in the home office and the field, and he established the district managers' retirement plan.

Desch remained popular with the field force by keeping their interest at heart. Their trust helped the company in the mid-1970s when the Internal Revenue Service insisted that American Family agents were employees for whom the company should pay Social Security tax. The field force lined up behind Desch, arguing successfully that agents were independent contractors. When Bob Koch named Desch president of the American Family Insurance Group in 1982, the agents applauded.

As an executive, Desch retained his gentle, supportive nature, preferring to build up people rather than dress them down. The approach earned Desch deep-seated loyalty from almost everyone he knew. But his strength was also his weakness, according to some. At times too kind hearted, Desch occasionally avoided confronting issues head on.

But he admired the aggressive, hard-driving state directors and emulated them by pushing to expand the company, both within its existing territory and by entering new states.

Desch died on April 12, 1985, following a battle with cancer. He was sixty four. The day of his funeral, friends and colleagues from across American Family's eleven-state territory filled Bethel Lutheran Church to capacity to pay their respects to one of the finest gentlemen ever to lead American Family.

Speaking at American Family's 1986 sales management conference, recently appointed president Dale Mathwich focused on his goal of making the company strong, growing, and friendly. That theme became American Family's motto and the framework for its strategic plan.

responsibilities of president until Desch's successor could be named. The following year, Koch selected Mathwich as president and COO effective April 1, 1986. "He had proven himself in everything he'd done—as an agent, district manager, state director, and vice president of marketing," Koch explained.

Mathwich reshuffled the senior management deck. He dissolved the EVP of administration post he had held and created two new EVP positions—field operations and finance. Mathwich chose Midland regional vice president Harvey Pierce to head field operations and investment vice president Paul King as treasurer and EVP of finance.

A few months after becoming president of American Family, Mathwich gave the keynote address at the thirty-third sales management conference in Oconomowoc, Wisconsin. Though he'd spoken to this group many times as vice president of marketing, this was his first opportunity as president. "I wanted to present my concept of how the company would succeed under my leadership," Mathwich recalled.

A firm believer in keeping things simple, Mathwich reduced his ideas to three key concepts: Strong, growing, and friendly. Each of these concepts represented a goal for American Family under his direction. "I'm asking each of you to adopt these goals," Mathwich said. "Then, working together, we'll move into an exciting and rewarding future." Mathwich's simple but powerful words struck a chord throughout American Family. The following year, the strategic planning team adopted "strong, growing, and friendly" as part of the

In memory of its late president, Floyd Desch, American Family established a $100,000 memorial fund to support the actuarial science-risk and insurance department at the University of Wisconsin-Madison.

corporation's objectives, crafting the five-year strategic plan around these three concepts.

American Family was poised to live up to Mathwich's vision. In 1986, new apps surpassed 1 million for the first time. Premium income exceeded $1 billion, and assets totaled more than $2 billion. AFLIC surpassed $10 billion of in-force life insurance. The following year, premium income increased 20 percent to $1.5 billion, and policies in force grew to 4.2 million. In 1988, American Family celebrated its third consecutive million-app year, its third consecutive $100 million operating gain, and an excellent capacity ratio of $2.06-to-$1.

Beyond the Tornado Belt

In 1983, American Family's five-year strategic plan called for an annual 5 percent increase in policies. Meeting such an ambitious goal required adding new territory. Mathwich, then vice president of marketing, and the planning and development team presented the strategic planning committee with an analysis of sixteen western states plus Kentucky and Tennessee. After Koch and Desch added Texas and California to the mix, Mathwich and the marketing division devised a plan for entering new territories. Drawing on his experience in Illinois and the company's history in Colorado, Mathwich laid out a plan for controlled growth. The strategy called for a state director and four district managers focused in a single metropolitan area. A central office from which rookie agents would work for the first ninety days and receive help from an on-site sales trainer would boost production. To gain an early foothold, American Family would enter the market with an aggressive advertising campaign and rates 10 percent below the major competition's. By gradually adding agents and district managers, the plan called for profitability in nine years.

In March 1985, the strategic planning team approved Mathwich's plan and selected

Between 1978 and 1982, just 10 tornadoes struck Arizona. During that same period, the eleven states American Family served averaged 137 twisters.

To keep up with the rush of applications submitted by Phoenix agents, Jim Andersen, American Family's lone underwriter in Arizona, put in twelve-hour days. Three others eventually joined him, but it was some time before the long hours let up. Andersen wasn't alone. More policies meant more claims, forcing adjuster Bob Vancil to put in long hours as well. American Family's plan called for a second adjuster during the first year. But with claims far ahead of planning, the company employed seven Arizona adjusters by December.

American Family entered Arizona with an aggressive advertising campaign and auto premiums 10 percent below its major competitors.

Arizona as American Family's twelfth operating state. Research showed that more than 160,000 people from the company's service area moved to Arizona between 1975 and 1980. Beyond the 3,000 to 4,000 policyholders this represented, it meant a ready-made market familiar with American Family. The weather that attracted these midwestern emigrants also attracted the company. Not only were there no blizzards, but the state suffered few hailstorms and tornadoes. After hearing the details, the board of directors approved the plan and the selection of Arizona on May 14, 1985.

To spearhead the effort, Mathwich chose marketing director Dave Wunsch as Arizona state director. Wunsch selected four district managers—Dan DeSalvo, Tom Holmen, George Novak, and Mike Campbell—to join him in Phoenix. An aggressive builder, Wunsch failed to follow the plan, preferring rapid expansion over controlled growth. An extremely competitive rate fueled his fire. Shortly after American Family opened its doors in Arizona on March 1, 1986, the state's established carriers filed a 15 percent increase in auto rates. American Family followed suit. Because American Family lacked a claims history in Arizona, however, the insurance commissioner rejected the increase—leaving the company with an auto rate 25 percent below the competition's. "We had what we referred to as a smoking rate, and we wrote business like crazy," said DeSalvo, now executive vice president of sales. With Wunsch's emphasis on quantity over quality, a large portion of this new business proved unprofitable—particularly for American Standard. Meanwhile, busy agents ignored the profitable homeowners market.

The low rates didn't attract policyholders only. The prospect of easy sales drew agents, including a number of American Family veterans from other states. In just nine months, the four district managers had forty-nine full-time and fifteen part-time agents—nearly three times more than planned. By the end of the year, Wunsch and his team had 41,000 policyholders—four times the projections.

The Arizona management team reviews floor plans for its new office. Pictured (from left) are district manager (DM) Dan DeSalvo, DM Mike Campbell, sales trainer Harold Young, DM Tom Holmen, state director Dave Wunsch, and DM George Novak.

The explosive growth challenged American Family's split-management structure, under which the marketing division managed the field force while the Midland Region handled the operating and service functions. After a few months, the company consolidated everything under Midland. "We started to slow Arizona's growth," Pierce, then Midland regional vice president, said. "The sales volume was exciting, but the number of claims disturbed many in the home office. They focused on the losses and thought that in five years we'd be buried under claims. It scared everybody."

Everybody, that is, except controller Brent Johnson. Pointing to Arizona's fast-growing policy count, he emphasized that American Family's plan was working. It was just ahead of schedule. "We hit our five-year policy count prematurely, so we're going to hit our five-year losses prematurely," he told Pierce and others.

In the fall of 1987, Wunsch stepped down as state director to become a district manager in Phoenix. Gary Hunter, Colorado state director for thirteen years, succeeded Wunsch. Hunter turned the focus from sales volume to profitability, which American Family achieved in Arizona in 1991, three years ahead of schedule.

Madison agent Chuck Webster (left), the first American Family agent to sell more than $1 million of life insurance in a year in 1966, remains one of the company's top representatives. Here, vice president John Reed presents Webster with an award for leading the company in life insurance sales in 1987.

Black Monday

After several years of price stability, the nation's economy began to heat up in 1987. In late summer, the stock market started a thousand-point slide that culminated in a 508-point plunge on October 19, 1987—Black Monday.

Because of its strong capacity ratio, American Family could afford an aggressive investment strategy. At the time of the crash, the company had nearly half its $2 billion of invested assets in the stock market—considerably higher than the 30 percent to 35 percent industry average. The remainder of American Family's investments was divided among bonds, mortgages and real estate, and cash equivalents. Despite the relatively large exposure, vice president of investments Tom King (no relation to Paul King) refused to panic, neither buying nor selling. By the end of the day, American Family had lost $57 million.

Tuesday morning, Tom King, Paul King, Dale Mathwich, and Bob Koch met for breakfast. The four men were not squeamish investors prone to panic-attack selling, and they quickly ruled out that option. Other than rising inflation, the market and the economy seemed sound. Rather than sell, they decided to sit tight—perhaps even pick up a few bargains. They also decided to tell employees of the loss and of senior management's response. With the market crash dominating the papers and newscasts, employees were sure to speculate about its effect on American Family. The facts, bad as they were, were better than rumors. After the meeting, Paul King wrote a candid memo telling employees of the company's $57 million loss. "That was one of the best things we could have done," Tom King said. "People were relieved to hear from top management, acknowledging the loss but telling them it was by no means crippling." In fact, American Family's capacity ratio stood at exactly $2-to-$1—compared to $1.89-to-$1 the day before—still among the healthiest in the industry. The market recovered by year's end, and with it American Family's investments, which turned a net profit in 1987.

In 1985, American Family revenues surpassed $1 billion for the first time. Noting the milestone, chairman Bob Koch said, "When I started in 1948, the company collected a little over $7 million in premiums. Now, we collect almost $7 million every Monday."

The October 19, 1987, stock market crash dominated the media, stirring up fears of a long bear market and possibly another Great Depression.

Addressing Government and Consumers

The turmoil of the early 1980s increased public resentment of insurance carriers and attracted more government scrutiny. To better respond to state and federal activity, American Family in 1983 split its law and government affairs division. Al Gruenisen, corporate secretary and vice president of the division, had been involved in government relations since the 1960s and assumed responsibility for the new government affairs division. Bert Hutchison, associate general counsel since 1969, became vice president of corporate legal. To gain support from American Family agents and employees, Gruenisen initiated a strong grass-roots program that kept people informed on the issues and urged them to contact their lawmakers. When Gruenisen retired in 1983, government affairs came under Hutchison. As the political battles heated up and the stakes got higher, Hutchison and assistant general counsel James Malinske expanded American Family's advocacy staff to make the company's voice heard in state legislatures and the halls of Congress.

Bert Hutchison   Ann Haney

During the early 1980s, most of the legislative activity regarding insurance occurred at the state level. A record number of insurance company bankruptcies caught the attention of Congress. Critics of the industry charged that state regulators were underfunded and ill-equipped to police large, multistate insurance carriers, prompting calls for federal solvency standards and igniting a four-year assault on the McCarran-Ferguson Act. Ironically, as dozens of insurance companies declared bankruptcy, consumer groups charged the industry with profiteering. Congress responded with the 1986 tax reform act, raising taxes on insurance carriers. The following year, the industry paid $2.8 billion in federal taxes—seven times more than it would have paid under the previous law. American Family's tax bill jumped from $2.6 million to $9.5 million.

Although insurers were by and large on the defense with Congress and state legislatures, the industry took the offensive on several issues—making air bags mandatory, raising the legal drinking age to twenty-one, strengthening drunken driving penalties, and maintaining the 55 mph speed limit. In 1986, insurers led the fight to reform a legal system gone awry. Despite the low regard many Americans had for the insurance industry, polls showed they supported the industry's bid for tort reform. Thirty-nine states enacted legal reforms that year, with more changes to follow. Despite the support of presidents Ronald

American Family and practically everyone in the insurance business believe in state regulation. It's closer to the people and problems, and it's easier to fix if necessary. In fact, state insurance laws are under constant reform. All this activity and progress taking place in the states shows that the McCarran-Ferguson Act is right to put insurance regulation in the hands of the states.

—Dale Mathwich

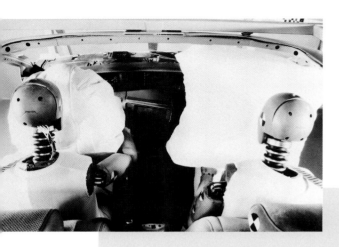

Reagan and George Bush, federal tort reform remained elusive.

American Family participated in these and other political battles through its government affairs staff, its own political action committees, and its support of the National Association of Independent Insurers and other trade groups. The company also addressed its own policyholders' dissatisfaction. The sheer size and complexity of insurance companies created an aura of impersonality. Callers often found themselves passed from one person to another as employees attempted to answer complex questions and com-

Used properly in conjunction with seat belts, airbags save thousands of lives each year.

Buckle Up for Safety

Today, everyone who gets in a car has the option of buckling their seat belt—which wasn't always the case. In 1950, Nash-Kelvinator unveiled a Rambler boasting the first factory-installed seat belts. Car buyers overwhelmingly rejected the innovation; many who bought the odd little car with a 100-inch wheelbase asked their dealers to remove the safety belts. Six years later, studies demonstrated the lifesaving value of seat belts. Heeding the facts, Farmers Mutual installed the safety devices in company cars and made them available to agents and policyholders. In 1962, Wisconsin became the first state to require all automobiles sold within its borders to have seat belts. Four years later, the National Traffic and Motor Vehicle Safety Act made seat belts a national mandate.

Continuing its crusade for safer automobiles, the National Association of Independent Insurers (NAII) and the Insurance Institute for Highway Safety (IIHS) urged automakers to install air bags in 1972. After five years of campaigning, insurers won the support of President Jimmy Carter, who approved safety standards that phased in mandatory passive restraints (air bags or automatic seat belts) by 1984. To promote air bags, American Family in 1979 offered a 30 percent discount on personal injury protection coverage for cars with passive restraints.

Carmakers continued to argue against the mandate. Manufacturers "feel a customer is not intrigued and won't buy a car with these accessories," explained Al Gruenisen, a member of the NAII committee on passive restraints.

Automakers found a sympathetic ear in the government-cutting administration of President Ronald Reagan. In 1982, the Department of Transportation (DOT) withdrew the mandate. A legal battle that wound up before the U.S. Supreme Court forced the DOT, under Elizabeth Dole, to implement a new standard in 1984.

Political maneuvering continued through the remainder of the decade, with insurers ultimately convincing carmakers and the DOT of the value of air bags. By 1993, 71 percent of new cars had factory-installed air bags, with 1998 set as the deadline for all new cars to be so equipped.

After airbags killed several children and frail adults, some people in 1997 began to question the value and safety of airbags. American Family and the IIHS, however, remain fully supportive of airbags. "If they are used properly in conjunction with seat belts, airbags save lives," said Dale Mathwich, American Family chairman and CEO and member of the IIHS board of directors. "Young children should always sit in the rear seat," Mathwich emphasized.

plaints. In 1983, American Family hired former Wisconsin insurance commissioner Ann Haney as director of its new consumer affairs department. Haney's staff handled all customer complaints, navigating the American Family maze on the policyholder's behalf. "We accept accountability for the call and see it through to completion," Haney said. "We save both the customer and American Family three or four phone calls." After resolution, the consumer affairs department coded each complaint by such factors as type of insurance, nature of complaint, location, and outcome. This transformed complaints into a management tool that helped identify trends, analyze policies and procedures, and make corrections. Today, under Vanessa Mosley, consumer affairs complies with regulations in thirteen states relating to consumer complaint handling. Staff members enter customer contacts into an electronic system that helps ensure the company provides timely response.

Jim Eldridge

American Family has always understood that quick claim response retains policyholders and often leads claimants to seek insurance through the company. In the 1980s, claims vice president Jim Eldridge established a policy of contacting injured people within twenty-four hours. "Establishing that initial contact is very important," Eldridge said. "They know we are handling the claim and will be talking to them." Without this immediate contact, people wondered what, if anything, was being done with their case, convincing many to seek out attorneys.

Another customer-focused development from the 1980s was Qwik Pay. A back-to-the-future approach, Qwik Pay enabled agents to pay small physical damage claims immediately—a 1980s version of Harvey Spriggs pulling eight dollars from his wallet to pay a farmer for a dented fender and asking the company to reimburse him. In the first year, agents paid 24,507 claims totaling $3.7 million. "Agents found having the insured in their office while working out the settlement was a more friendly approach," said Annette Zacher, strategic research director. "They could ask questions, discuss their coverages and how the claim was settled, plus receive a draft, all at the same time."

In 1986, American Family became one of the first insurance companies to adopt a windshield repair program, saving an estimated $47 million in the first eight years. Pictured here, Larry Farino (left) and Toby Nechkash from Auto Glass Specialists Inc. of Madison demonstrate the repair process.

American Family chairman Bob Koch displays his 1989 Distinguished Alumni Award from the University of Wisconsin.

A few years later, American Family brought the settlement of larger claims closer to its customers by building service centers in areas with a concentration of American Family policyholders. Under the old system, claims adjusters served widespread sales districts from a single site. In the Minneapolis/St. Paul area, where the service-center approach was introduced in 1988, that meant traveling back and forth across the entire metro region. Service centers dispersed adjusters, giving policyholders faster, more reliable service while saving the adjusters time and the company money.

Although American Family and many other insurance companies continued to get high marks from their policyholders, the public as a whole grew increasingly hostile toward the insurance industry. Hostility erupted into open rebellion when California voters approved Proposition 103 on November 4, 1988. Prop. 103, the "Voter Revolt Initiative," rolled auto rates back to 1987 levels. Within weeks, other states began debating similar measures. Following passage of Prop. 103, the NAII asked board member Bob Koch to chair a special committee charged with mapping out a communications plan that would go beyond the association's traditional work with the media. The committee developed Talking Points, a program to help the entire industry speak with one voice to Congress and the public. Through Talking Points, the NAII provides timely, concise information that its members disseminate through magazine and newsletter articles, speeches, and premium stuffers.

Koch completed his NAII work shortly before stepping down as chairman and CEO of the American Family Group on December 31, 1989, the group's fourth consecutive million-app year. Following the tradition set by Pete Miller, he continued on the board until his seventieth birthday in 1995.

A gifted leader, Koch inspired the company's agents and employees to make the best use of their abilities, resulting in phenomenal growth. When he became president of the American Family Group in 1977, American Family Mutual, with assets of $596 million and total revenue of $448 million, didn't rank among the top twenty property/casualty insurers. When Koch retired, the company, operating in just twelve states, had $3.3 billion in assets, annual revenue exceeding $2 billion, and was the eighteenth-largest property/casualty insurance carrier in the nation.

*The success of a company is
in direct relation to the cooperation,
loyalty, and hard work of all.*

—HERMAN WITTWER

TEAMWORK AND TECHNOLOGY

Herman Wittwer founded Farmers Mutual to provide farmers with low-cost auto insurance. He also understood that quality service was essential to retaining members. So he set a high standard for prompt, courteous service. Every application was to be processed into a policy and placed in the mail on the day it arrived. Every letter, every telegram, every phone call that required a response was to receive one on the same day. To achieve this daunting goal, Wittwer and his partner Richard Kalbskopf joined the staff each morning around a large wooden table to open and sort the mail.

Like their policyholders, Farmers Mutual employees believed in working hard. With the exception of lunch, staff remained at their desks the entire day. Only the receptionist received a coffee break. Once in the Boyd mansion, however, employees enjoyed brief morning and afternoon breaks.

Each afternoon, they met again at the table to stuff and stamp envelopes. The pace was hectic. Many evenings after supper, accountant Harold Frank and his wife Maybelle returned to the office to post the day's entries in the ledger. Often, they found Wittwer at his desk tending to his fledgling company.

The combination of low premiums and responsive service appealed to many Wisconsin farmers. By December 1929, Farmers Mutual had more than 4,500 policyholders and fifteen employees. To maintain service, the home office had to become more efficient. Wittwer organized the staff into nine departments—accounting, underwriting, policy writing, statistical, mailing, supplies and purchases, agency, stenography, and claims. Still, everyone met around the mail table at the beginning and end of the day.

Turning to office machines for additional help, Frank purchased a

Start the Presses

Through the 1930s, Farmers Mutual's printing capacity consisted solely of the stenography department's mimeograph machines churning out blurry, blue-ink copies. In the 1940s and 1950s, tabulating machines that read information off punch cards printed premium notices and certificates. The cost-cutting magic of photocopying came to Farmers Mutual in 1958 when Bob Kelliher bought a photocopy machine to reproduce policies. The delicate piece of equipment required daily cleaning and polishing and top-to-bottom maintenance every six months. A few years later, the company upgraded, leasing two Xerox 914s that cranked out 19,000 copies a month.

To save money on its ever-increasing printing costs, Farmers Mutual purchased a Multilith press and formed a printing department under the leadership of Dick Kopp, who later joined the field force, earning rookie of the year in 1964 before going on to become a leading agent and district manager. As the company grew, so did the print shop. By the mid-1970s, the department, under Bob Beyler, had two composing machines, an electrostatic camera burning 19,750 master plates a year, and five presses producing 15.5 million impressions annually. Other machines collated, cut, folded, and bound manuals, circulars, booklets, and brochures.

In 1994, printing and graphics supervisor Al Lewis oversaw the print shop's move from its 17,000-square-foot home on Darbo Drive to a building more than twice that size near the company's new national headquarters on the outskirts of Madison.

Today, the print shop boasts ten presses, including a huge four-color web press. The shop can handle orders as small as fifty impressions or as large as 2 million. Smaller jobs automatically come to the shop, but Lewis' staff has to bid on the larger ones. "In order to get the job, we have to come up with the lowest bid," Lewis said.

That usually isn't a problem. "Because we don't have to build in a profit margin," Lewis explained, "we're usually 35 percent to 40 percent under commercial bids."

The savings are so substantial, it's almost like printing money.

Burroughs bookkeeping machine in December 1929 and postponed hiring another accountant. A second device helped cut costs in 1932 when Farmers Mutual converted to a semi-annual, semi-direct plan. By renting a Hollerith punch-card machine once a month, Farmers Mutual issued renewal certificates produced at the rate of 1,000 per hour. These replaced new policies the company issued annually, typed by the policy writing department at the rate of eight per hour. A few years later, the Wisconsin insurance department asked insurers to provide detailed breakdowns of their premium revenue, forcing Farmers Mutual to purchase its own Hollerith in 1935.

Invented in the 1880s by Charles Hollerith, the punch-card machine stored basic information in the form of coded punches on stiff paper cards. The punch holes allowed wire brushes to touch a metal cylinder, creating an electric current that told the machine to add, subtract, print, etc. Due to its ability to store and process large volumes of data, the punch-card machine—and its descendent, the computer—became essential tools for success in the insurance industry.

Farmers Mutual installed its first International Business Machines (IBM) system in 1941, starting a relationship that continues today. Supervised by Bob Kelliher, the new punch-card system included an alphabetical tabulator, a reproducer, an interpreter, a sorter, and three keypunches. A year later, the United States entered World War II, and nine Farmers Mutual employees, including Kelliher, entered the armed forces. Many Farmers Mutual employees who stayed at home spent their mornings at the company and their afternoons working in the defense plants. The IBMs helped the short-staffed home office keep up.

Bob Kelliher inspects one of Farmers Mutual's new International Business Machines installed in 1941.

Father Knows Best

Paternal by nature, Wittwer took a personal interest in his employees. He looked after them both on and off the job and, like a father, had high expectations. Employees responded with loyalty to Wittwer and dedication to his company. As his company grew, management reflected Wittwer's paternal instincts. In 1934, Farmers Mutual provided company-paid life insurance. In 1947, it added health coverage, and two years later a pension plan. Employees also enjoyed ample vacation and sick time, paid holidays, and company-paid recreation. But rules were strict and rigidly enforced. An indiscretion, even in one's private life, could result in a reprimand. Small infractions, including napping at your desk or "intentional waste," could lead to dismissal.

Following World War II, employment at Farmers Mutual doubled to 250 people. To relieve some of the burden on Harold Frank, Wittwer hired Bill Hoppe as the company's first personnel director. With Farmers Mutual swimming in applications, production was paramount. Hoppe hired efficiency experts to measure the work flow and set performance levels. Employees wrote down every task they completed, and supervisors spent much of their time making sure their staff met the standards. Bells became part of the company's culture with the construction of an addition to the Boyd mansion in 1947. For the next twenty-one years, bells ruled employees' lives. They were to be at their desks and working when the bell started the day and to stay there until the bell signaled a coffee break or the end of the workday.

The addition and the frenzied hiring of new employees strained Farmers Mutual's family-like atmosphere. New people came in every week, others left. Some worked in the main building, others in the addition. By 1951, 350 people worked at Farmers Mutual—many of them strangers to each other. But in December, they all moved to the new headquarters on East Washington Avenue. Twice the size of the Wisconsin Avenue office, the new building nevertheless brought people together under one roof. Thanks to the efforts of everyone from Wittwer to custodian Ray Sather, the company's family

A game of cards in "the Coke room" of the old Boyd mansion helps pass the time during lunch at Farmers Mutual.

atmosphere returned.

Women, known as "the girls," comprised nearly three-fourths of home-office staff. From 1942 on, personnel assistant Helen Esser, the only woman with an office, hired all the female employees. Although they didn't

Helen Esser

JoAnn Sprecher

report to her, Esser handled their personnel issues. So in 1955, when JoAnn Sprecher sought permission to return to work after having her first child, she had to see Esser. "No," Esser said, "a mother should be home with her children." Sprecher wasn't satisfied and took the issue up with her boss, controller Henry Harvey. He agreed with Sprecher, giving her a four-week leave of absence—the first such concession to working mothers at Farmers Mutual.

Male applicants interviewed with Norb Vanden Heuvel, who became assistant personnel director under Pete Miller in 1954 and personnel director in 1957. With a master's degree in personnel and marketing, Vanden Heuvel represented a new era in employee management. During his tenure, Vanden Heuvel introduced many innovations, including annual cost-of-living increases in the 1960s and 1970s, merit pay in the 1980s, peer assessment, flexible hours, and a host of new benefits.

Bob Kelliher (left), Hugh Wallace (center), and Irving Maurer welcome the RAMAC 305, which Farmers Mutual first leased in 1959 for $250,000.

Enter the Computer Age

As the volume of Farmers Mutual's business grew, so did the demand for faster data processing. In 1959, with the company handling 664,000 policies and $26.5 million in annual premiums, Kelliher recommended leasing IBM's RAMAC 305, an early business computer, for $250,000 a year. Like the previous IBMs, RAMAC used punch cards to enter data. Unlike earlier machines, this primitive computer had "memory" in the form of magnetic disks that held up to 10 million characters.

The promise of faster data processing convinced Farmers Mutual to lease RAMAC. But the by-product of data processing—information—proved equally valuable. Using RAMAC's ability to sort and analyze data, Farmers Mutual refined its underwriting classifications. RAMAC, however, couldn't handle the

John Sather loads an electronic vehicle (far left) capable of carrying thirty pounds of mail through the ceiling to waist-level loading stations located throughout the national headquarters. From there, staff transfer mail to "mailmobiles" (near left) that drive independently along preprogrammed routes. Jim Meyer picks up mail from a mailmobile.

Neither Rain, nor Sleet...

The sheer, relentless volume can seem overwhelming. Each day, American Family receives up to 50,000 pieces of mail and sends up to 140,000 pieces, placing it among the largest mail rooms in Wisconsin. Keeping up is essential. Many states require that insurers send premium notices a certain number of days before payment is due. And delays in mailing notices mean delays in receiving premiums. "If we don't get the mail out on time, the company could lose thousands of dollars a day in lost investment income," explained mail department supervisor Vonnie Ryan.

Beginning in the late 1940s, the responsibility for outgoing mail came under the print shop, where punch-card machines printed premium notices

and certificates. But in the mid-1970s, American Family consolidated all incoming and outgoing mail responsibilities under Ryan's mail department. With incoming mail exceeding 14,000 pieces a day, American Family received its own ZIP code in 1977. Eight years later, the company received a second ZIP code, routing the more than 10,000 premium payments received each day directly to the money processing center in the Great Lakes regional office. This cut in half the volume of mail sorted at the home office.

In 1978, the federal government added two cents to the price of a first-class stamp, raising postage rates to fifteen cents per ounce. To cut the cost of mailing, American Family purchased an automated inline mailer (AIM) machine designed specially by the Bell & Howell Company. More than just a stuffing machine, AIM read ZIP codes on outgoing property and casualty premium notices, marking the first envelope in each new ZIP. An operator then bun-

dled the premium notices by ZIP, saving two cents apiece—$35,000 a year. Five years later, the mail automated processing system (MAPS) expanded presorting to include life insurance premium notices, AmPlan notices, and lapse notices, saving $360,000 a year. By the early 1990s, presorting saved the company $1 million annually.

Meanwhile, bar-code technology also has reduced the time required to issue policies. At one time, policywriters assembled policies by hand. Today, the Mailstar and VELO-BIND machines read bar codes that tell the machines to collate, bind, insert, seal, and stamp outgoing policies in seconds.

With a mountain of mail to process, every second counts. So Bell & Howell staffs two on-site employees at American Family to service the mail machines. Because millions of premium dollars ride on each day's mail, Ryan said, "It's important to keep the machines running."

more than 1,100 new categories it helped create. So in 1963, Farmers Mutual installed two IBM 1400-series computers. The 1400s' principal advantage was programmability. Instead of rewiring RAMAC's computer boards, programmers used punch cards, each containing a single command, to tell the computer what to do. "You'd feed these cards into the machine and test the program by going through each step individually," recalled Don Breitenbach, one of the company's early systems experts.

As senior managers grew more interested in the information computers could provide, Farmers Mutual established an electronic data processing department, with George Riege as director. Administratively, data processing moved from office administration to finance and back before president Pete Miller created the management information systems (MIS) division in 1971. To head the new fifty-five-employee unit, Miller tapped controller Breitenbach, promoting him to vice president of MIS. Breitenbach, who never acted the role of a vice president, drove an old pickup and insisted on being treated like one of the gang. Yet, as head of MIS, he wielded tremendous power, determining which projects got priority and which waited.

Taking the Punch Out of Punch Cards

Punch cards were the only way to enter information into the computer until 1967 when American Family bought an OCR Page Reader, which "read" printed information into the computer. Five years later, the company installed its first CRT (cathode ray tube) terminals, allowing people to type information directly into the system. Taking advantage of the new technology, health lines and American Family Financial Services began working on line in 1976—but they maintained paper files as a backup.

Three years later, the company introduced the claims on-line processing system (COPS) to all lines. The sudden surge in volume overwhelmed American Family's two IBMs. "There were many days when you were surrounded with all your files because the system was down, and you couldn't input the draft," recalled claims vice president Darnell Moore, then a branch

Introduced in October 1974, the Family Album, *was American Family's first publication designed solely for employees. Produced by public relations manager Kathryn Gibson, the monthly magazine carried news about the home office, regional and branch offices. As American Family grew, public relations experimented with regional publications and a "community newspaper" to augment* Family Album. *In the spring of 1997, American Family's employee publications came full circle when the company folded regional news back into the* Family Album.

claims manager in Schaumburg, Illinois. "You had to handwrite a draft, stick it in the file, and input it later whenever the system came up."

Breitenbach called IBM to see about an upgrade. But IBM, easily the most popular computer company at the time, had a backlog of orders. Unable to wait, Breitenbach turned to a new outfit named Amdahl. The company quickly delivered an Amdahl 470-V6 to replace one of the IBMs. When the computer giant learned of the switch, several top executives visited American Family president Bob Koch to convince him to stick with Big Blue. Koch stood behind Breitenbach, even though it meant leaving the security of IBM to become one of Amdahl's first customers.

On-line processing meant the end of punch cards and keypunch operators. Since all application and claims information was captured electronically, on-line processing also signaled the demise of the history card department, which kept handwritten claims histories on all policies. But these changes didn't force anyone out the door. Constant growth at American Family created a continual demand for employees, and the company found positions for everyone who wanted to stay.

COPS served American Family through the 1980s, but in 1991 a team led by Moore, who was by then vice president of claims, information services vice president Rod Christenson (Breitenbach's successor), and health lines operations director Bob Powers began work on the claims on-line computer

Darnell Moore

The nucleus of the PLUS working committee—Bob Johnson (seated), Art Massmann (left), and Howard Boersma—test the personal lines underwriting system.

When twenty-five-time-hall-of-fame-agent Everette Pierre retired in 1997 after forty years in Clintonville, Wisconsin, he opened the door for Sheila Link, one of many underwriters who became agents after the company began downsizing the division in 1993. Link (center) cuts the ribbon held by district manager Lisa Ritchie (right) and office manager Ronda Olson. Joining them are the members of the Clintonville Chamber of Commerce.

enhanced processing tool (CONCEPT). The new system replaces CRTs with powerful personal computers (PCs) that process claims on the desktop, reducing dependence on the mainframe, according to claim administration director Bob Kovich. Rather than attempt to implement a new claims system in one step, American Family is rolling out CONCEPT in stages, with the first pieces introduced in early 1997.

Electronic Underwriting

With claims processing successfully on line, American Family began to consider other computer applications to increase productivity. In 1982, Breitenbach, corporate research director Alan Hunter, and underwriting vice president Jim Klokner headed a committee to develop a computer-assisted underwriting program. Two years later, Minnesota South tested the personal lines underwriting system (PLUS). Using PLUS, claims personnel enter application data directly to the computer. The system screens applications, issuing policies to those who meet American Family's underwriting requirements. Only apps that don't readily fit one of American Family's categories are referred to underwriters for personal attention, giving underwriters more time to make the most difficult decisions.

PLUS also allows agents to do more risk selection, providing clients with faster, more personal service. Agents' ability to accurately select and classify

In 1979, employee development instructor Nancy Yugo learned that a few companies were experimenting with programs to help workers find and access community services. The idea struck a chord. With vice president of personnel Norb Vanden Heuvel's support, Yugo began American Family's employee assistance program (EAP) as a pilot project with nearly forty volunteer employees in Madison, Wisconsin. Today, American Family contracts with half-a-dozen professional services to administer EAP, providing referrals to between 150 and 250 employees and family members a year throughout its thirteen-state operating area.

risks got a boost in March 1997 with GIROS (generic interactive report ordering system). GIROS enables agents to check an applicant's driving record in twenty-two states and claims history with other insurers while the person is in the office. This eliminates delays and avoids cancelations or reclassifications created by the later discovery of accidents or traffic violations, saving the customer, agent and company time, money, and frustration.

Emphasizing the need to drive down costs, president Harvey Pierce in 1990 asked Klokner, now executive vice president of administration, to reconsider the structure of the underwriting division. Klokner, one of the company's first resident underwriters, initially resisted any change. As technology advanced, however, Klokner also saw the opportunity for cost savings. Through a process improvement team, he and Pierce initiated a seven-year program to bring underwriters out of the field and back into the regional headquarters and select branch offices by the year 2000. American Family again avoided layoffs by retraining underwriters to work in growing areas of the company.

Milwaukee agents Mike Voss (seated) and Dennis Beaudry test the DEFACTO system in 1983.

On-Line Agents

To reduce paper flow between the home office and the field, Rod Christenson in the marketing division and John Stassi in MIS worked with Wang Laboratories on a computer system to connect agents to the home office. DEFACTO (data entry from agent's computer to ours) went on line in 1983 with primitive Apple computers in five test sites, serving fifteen agents. Although some agents found DEFACTO useful, others were disappointed by its emphasis on processing and transferring information rather than sales and marketing. "It didn't do much," recalled Dan DeSalvo, now executive vice president of sales. "It was limited in function and not widely accepted." Acceptance grew as DEFACTO offered additional marketing-related programs. District managers were hooked up to the company beginning in 1987, and by 1989 most of American Family's field force were wired to the home office.

Attracted by ACCESS, a powerful DOS-based system,

American Family began migrating back to IBM in 1993. Although it offered new features, the system demanded a great deal of computer knowledge. Frustrated by ACCESS, agents asked the company to adopt a Windows-based, point-and-click system. In early 1997, a small group of agents began testing the agency data system (ADS). Operating on Windows 95, ADS is easier to use and offers a variety of new features, including a contact management program, price-quoting capabilities, and compatibility with most off-the-shelf software.

While computers have revolutionized communications between the agents and the home office, telephones remain an essential aspect of the home office/field force relationship. In the early years of Farmers Mutual, one receptionist handled the switchboard, routing calls to the few phones scattered around the building. Agents and policyholders calling long distance reversed the charges. As the volume increased, the company added operators to the central switchboard, then "mini switchboards" that served certain divisions.

By the mid-1970s, American Family's annual phone bill surpassed $1 million. To cut costs, vice president of administration Bob Amundson installed a toll-free WATS line (wide area telephone service) in 1977, slashing thousands of dollars from the monthly phone bill. By 1982, American Family had twenty-seven WATS lines handling a total of 1,900 calls a day at the home office and regional centers. Agents complained about time spent on hold, and WATS line charges exceeded $1 million. To improve service and reduce costs, American Family installed a system that allowed agents to talk directly to computer operators who could quickly answer basic status questions during business hours. Beginning in the late 1980s, Infobot offered agents prerecorded answers to basic questions around the clock.

By 1994, 1-800 calls totaled more than 1 million minutes a month, costing nearly $90,000. American Family telecommunications manager Cary Pierce installed a 1-700 system, cutting a penny a minute off the 1-800 calls. The

Using American Family's first push-button phones, Maxine Jensen (left), Donna Gehrke (center), and Nancy Clapper handled hundreds of calls a day at the home office switchboard in 1977.

Bob Amundson

1-700 "virtual network" offers additional services such as desk-to-desk dialing throughout the company and monthly reports detailing the number of calls each agent makes, the total time, and cost to the company. Given to district managers, these reports represent another tool to help them manage their agents. The 1-700 service also allows agents to benefit from American Family's volume discount on all their long-distance calls. Currently this feature saves American Family's 3,600 agents $20,000 a month on long distance charges.

To better serve its customers, American Family also maintains separate 1-800 numbers for service and claims calls.

Norb Vanden Heuvel

Saving for Retirement Through Investment and Thrift

Farmers Mutual/American Family employees have benefited from the security of a company-paid pension plan since 1949. But in the 1970s, double-digit inflation caused many Americans to wonder how they would save the millions of dollars financial planners warned would be necessary for retirement. To help employees save for their future, vice president of personnel Norb Vanden Heuvel in 1972 proposed a mutual fund to which employees could make voluntary contributions. Each year, American Family would make a matching donation based on the company's profitability. The board of directors loved the idea, and in January 1973 American Family unveiled its investment and thrift (I&T) plan. It was an instant success as 603 employees, 94 percent of those eligible, signed up. That year, the company invested the maximum amount—300 percent of employee contributions—totaling $574,000.

Because American Family's contribution depends on the group's profitability, the I&T program gives employees an incentive to keep costs down and profits up. In the 1990s, employees have shared in American Family's success. Between 1992 and 1995, the company kicked in the maximum amount each year, totaling $58.8 million. Catastrophic storm losses, however, cut deeply into 1996 profits, reducing the company's contribution to 33 percent. Today, with assets standing at $280 million, the I&T fund provides current and future retirees with security and peace of mind far beyond what Vanden Heuvel envisioned in 1972.

CASH Back?

In the fall of 1985, executive vice president of administration Dale Mathwich sat down with vice president of MIS Don Breitenbach and controller/vice president of finance Brent Johnson to consider a new billing system. Then twenty years old, AmPlan lacked the flexibility that customers and agents demanded. Johnson appointed John Bornick as project administrator. After Bornick and vice president of corporate research Nancy Johnson completed the market research, a steering committee composed of eight vice presidents set high goals for the new system, called CASH (customer account service handling). The committee envisioned a flexible, efficient, easy-to-use system that consolidated all billing and money-processing systems.

This vision of billing nirvana affected nearly 4 million policies at the time, making it the single largest computer project ever undertaken by American Family. The complexity of the insurance business, the number of variables that can

Paul King   Tom Mooney

change a policyholder's premiums, and the fact that insurance is a prepaid product made the project even more demanding. Rapidly advancing computer capabilities further complicated the process, as the technology on which decisions were based quickly became outdated or failed to do what was promised.

After several delays, American Family introduced CASH in 1991, starting with casualty PLUS accounts in Iowa. Gradually, the company added casualty PLUS accounts in all remaining states except Wisconsin. CASH lets people customize premium payments, allowing them to pay the full amount, the minimum amount due, or any figure in between. But after more than ten years in the making, the system remains a disappointment.

While the scope of the CASH project has been daunting, the highest hurdle has been the lack of central authority to implement the system. To correct this, president Harvey Pierce asked executive vice president of finance Paul King to oversee the project in January 1997. "CASH was a significant step forward for American Family, and it's important to note that many of our customers really like the system," King said. "At the same time, there are customers and agents who have experienced problems with CASH, and it still is not fully implemented." King's mandate is to have a customer billing system fully implemented—save for business, life, and health lines—by the end of 1998. To help achieve this goal, he hired sales development director Tom Mooney as program management director.

The Changing Complexion of American Family

Women have long comprised the majority of employees in American Family's home and regional offices. Many of these women, such as Esser and Sprecher and executive secretary Mary O'Connor, garnered considerable

Kick the Habit

In 1978, an employee attitude survey ignited a hot debate over smoking at American Family. Vehement nonsmokers urged management to ban smoking in the workplace, while smokers defended their right to light up. Vice president of personnel Norb Vanden Heuvel struck a compromise, segregating the cafeteria into smoking and nonsmoking sections and encouraging individual departments to do the same wherever practical.

The issue smoldered for eight years until new studies documented the health risks related to second-hand smoke. In 1986, American Family initiated a gradual program to end smoking in all corporate offices. On March 31, 1986, American Family restricted smoking to segregated break rooms and areas of the cafeteria. Three months later, smoking was completely banned from all American Family buildings.

Mary O'Connor

Ruth Kutz

authority. But none of them found their way into senior management. Early in the 1970s, while Americans debated the Equal Rights Amendment and the Equal Employment Opportunity Act, marketing vice president Floyd Desch convinced the company to initiate an affirmative-action program to increase the number of women and minorities in the field force and management ranks.

In 1979, money center specialist Ruth Kutz became the first female junior officer in the company, succeeding Art Babler as assistant treasurer. Kutz, a graduate of the Madison Area Technical College and later the University of Wisconsin-Madison, joined the company as a stenographer in 1945. After a brief hiatus to start a family, Kutz returned to Farmers Mutual as money center specialist. For almost twenty years, she handled all the details surrounding American Family's investments. "Still, it was a shock when Pete Miller and Bob Koch asked me to become assistant treasurer," Kutz said.

About this time, Vanden Heuvel was contemplating changes in employee training, then conducted separately within each division. As computers eliminated some jobs and created others, demand for training grew. Vanden Heuvel recommended a centralized training department. Koch and Miller agreed, and in 1981 American Family consolidated claims, underwriting, and clerical training along with employee development and media production under the new corporate training and development department. (Because of their particular needs, marketing and I/S continued their own independent training programs.) To direct the new department, Vanden Heuvel selected Nancy Johnson, a product

Saying Yes to Family Members

Although Farmers Mutual/American Family has long prided itself on its close family atmosphere, for many years the company's management was wary of hiring close relatives of any employee. As the company grew and opportunities multiplied, American Family lifted the ban on hiring siblings, provided one didn't report to the other or the same supervisor.

The State of Wisconsin forced further liberalization of the company's nepotism policy in the mid-1980s when the Department of Industry, Labor, and Human Relations ruled that refusing to hire an employee's spouse amounted to

discrimination based on marital status. In the shadow of this interpretation, American Family in 1986 changed its policy companywide to allow hiring spouses—again as long as one does not report to the other or the same first-line supervisor. The change created no significant problems, and in 1990 American Family dropped its prohibition on hiring the parents and children of employees and district managers.

Today, many of American Family's 6,800 employees share family ties, reflecting the trust and commitment that many of these families have placed in the American Family Group.

training specialist in the marketing division since 1977. With undergraduate and graduate degrees in education from the University of Wisconsin-Superior and several years' teaching experience, Johnson had the ideal background for the new position.

Vicki Chvala   *Nancy Johnson*

Uniting the five distinct areas, however, proved a challenge. "The underwriting trainers saw themselves as underwriters first, trainers second. The claims trainers saw themselves as claims people first, trainers second," Johnson recalled. To forge the twenty-six people into a unified team, she moved them together in one area—except for the media center—then focused on developing them as trainers first and foremost. Shortly after Johnson established a strategic plan for her new unit, Koch and Desch asked her to succeed Alan Hunter as vice president of corporate research. Johnson accepted, becoming American Family's first female vice president on November 1, 1983.

In addition to leading American Family's extensive research efforts and chairing the strategic planning team, Johnson introduced American Family to the quality improvement concept. The new approach brought together teams of people representing the various stages of a process to analyze how and why something is done a certain way. "A step either adds value or cost to a process," Johnson explained. "If there isn't a good reason for doing something, you stop doing it."

Launched in 1989, the process improvement program has streamlined scores of routines at American Family. Recognizing the growing importance of the program, Johnson reorganized her division in 1992, creating the improvement resources

The management training unit of the new corporate training department included (from left) Teri Lawson, Nancy Yugo, Lee Kessenich, and Charlie Cook (not pictured).

In 1987, American Family's sixtieth year, the company hired its 5,000th employee. A year later, 5,600 people worked at American Family. Despite the increase in payroll, the company's expense ratio stood at a lean 30 percent.

department under Jim St. Vincent and the strategic research department under Annette Zacher.

When Johnson left the corporate training and development department in 1983, Vicki Chvala succeeded her as director. Chvala joined the company in 1979 as a part-timer in American Standard's rating/change department. The restrictive environment caught her off guard, making Chvala question her future with the company. "We couldn't take unscheduled breaks. We couldn't receive personal calls at work unless it was an emergency," Chvala recalled. But the former teacher took an interest in American Family's training program and transferred to human resources, first as employee development specialist, then manager. As director of corporate training and development, Chvala

More Elbows, More Room

When Farmers Mutual moved into its new 90,000-square-foot office at 3099 East Washington Avenue in late 1951, Herman Wittwer believed his thriving company—with more than a quarter million policyholders—had finally found a permanent home. That, of course, wasn't the case. Today, the American Family Insurance Group serves more than 6 million policyholders in thirteen states, requiring a bit more space than that three-story office building provided. In fact, American Family now owns and leases 117 properties in more than eighty communities, providing 3.8 million square feet of elbow room—equal to 179 football fields.

Of the 3 million square feet of space the group owns, more than half is located in Madison, Wisconsin—home of American Family's national headquarters (NHQ) and its Great Lakes regional office. Large regional complexes in Eden Prairie, Minnesota, and St. Joseph, Missouri, account for another 444,443 square feet of owned space.

The largest building is NHQ, totaling 840,000 square feet—nine times larger than the 1951 home office. The smallest sites include eight drive-up claims centers sprinkled around Colorado and Arizona, each consisting of an economical seventy-five square feet. While most of American Family's 6,800 employees work in a few mammoth buildings, helping policyholders after a claim is best handled in the field. That's why American Family's claims division employs 2,700 people, many of whom work in forty-nine

drive-in or drive-up claims centers and six total loss centers strategically located throughout its service area.

While American Family leases 764,000 square feet of office and storage space, the company also plays the role of landlord. In 1986, after constructing the 80,000-square-foot Gateway Building in Omaha, Nebraska, American Family began renting space to others. Today, two-thirds of the Gateway Building is occupied by companies outside the American Family Group. The 1992 advent of the American Center, with its 400 acres of prime office park property on the outskirts of Madison, signaled a new era for American Family as a real estate developer.

fleshed out Johnson's blueprint for the department. She developed a course catalog for training programs, implemented an automated enrollment process, founded the professional development library, and launched computer-based training.

When Vanden Heuvel retired in 1988 after more than thirty years as vice president of human resources, Chvala succeeded him. While replacing a long-tenured executive is always difficult, doing so in this case was particularly hard because Chvala's mentor was so widely respected. "In the human resources profession, Norb was looked upon very highly," Chvala said. "He was always pushing new, innovative ideas."

Nevertheless, Chvala initiated fundamental changes at American Family. "We began shifting away from a paternalistic view of employees," she said. "The worker has changed and wants more freedom to make choices and decisions." To that end, Chvala eliminated many punitive employee programs, replacing restrictions with guidelines. "When we rewrote the manual, if my staff couldn't tell me why we had a certain rule we got rid of it," Chvala said. "That scared many people, because that was how they policed the company."

American Family's group hiring program is another change implemented by Chvala. Beginning in 1989, human resources asked claims managers to project the number of claims representatives they would need in the coming six months. Human resources then hired enough people to meet those needs and trained them together in an intense ninety-day course called EXCEL. "It was a more proactive process than we had in the past," said claims vice president Darnell Moore. "Now we have people ready to move into the field immediately rather than six months or a year later."

Moore represents another change in American Family's corporate culture. After earning graduate degrees in sociology and psychology from Northwest Missouri State University in 1971, Moore joined American Family as a claims

Karen Laatsch holds the ladder while Brian Klupper measures shingles on a model house in preparation for an EXCEL training session.

representative in St. Louis. He advanced to branch claims manager in Schaumburg, Illinois, in 1980 and regional claims manager for Illinois and Indiana in 1985. Five years later, he moved to the Wisconsin Region in Madison. On November, 17, 1990, Moore succeeded Jim Eldridge as vice president of claims, becoming the company's first African-American officer.

Today, claims representatives are recognized as frontline public relations ambassadors, putting a human face on the company when policyholders need it most. To improve this vital link to policyholders, Moore has given adjusters and managers more authority to settle claims quickly. "We're empowering people to perform their jobs rather than restricting them, which hinders customer service, harms productivity, and drives up costs," Moore explained.

Under Moore's leadership, American Family developed the customer repair program, which speeds up auto repairs by allowing preapproved repair shops to immediately order parts and begin repairs. Besides improving service, the program cuts costs by reducing the need for customer service centers. Moore's division also established total loss centers, which provide faster settlements on cars that are no longer operable. And Dick Haas, vice president of office administration, worked with Moore's division to outfit the insurance industry's only disaster response trailer, a satellite-linked mobile claims office that provides on-site service following catastrophes such as tornadoes and hailstorms.

Through the minority internship program, Karen Stewart (left), a senior majoring in accounting at the University of Missouri-Columbia, works with district casualty claim manager Joelene Wentz in the St. Louis claims department.

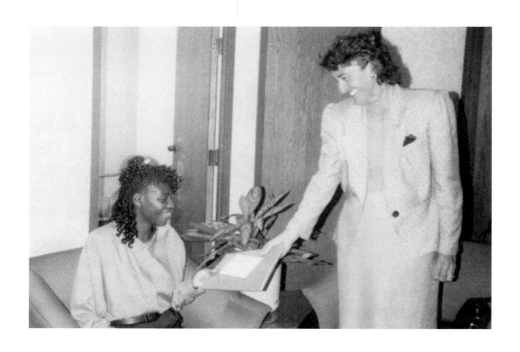

To ensure that others follow Moore, Chvala, Johnson, and Kutz, American Family has initiated and participated in numerous programs designed to increase the number of women and minorities in management positions. One of the most significant has been the partnership for equal opportunity producing leadership excellence (PEOPLE) plan introduced in 1990. More than a cultural-diversity awareness program, the PEOPLE plan sets realistic goals based on U.S. Labor Department statistics for hiring and promoting women and minorities in American Family's corporate offices.

In one sense, the PEOPLE plan was a necessary business decision. Today, racial and ethnic minorities represent 25 percent of the U.S. population. That figure will exceed 50 percent by 2060. To understand and serve the needs of

The CAT's Meow

It didn't have long to sit around looking impressive. Two days after American Family unveiled its disaster response trailer, the claims-office-on-wheels was rolling toward Iowa. A hailstorm had battered Dubuque, causing millions of dollars in damage. By 8:30 that night, CAT trailer drivers Lloyd Chadwick and Tim Murray had the trailer hooked up and ready for action. As other insurers scrambled to set up temporary centers, American Family's CAT team, led by Kansas City property claim manager Calvin Cole, processed more than 1,000 claims in three days.

The only one of its kind in the insurance industry, the fifty-two-foot disaster response trailer represents an innovative partnership between American Family and MCI Telecommunications Corp. In 1993, Cary Pierce, American Family's telecommunications manager, approached MCI about developing a mobile claims office. Working with a team of CAT program administrators led by property claims administrator Jerry Marvin, MCI built the self-contained catastrophe headquarters and delivered it in August 1994.

American Family's disaster response trailer is the only one of its kind in the insurance industry.

The half-million-dollar CAT trailer contains five computer workstations, two printers, telephones, and a fax machine/copier. One challenge CAT teams often face is the inability to get phone service connected quickly. To avoid that problem, the CAT trailer carries its own satellite dish, which connects the trailer to the home office, allowing voice communications as well as e-mail and access to the mainframe computers. The CAT trailer also has its own generator that runs off an 80-gallon diesel tank, providing up to thirty-three hours of power.

Based in Madison, the disaster response trailer can travel to most catastrophe sites within twenty-four hours. Travel time to CAT sites in Colorado and Arizona is a little longer. The trailer provides a home for immediate, short-term claims service while the company sets up a catastrophe center in a storefront or motel. "We can marvel at the technology in this vehicle," Pierce said. "But to the policyholder, the trailer means one thing: Their claims will be taken care of swiftly and efficiently, and their lives can hopefully get back to normal a little sooner. That's the bottom line."

(Above right) Under American Family's minority internship program, four students entering their last year of computer training spent the summer of 1992 in American Family's information services division. The group includes (from left) Demetrius Williams, Jan Basha, Phuong Dao, and Dennis Law. (Above) Yang Lu, who prefers to be called Evelyn, is a native of China living in Madison. She won American Family's 1992 minority scholarship to the University of Wisconsin-Madison.

an increasingly diverse population, American Family must itself become more diverse. But the roots of the PEOPLE plan are embedded deep in American Family's corporate culture. Beginning with Wittwer and Kalbskopf, the company has felt an obligation to be more than a strong, growing, and friendly business providing jobs and opportunity. "The PEOPLE plan is a matter of corporate responsibility," explained president Harvey Pierce, the PEOPLE plan's most powerful advocate. "We have a moral obligation to provide equal opportunity in the workplace. The PEOPLE plan provides direction for us to fulfill that obligation."

In addition, American Family has a minority intern program, minority scholarship program, diversity training, education programs for minorities and people with disabilities, and a minority pre-employment program.

A New Home for the Twenty-First Century

Despite rapid advances in labor-saving technology, American Family added several hundred employees to its home office staff in the mid-1980s. By 1986, the company had more than 2,000 employees in five buildings scattered across Madison's east side. And projections showed that figure more than doubling by 2007. "We're going to have a problem pretty soon," director of corporate facilities Loren "Buzz" Buchanan told John Scharer, vice president of office administration.

Chairman Bob Koch, president Dale Mathwich, and the strategic planning committee agreed. Since the current East Washington Avenue site was too cramped for further expansion, Scharer began touring the Madison area in search of a new location. Madison Mayor Paul Soglin and the city council urged American Family to move downtown. But the area offered little parking and inadequate room for future growth. Instead, the company settled on land in the Town of Burke, just northeast of Madison at the intersection of Interstate 90/94 and Highway 151. At Mathwich's urging, American Family bought more than 500 acres in late 1987, far more than the 130 acres originally sought. "I felt we should give future generations enough land to expand," Mathwich explained.

After Burke proposed placing a garbage dump nearby, Scharer and others began to worry about how the surrounding acreage would be used. To ensure appropriate development, the company bought additional parcels, ultimately owning 876 acres of land. Working with Bowen, Williamson, and Zimmerman as its master planner, American Family set aside 75 acres of rolling prairie and woodland as a nature preserve. The company allotted 400 acres for development as an office park and

An Office Park for the Future

As interested in the quality of its business as the quantity, American Family Insurance has grown to become the nation's fourth largest mutual automobile insurance company. Today, the corporation is applying that same steady, conservative approach to developing the American Center, Wisconsin's largest office park. "We could develop this much faster than we are," said Tom King, vice president of investments. "But we're not typical developers just interested in pushing the next lot."

In fact, American Family has turned away prospective tenants that didn't fit its vision for the American Center. It's a vision guided by strict building covenants established under a development agreement hammered out over a two-year period with the City of Madison. That vision includes corporate offices and convenience retail stores—no factories, warehouses, or apartment complexes allowed. Comprised predominantly of brick buildings set far back from the street, the American Center will provide ample greenery and landscaping, winding walkways, and plenty of open spaces.

After American Family's national headquarters, the first building erected in the American Center was the State Capitol Credit Union in 1994. Two office buildings and a day-care center followed. In 1997, Cellular One completed construction of a regional office, a Woodfield Suites Hotel opened its doors, and the University of Wisconsin Hospitals and Clinics broke ground for an outpatient clinic.

"Fifteen years down the road, there will be about 20,000 people working in the American Center," King said. "To some developers, that may seem slow. But because we're American Family, we can afford to wait."

the remainder for the national headquarters (NHQ) and future expansion.

American Family's plans angered the Madison mayor and city council, Burke leaders, and environmental groups concerned about urban sprawl. But after long, difficult negotiations—and even some talk of leaving Madison altogether—the company reached agreements that satisfied all sides. To provide essential services to the new site, the City of Madison annexed the property. And working with American Family, the city streamlined its approval process for new construction in the planned office park, the American Center.

To ensure the NHQ met the needs of current and future employees, Nancy Johnson, vice president of corporate research, headed a workplace committee comprised of fifty employees to provide input on the building's design. The committee first met in 1988—even before an architect had been selected—and continued to meet through completion of the building in 1992. "We began by asking: 'Who is American Family? What is our culture?'" Johnson said. "Then we asked what kind of building a company like that should have." The committee described American Family as

1992

strong, successful, dependable, conservative, friendly and honest. As for the building, members felt the design should be straightforward, modest, unassuming, significant without being monumental.

Using the information from the workplace committee and the executive building committee, Madison architects Flad & Associates designed a complex based on the movement and relationship of employees and their functions. So vital and time consuming was the project that Mathwich named Scharer vice president of national headquarters development in 1989. Working with real estate manager Jeff Weerts, director of planning and construction Paul Easton, and Bill Batterman of Durrant Engineers, Scharer spent the last three years of his tenure directing the construction of the NHQ.

Groundbreaking occurred May 21, 1990, with construction managed by M. A. Mortenson, Inc., of Minneapolis. American Family worked with Mortenson and its subcontractors on an aggressive work-safety program that resulted in a record 400,000 injury-free hours during construction of the complex.

Mathwich and Wisconsin secretary of development Robert Trunzo cut the ribbon on the $80 million building October 1, 1992. The following day, information services began moving in. The first occupants found themselves in a large, empty building with no cafeteria and few services. But as more divisions relocated to the NHQ, additional services followed. Finally, in the spring of 1993, the move was complete. American Family celebrated with an open house on June 12 and 13. More than 7,000 people—including 200 retirees; nearly 4,000 employees and field staff; government,

John Scharer   *Dick Haas*

The colonnade symbolizes American Family's mission to be a strong, growing, and friendly company. The gentle, curving arch is like a front porch, welcoming visitors. Built of stone, it signifies American Family's enduring strength and protective service. Reaching skyward, the columns arrive at a level, then grow some more, representing American Family's controlled growth.

Making the Money Grow

When Herman Wittwer handled Farmers Mutual's investments, his strategy was simple: Buy high-quality bonds and hold them to maturity. Many people scoffed at this conservative approach. But when the stock market crash forced many of the more speculative insurers out of business, Farmers Mutual suffered only one bond default. The company's conservative approach had changed little by 1961 when Fred Morton joined Farmers Mutual as its first vice president of investments. More than 92 percent of its $36.8 million portfolio rested in high-quality "A" bonds. Treasurer Hugh Wallace had placed less than 7 percent in stocks, and 1 percent in mortgages.

Today, with vice president of investments Tom King at the helm, American Family's $6.8 billion portfolio is far more diverse, and the strategy more complex. But Wittwer's unwillingness to gamble with policyholders' money continues to guide King and his seventeen-person division. "We're more interested in return *of* principal than return *on* principal," King said.

Bonds still represent the bulk of American Family's investments, accounting for $4.5 billion—66 percent of invested assets—in 1996. Bond yields, however, have remained low throughout the 1990s. Rather than settle for record-low returns, American Family has ventured beyond traditional municipal and corporate bonds into

Investments vice president Tom King (left) and fixed asset investment director Phil Hannifan discuss American Family's market strategy.

home equity loans and highly rated securities backed by commercial assets. "By doing our research, we're able to earn higher yields while maintaining security," said Phil Hannifan, fixed asset investment director.

Stocks represent the company's second largest investment tool. Managed by equity investment director Richard White, American Family's stock portfolio emphasizes large, stable companies that provide security as well as growth. In 1996, American Family's capital gains totaled $270 million. New purchases added another $170 million, bringing the company's stock holdings to nearly $1.5 billion. White also manages American Family's pension and 401(k) plans, accounting for several hundred million dollars.

Alternative investments director Bart Richardson manages a smaller, more aggressive tool. His investment options include such exotic vehicles as derivatives and hedge funds. Richardson's strategy focuses on venture capital and buyout funds. Carefully studied and cautiously approached, these investments offer high yields in return for additional risk.

Commercial loans provide another small but aggressive complement to American Family's larger investments. Through a national network of mortgage brokers familiar with American Family's goals, investment real estate director Al Donsing provides loans to fund shopping centers, office buildings, and industrial sites. These include loans to companies interested in building at the American Center, the 400-acre, American Family-owned office park adjacent to the company's national headquarters.

Venture capital, buyout funds and commercial loans may seem to stretch American Family's conservative investment philosophy. But in today's complex market, the small percentage of money American Family puts to work in these investments provides essential diversification. In 1996, that strategy earned American Family $600 million in investment income—an 11.3 percent return. "We're long-term investors with a conservative, diversified strategy that protects our financial strength while helping us grow," King said.

industry, and community leaders; and scores of Madisonians drawn by music and the aroma of 6,500 hot dogs—attended the NHQ's grand opening.

The move to the NHQ spawned many cultural shifts throughout American Family. One such change involved the company's flex time policy. Since 1973, American Family employees enjoyed a summer work schedule that compressed the company's work week into four and a half days, giving them Friday afternoons off. Amid calls to extend summer hours year round, Vanden Heuvel introduced flex time in 1977, making the company a leader in alternative work schedules. Flex time allowed employees to set their own schedules, beginning anywhere between 7:00 and 9:00 a.m. and ending between 3:00 and 5:00 p.m. The majority of American Family's employees chose to start early, leaving the office nearly deserted by 4:00 p.m. This made it difficult for employees and customers in Colorado and Arizona to get service after 3:00 Mountain Time. The problem was particularly acute during the summer when the home office closed at noon on Friday. With American Family's plans to expand both east and west, the NHQ needed to extend its office hours.

After testing alternative work schedules in its branch claims offices, Vicki Chvala took the concept companywide in March 1993. The new approach offers employees the same flexible start and stop times, but requires managers to be certain their areas have adequate coverage during the core hours of 8:00 a.m. to 5:00 p.m. In addition, salaried employees—not subject to federal regulations concerning overtime—may select a five-day/four-day option, allowing them to work slightly longer days in exchange for an additional day off every two weeks.

Distances in the sprawling NHQ created other cultural shifts. Because many employees were a long walk from the cafeteria, management stretched the

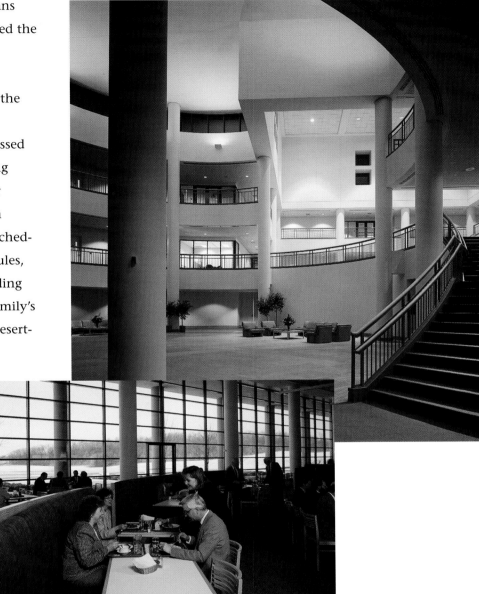

(Top) The three-story open rotunda provides a focal point for employees and visitors. (Bottom) The 800-seat cafeteria offers a view of the small pond and 75-acre nature preserve. Phyllis Buskager, Joan Laeser and Jim Smith (seated) enjoy lunch-time conversation with Mary Vertacic.

Construction of the national headquarters required American Family to change the name of its home office on East Washington Avenue. In the American Family tradition, the company sponsored a contest, offering fifty dollars to whoever submitted the winning entry. Six people suggested the Capital Building. Through a random drawing, AmPlan processing coordinator Sharon Mick won the fifty dollars and the honor of renaming the building.

half-hour lunch break to forty-five minutes and tacked fifteen minutes onto the end of the day, pleasing some employees and disappointing others. Distances also led to the elimination of formal coffee breaks. The traditional midmorning and midafternoon trips to the cafeteria simply weren't practical in the new complex. Besides, the nature of work at the home office had changed dramatically over the years. No longer did supervisors ride herd over employees, keeping them at their desks until the bell rang. In the 1990s, employees are thinkers and planners, free to move about, encouraged to communicate. To enhance this environment, break rooms complete with vending machines are scattered throughout the NHQ. Now employees in all American Family's offices are able to take food and drink to their desks or into conference rooms. Though the change provided employees with more flexibility, sixty-year-old traditions die hard.

For some people at American Family, the sheer size of the NHQ, which encompasses 840,000 square feet, symbolized a challenge to the company's family-like culture. To compensate, interior architects PHH Environmentalists approached the complex as a "city," clustering workstations into "neighborhoods" to create open, productive relationships among employees. Nevertheless, some people initially considered the NHQ with its 1,100 employees too large, too impersonal. Others found it confusing, easy to get lost in. Still others felt the home office had lost its friendly familiarity.

Mathwich and other executives acknowledge that growth has made it more challenging to maintain the company's family atmosphere. "There's a point where you cannot know everybody, when you're spread too far out and just don't see people often enough," Mathwich said. But like Herman Wittwer before him, Mathwich still strolls the halls, comfortably greeting by name many of the employees in the complex. Similarly, when he visits any of the five regional offices or other facilities, he makes a point of stopping to talk with employees in the building, a task that can take several hours. But it's a labor of love for Mathwich. "I work hard to keep us on a first-name basis," he explained. "That's an important part of our corporate culture that we want to maintain."

Chapter Nine

*We view ourselves in terms of what we feel
we are capable of achieving. Others view us
in terms of what we have done.*

—HENRY WADSWORTH LONGFELLOW

STRONG, GROWING, AND FRIENDLY

On January 1, 1990, Dale Mathwich and Harvey Pierce took charge of American Family as chairman and president, respectively. Prospects for the year were bleak. Stiff competition coupled with public outrage over the cost of insurance prevented necessary rate increases, leading to a $100 million underwriting loss on auto and homeowners business in 1989. A bull market and strong profits from American Family Life helped the group squeeze out a $63 million operating gain—but without profits from its main lines, the gain seemed a hollow victory.

Mathwich and Pierce dedicated themselves to returning American Family to true profitability. Both men had spent much

Once a farmers-only company, American Family is building its presence in urban areas.

Shown here in 1990, chairman Dale Mathwich (left) and president Harvey Pierce led American Family through a challenging year.

of their careers in the field and understood the need for growth. But with many years of management between them, they were well aware of the essential ingredient of continued success—profit. Profit pays the bills for future expansion, provides the necessary cushion for unexpected catastrophes, and undergirds the security that insurance companies represent. As Herman Ekern told the company's charter members at its first policyholders' meeting, "An insolvent insurance company is of no service to anyone."

Mathwich and Pierce approached their new roles in dramatically different manners. Like Bob Koch before him, Mathwich was a detail person who rolled up his sleeves and involved himself in all aspects of the company. Pierce took a more global approach, setting direction but leaving the details to others. Despite their different styles, the two men worked well together. "I liked the way he thought, his rationale, his expertise," Mathwich said. And he liked Pierce's directness. "Harvey will give you

Quake, Rattle, and Roll

In the fall of 1990, unknown biophysicist and inventor Iben Browning predicted a December 3 earthquake in one of three areas—Japan, California, or along the little-known New Madrid fault in the central United States. Although seismologists ridiculed Browning's prediction, they conceded that a major quake along the New Madrid fault, stretching from Mississippi to central Illinois and Indiana, was likely within the next forty years. Smelling a story, the media ignored quake-prone Japan and California, turning instead to the Missouri boot heel.

Within days of Browning's prediction, insurance agents in the St. Louis area, including nearly fifty American Family agents, were awash in requests for earthquake coverage. The number of American Family policyholders with earthquake riders in eastern Missouri jumped from 3 percent before Browning's prediction to 95 percent by the end of the year. As applications for earthquake coverage rolled in, American Family officers began to worry. After a sleepless night, chairman Dale Mathwich called together president Harvey Pierce and the executive vice presidents. "This thing could break the company," Mathwich said. "Let's find out what our exposure is."

Working with American Family actuaries, underwriters, and a topnotch consulting firm, vice president of underwriting Alan Hunter set American Family's maximum probable loss above $2 billion—more than twice the balance in policyholders' surplus.

As the insurance industry and government officials prepared for a disaster, so did American Family. Hunter and controller Brent Johnson put in long hours developing a plan to lower American Family's exposure. At the same time, Jim Eldridge, then vice president of claims, set in place procedures to respond in the event of a quake.

December 3 passed without a rumble. But the threat of a quake his opinion whether you like it or not. He doesn't condition his response with a lot of political muttering, which is good at this level of management."

Working with executive vice president (EVP) of finance Paul King and vice president of actuarial Brad Gleason, who succeeded Lyle Sorenson in 1990, Mathwich and Pierce began raising rates where appropriate, confident that other companies would follow their lead. They also eyed expenses, stressing cost control as a matter of survival in the extremely competitive environment of the 1990s. Both men promoted American Family's process improvement program as a means to control costs and become more efficient. To lead by example, Mathwich and Pierce applied process improvement to senior management. Working with the four EVPs—King, Jim Klokner in administration, Bert Hutchison in corporate legal, and Clayton Nelson in operations—they analyzed how the executive staff made decisions. Of the five decisions they reviewed, the chairman had made four and the president one.

Through a training program with insurance carrier USAA, American Family property claims examiner J. R. Reeder inspects earthquake damage to a Los Angeles home in 1994.

remained, and American Family went ahead with Hunter and Johnson's earthquake exposure reduction program. Patterned after earthquake coverage in California, the plan raised rates on earthquake riders and increased deductibles from the current 2 percent to 10 percent on homes in Illinois, Indiana, and Missouri. Eventually, the plan also called for retrofitting brick homes to meet earthquake standards. To further reduce exposure, American Family put the brakes on production in the area, leaving vacancies created by retiring agents unfilled.

The program wasn't popular in the field, and in January, Mathwich, Pierce, and ten American Family officers held a town meeting in St. Louis. "There are 8,000 careers and the security of nearly 5 million policyholders at stake," Mathwich told the agents during the highly emotional meeting. "We've got to protect our people."

With continued support from Midland vice president Russ Lemons and Missouri East state director Al Meyer, the agents accepted the changes. "We spent a month crying in our beer," Meyer recalled. "Then we decided as a team that we weren't going to focus on what we couldn't do but instead focus on what we could do." So Missouri East agents turned to life insurance, eventually becoming the company's leading life insurance producers.

Today, thanks to the earthquake exposure reduction program and American Family's financial strength, a major quake along the New Madrid fault would shake the company but not shatter it. Nevertheless, American Family supports the Natural Disaster Protection Act, which would establish a federal disaster reinsurance program, financed by insurance companies. "We don't have a problem now," Mathwich said. "But for the greater good of the industry and the solvency of smaller companies, Congress should pass the bill."

Debuting in January 1992, these three commercials represent a dramatic shift in American Family television advertising. Rather than use actors, as the company's TV spots had done for more than twenty-five years, Three Generations *(top),* Classic Cars *(middle), and* Pictures *used actual policyholders telling real stories in their own words. It's an approach that American Family continues to use today.*

Mathwich and Pierce preferred a more democratic style of leadership, and they began the difficult process of pushing authority down the management ladder. "Dale deserves a great deal of credit for that," Pierce said. "He has allowed more change to occur in this company than anybody I've seen in his position."

Part of that change was to allow the president to manage the organization. "You're the chief operating officer," Mathwich told Pierce. "I expect you to run the company." Despite his penchant for detail and hands-on approach, Mathwich began to step back from the day-to-day operation of the company. Still, Pierce regularly discussed major issues with Mathwich before making final decisions. This freed up Mathwich to spend more time as American Family's ambassador to industry and community groups and meet with agents, employees, district managers, and state directors.

Using the process improvement concept, each division took a fresh look at long-accepted processes and initiated fundamental changes aimed at ultimately reducing operating expenses to less than thirty cents for every dollar of premium. New vice president of claims Darnell Moore, for example, implemented numerous changes including the claims 2001 project and the customer repair program, which began as a pilot project in Minneapolis/St. Paul in 1992. Under the program, American Family preapproves certain body shops. Claimants and policyholders who have repair work done at these shops can avoid getting estimates or making a trip to an American Family claims center. The program, which has expanded to other areas, has improved customer satisfaction and decreased American Family's reliance on costly drive-in claims centers.

Though process improvement and necessary rate increases would have a dramatic impact on American Family's profitability in the years ahead, they came too late to salvage 1990. Like watching a train wreck in slow motion, American Family officers and board members tallied the underwriting losses at each quarterly meeting: $24.9 million the first quarter, $92 million the second, $169 million the third, and $228 million the fourth. At the February 7, 1991, board meeting, treasurer Paul King reported that the American Family Group turned in a combined underwriting loss of $235 million for 1990. To make matters worse, a sharp recession beginning early in the year knocked the wind out of the stock market, adding a $13 million capital loss to the group's balance sheet.

Despite record profit from American Family Life and larger than projected earnings from American Family Financial Services (AFFS), the group suffered a $48.6 million operating loss, forcing American Family to dip into policyholders' surplus for the first time in sixteen years.

"That's the way Dale and I came into this," Pierce said. "It was a real wake-up call."

Strong

Everyone in the company heard the call. Working with the EVPs, Mathwich and Pierce redoubled their efforts to reverse the trend. In 1992, American Family lowered its combined ratio eight points to 105 percent, giving the group a $97 million operating profit. After adding $158 million to surplus, American Family ended the year with a $2.10-to-$1 capacity ratio—beginning several years of record growth and profit for American Family.

Financial strength was a concern to more than just American Family. In 1990, the bottom fell out of the junk bond and real estate markets, forcing several large life insurance companies into insolvency. Although the vast majority of life companies remained financially strong, Congress couldn't resist weighing in on the high-profile issue. Warning that insurance company insolvencies could rival the savings and loan crisis, some lawmakers called for federal oversight of the industry, leading to yet another attack on the McCarran-Ferguson Act. "The reaction from Congress and the regulators was an over-reaction," said Jim Eldridge, who succeeded Hutchison as EVP of corporate legal in 1992. "So we had to suffer along with the other companies that were strong and solvent."

Rather than sink money into high-risk, high-return investments to pay higher dividends on its life insurance products, AFLIC vice president Pete Walton and investments vice president Tom King preferred to set consistent returns based on a conservative, secure portfolio. As sinking markets dragged down other carriers, American Family Life celebrated its most profitable year in its thirty-two-year history, prompting *U. S. News & World Report* to list

In 1991, at the suggestion of regional vice president Joe Tisserand, American Family renamed the Wisconsin Region, which also included Illinois and Indiana, the Great Lakes Region.

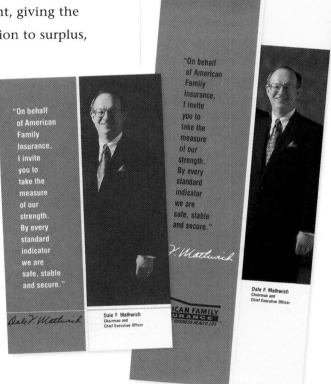

To assure policyholders of the company's financial health, American Family produced a special insert (top) along with its 1991 financial statement. Sent to all policyholders, the insert provided an easy-to-understand summary of American Family's growth over the previous five years.

A History of Giving

Busy though he was, Farmers Mutual/American Family founder Herman Wittwer joined sixty Madisonians in the fall of 1926 to begin the Madison Civic Symphony Orchestra. Music was important to Wittwer, and he continued to support and play in the orchestra. Since then, Farmers Mutual/American Family and its employees have given back to the communities that helped the company grow and prosper.

Over the years, community groups have often turned to American Family for contributions. Aware of the company's obligation to support the communities it served and their responsibility to use policyholders' money wisely, the board of directors carefully weighed each request. Finally in 1966, the board set a contributions formula and appointed a committee to make recommendations for using the funds. Through the efforts of the contributions committee, American Family has developed a philosophy of "giving a little to a lot," enabling the company to support hundreds of organizations that provide basic human services, education, health and welfare services, and arts and cultural experiences.

In 1996, American Family contributed more than $1.1 million to charitable and community projects companywide. In Madison, the United Way received the largest contribution,

$146,000, with employees contributing an additional $252,000. American Family sponsored the Taste of Madison, the Martin Luther King Junior Birthday State Celebration, the Special Olympics, and the American Cancer Society Run/Walk. In-kind printing by American Family's print shop for various organizations accounted for $50,000.

But money is only part of what American Family gives back to its communities. The time and talent American Family's 6,800 employees and 3,600 agents offer is impossible to tally. From serving as Boy Scout leaders to sitting on government advisory panels, American Family people are there every day giving of themselves to make their communities a little stronger, a little better place to live.

(Top) An American Family sponsored event raised money to support a Kansas City program for disadvantaged school children. Pictured (from left) are Kansas City Metro state director Dave Clark, agents Gary Hubert and Bill Petty, Project SOS board member Burt Darling, Royals Alumni Association member Al Fitzmorris, and SOS board member Bruce Re, along with two Kansas City children. (Bottom) President Harvey Pierce congratulates a Special Olympics participant on his performance.

American Family Life among the nation's ten strongest life insurance companies in 1990. Capitalizing on its strength, AFLIC set a new application record in 1991, pushing the number of policies in force beyond the half-million mark. Application records followed in 1992, 1993, and 1995, driving policies in force over 650,000.

The American Family Group continued its ascent in 1992. The group turned in the first of four consecutive $200 million operating gains; policyholders' surplus stood at $1.1 billion; and all-lines policies surpassed 5 million. That year, AFFS turned a record $4.5 million profit. Recognizing the growing importance of Financial Services, Mathwich promoted Gary Switzky to vice president of American Family Financial Services in May 1992. Switzky's promotion not only gave AFFS direct representation on the executive staff but represented a degree of respect that some in Financial Services felt was long overdue.

As a group, American Family celebrated its best year in history in 1993, posting a record $169 million addition to surplus. Meanwhile, loan volume in Switzky's Financial Services company surpassed $100 million for the first time in seven years.

The most serious debate over national health reform in twenty years dominated Congress in 1993 and 1994, placing the future of American Family's health lines in jeopardy. With input from a high-profile task force, President Bill Clinton proposed a radical national health reform plan that would have herded Americans into giant managed care networks, making American Family's individual policies obsolete. So important was the

Peter Walton   Gary Switzky

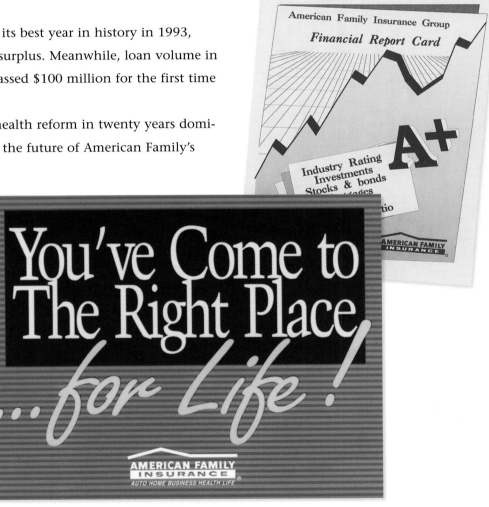

Public concern about the solvency of life insurance companies prompted American Family to publish this financial report card (top right) in 1991, highlighting American Family's financial strength. The company launched the "You've come to the right place" slogan in 1992.

Dale F. Mathwich

In Touch with the American Family

An article in the August 1956 *Nation's Business* caught Dale Mathwich's eye. Ranking the best careers for young executives, the magazine placed insurance above banking. Mathwich, a banker by day and insurance agent by night, read the article twice—then called Farmers Mutual district manager Frank Feivor. Mathwich signed his exclusive agent agreement with Farmers Mutual on October 3, 1956, and soon started his own agency in New London, Wisconsin.

Born August 8, 1934, Dale Mathwich grew up on a dairy farm east of Wausau, Wisconsin, where Reuben and Olga Mathwich and their three children weathered the Great Depression by providing for themselves. Born with his left foot turned at a 90 degree angle toward his right, young Dale couldn't run like other kids. But it didn't slow him down. He woke early every morning to do chores before school. In the summer, he picked rocks from the fields, helped make hay, and even played a little baseball when he got the chance.

After graduating from Birnamwood High School in 1952, Mathwich attended the University of Wisconsin—Madison's agriculture program on a scholarship that paid his tuition the first year but left him to pay his living expenses. Unenthusiastic about his studies and tired of being poor, Mathwich left the university before his junior year to work for a banker and insurance agent in Birnamwood.

When Mathwich committed his full time to Farmers Mutual in late 1956, the company was suffering one of the most contentious periods in its history. Angered over the shift to exclusive representation, many agents left the company, and poison-pen letters circulated

President 1986-1990
Chairman and CEO 1990-Present

Dale F. Mathwich

widely. Mathwich paid little attention, focusing instead on building his agency. He married Lila Pohl in 1958, bought a house, and began raising a family.

In 1960, Mathwich accepted a district manager position in Rockford, Illinois. These were lean years for Farmers Mutual and the Mathwichs. Frustrated by some of management's decisions, Mathwich nearly quit. But regional vice president Joe Nicolay convinced him to stay. "Dale was diligent, sincere, hard working," Nicolay said. "I knew the situation would change and Dale would really take off."

Mathwich dug in, steadily developing American Family's largest district in Illinois,

growing from three full-time agents to fourteen by 1969. Mathwich's determination was just what Illinois needed, and Nicolay appointed him Illinois state director in January 1970. Over the next ten years, Mathwich quadrupled the number of American Family agents in Illinois and increased annual premiums from $2.7 million to $34.9 million.

Mathwich moved to Madison in October 1979 as director of marketing, later vice president. He modernized the company's commission structure, developed American Family's plan for opening up Arizona—which became the model for entering Ohio—and established American Family Brokerage Inc.

Mathwich advanced to executive vice president of administration in 1985 and president on April 1, 1986. Shortly thereafter, he coined the company's current slogan, "Strong, growing, and friendly." As president, Mathwich balanced his hands-on, self-sufficient nature with a democratic management style successfully involving himself in all aspects of the company without hoarding control. In this manner, he engineered American Family's remarkable growth spurt in the late 1980s. Mathwich became chairman and CEO on January 1, 1990, overseeing record growth and unprecedented financial strength.

Active in the industry, Mathwich chaired the National Association of Independent Insurers and the Insurance Institute for Highway Safety in 1995, taking strong roles in managing dramatic changes in both organizations. Closer to home, Mathwich served as campaign chair of the Dane County United Way in 1993, leading a $7.5 million fund drive, and United Way board chair in 1994.

outcome that health lines underwriting manager Marty Brewer worked full time with American Family's government relations staff tracking state and federal proposals.

A coalition of employers, insurance companies, and health care providers helped defeat the plan in 1994. The national debate over controlling health care costs readied consumers for American Family's Premium Care Health Plan. Introduced in 1994, the plan combined lower premiums with higher deductibles and copayments. The new policy enjoyed immediate popularity, attracting more than $17 million in premiums that year and helping health lines, after several dismal years, log its best year ever. The excitement, however, was short-lived. The company stopped selling major medical policies in Minnesota after the legislature passed a health reform plan that relied exclusively on managed care organizations. American Family resumed sales of major medical policies in Minnesota in 1997.

In 1991, American Family Financial Services (AFFS) held a "money sale." With interest on consumer loans surpassing 11 percent, AFFS offered a limited number of loans at 7.99 percent and 9.99 percent. Consumers quickly snapped up $63 million in loans. "We did a year's worth of business in one week," AFFS vice president Gary Switzky said. "Any way you look at it, the money sale was one of the most successful campaigns in our history."

The More Things Change, the More They Stay the Same

Memorability is the hallmark of good advertising. The jingle that sticks in your head, the image that catches your eye, the slogan that rings true, all help create an identity for the advertiser. Thanks to consistent, high-quality advertising directed by Bob Salisbury and his successor Annette Knapstein, American Family's red, white, and blue logo and slogan, "All your protection under one roof," have remained synonymous with strength, growth, and friendly, responsive service for more than thirty years.

Under Knapstein, who succeeded Salisbury in December 1990, American Family remains committed to the same core programs—such as television advertising, cooperative advertising,

and direct marketing—that helped the company become the eleventh largest property/casualty group in the nation.

But advertising hasn't stood still. On the contrary, a lot has changed under American Family's roof. The advertising department, now called integrated marketing, includes twenty-two employees with responsibilities for an in-house advertising agency, television advertising, co-op advertising, yellow pages advertising, urban advertising, direct marketing, print collateral material, and some field communications. Integrated marketing also coordinates the development of American Family's Internet home page, which went on line in April 1996 and continues to evolve.

Previously, advertising followed the

keen instincts of Salisbury and promotions director Charlie Ambrosavage. Today, however, careful research precedes every marketing effort, and data tracks the success of each program. "Our advertising is data driven and market driven," Knapstein explained. "To continue, a program has to be profitable for both the agents and the company."

Chairman Dale Mathwich and president Harvey Pierce are so convinced in the power of American Family's advertising that integrated marketing's budget got a 60 percent boost in 1997. "We support every aspect of the corporate vision," Knapstein said. "They must believe it's worth the investment."

Annette Knapstein

Board of Directors

Front row (from left): Dr. Beverly S. Simone, president, Madison Area Technical College; Rockne G. Flowers, president, Nelson Industries, Inc.; Dale F. Mathwich, chairman and chief executive officer, American Family Insurance Group; Barbara A. Parish, president, Wis-Pak, Inc. Second row (from left): Richard R. Renk, chairman, Wm. F. Renk & Sons; Albert O. Nicholas, president, Nicholas Company, Inc.; Carl A. Weigell (deceased)*, chairman, Motor Castings Company; Harvey R. Pierce, president and chief operating officer, American Family Insurance Group; Dr. David Ward, chancellor, University of Wisconsin-Madison; Dr. Robert E. Walton, chairman, World Dairy Center Authority Board.
*Mr. Weigell died of cancer on February 8, 1997.

Officers

Seated (from left): Paul L. King, executive vice president (EVP), finance, treasurer; James R. Klokner, EVP, administration; Harvey R. Pierce, president and chief operating officer; Dale F. Mathwich, chairman and chief executive officer; Daniel R. DeSalvo, EVP, sales; James F. Eldridge, EVP corporate legal, secretary. Standing (from left): Bradley J. Gleason, vice president, actuarial; Ralph E. Kaye, vice president, sales, Valley Region; David N. Krueger, vice president, sales, Great Lakes Region; David R. Anderson, vice president, infor-

mation services; J. Brent Johnson, vice president, controller; Vicki L. Chvala, vice president, human resources; Clayton H. Nelson, vice president, sales, Mountain Region (retired May 31, 1997); Gary M. Switzky, vice president, American Family Financial Services; Darnell Moore, vice president, claims; Thomas S. King, vice president, investments; Alan E. Meyer, vice president, marketing; Nancy M. Johnson, vice president, corporate research; Alan F. Hunter, vice president, underwriting services; Joseph W. Tisserand, vice

president, American Family Life Insurance Company; Richard J. Haas, vice president, office administration; Russell W. Lemons, vice president, sales, Midland Region; Peter B. Walton, vice president, sales, Northwest Region. Not pictured: Don Alfermann, vice president, sales, Mountain Region (elected effective June 1, 1997), and Jerry Rekowski, vice president, commercial lines, (elected effective September 1, 1997).

Managed care's growing popularity continues to drive down American Family's health care policy counts. The line, however, remains profitable, thanks to strict cost controls, the success of its preferred provider organization—established in 1987—and the vigilant scrutiny of health care claims by the medical services unit. American Family's Medicare supplement policy and the Limiterm policy for people between jobs remain popular. After considering research by health lines director Bob Powers, American Family will soon offer long-term-care insurance.

The increasing political pressure on insurers convinced Mathwich that American Family should take a more visible role in advocacy and public relations. In 1992, corporate secretary and general counsel Jim Eldridge reorganized the public relations department. In addition to consumer affairs, corporate communications, and corporate contributions, the PR department assumed responsibility for the media production center. To direct the revamped department, Eldridge hired Rick Fetherston, a veteran television news anchor in Madison. Fetherston, who completed his law degree during his first year at American Family, also taught journalism at the University of Wisconsin—Madison and has strong ties to media outlets throughout American Family's service area. As public relations director, he develops strategic approaches for American Family's communications with policyholders, the media, agents, employees, and state regulators.

To improve American Family's government relations efforts, Eldridge hired top-notch lobbyist Mark Afable as associate general counsel in the government affairs division. Before joining American Family in 1994, Afable lobbied for Allstate and the National Association of Independent Insurers (NAII). Today, Afable directs seven lobbyists covering all state legislatures in the company's operating territory.

Mathwich also pushed for broader involvement in the NAII. Since the days of Irving Maurer, American Family's chairman served as the company's representative to the association, with others occasionally sitting on special committees. But Mathwich believed that American Family, as the eleventh largest property/casualty group in the nation, needed to become

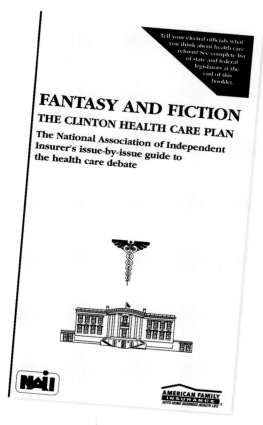

Using material from a National Association of Independent Insurers (NAII) white paper on President Bill Clinton's health reform plan, American Family produced this *Fantasy and Fiction booklet and distributed it to the company's agents and employees.*

Mark Afable   Rick Fetherston

more of a leader. "Now we're on all the principal committees," Mathwich said. "We're involved in the plans, we're involved in the legislation, we're involved in the lobbying."

Recognizing Mathwich's commitment to the association, NAII members elected him vice chairman of the board in 1994 and chairman in 1995—the association's fiftieth anniversary. With sixteen-year president Lowell Beck and several senior managers retiring during this period, Mathwich found himself deeply involved in transition planning during those two years. In 1995, Mathwich also served as chair of the Insurance Institute for Highway Safety (IIHS), which had recently opened its new, state-of-the-art testing facility outside Charlottesville, Virginia.

Though political debates consumed a great deal of management's attention, American Family posted yet another "best year ever" in 1994. The number of agents representing the company exceeded 3,000 for the first time since 1950, and policies in force grew to 5.5 million.

American Family continued to shatter records in 1995. The group turned a $227 million profit on revenues of $3.1 billion and added a record $363 million to surplus, giving American Family a remarkable capacity ratio of $1.42-to-$1.

Tornadoes, wind- and hailstorms in 1996 caused a record $240 million in catastrophic storm claims—$100 million above projections. American Family's ability to handle these unexpected losses served as a testimony to its strength. With the help of $270 million in capital gains, American Family added an impressive $322 million to policyholders' surplus, bringing the balance to just over $2 billion. Policies in force jumped 5 percent and premium income 6 percent—twice the rate of the property/casualty industry as a whole.

The process improvement changes that Mathwich, Pierce and the EVPs initiated during the gloomy days of 1990 were paying off. Productivity increased 21 percent between 1990 and 1996, and the group's expense ratio stood at a lean 32.2 percent at the start of 1997. As American Family focused on being a

Between 1979 and 1994, only nine of the nation's top thirty-five property/casualty insurance companies held the combination of claims paid and operating expenses to less than $1.05 for every $1.00 of premium collected: AIG, American Family Insurance, Chubb, GEICO, Gen Re, Hanover, Progressive, SAFECO, and USAA.

American Family chairman Dale Mathwich (right), who chaired the Insurance Institute for Highway Safety (IIHS) in 1995, dons a crash helmet for a test at the IIHS state-of-the-art testing facility near Charlottesville, Virginia.

low-cost producer, growth followed. The number of policies grew by a third, from 4.6 million in January 1990 to 6.1 million seven years later. With that growth has come unprecedented financial strength. American Family opened the decade with $3.3 billion in assets; seven years later, the group had amassed assets of more than $6 billion. Policyholders' surplus at the beginning of 1990 totaled $367 million; at the beginning of 1997 surplus exceeded $2 billion. In January 1990, American Family had an enviable corporate capacity ratio of $1.93-to-$1; at the beginning of 1997 the capacity ratio stood at $1.29-to-$1—the strongest in the company's seventy-year history—ensuring that American Family can weather any storm and still meet its obligations to its policyholders.

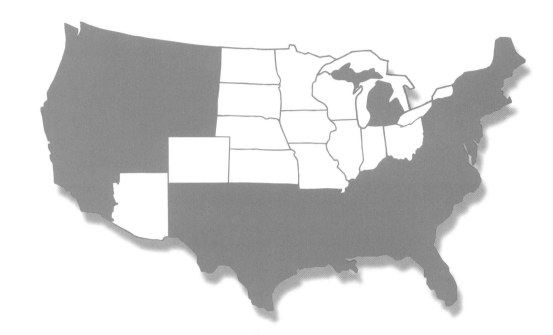

American Family put its financial strength to work in the 1990s. In addition to entering several large metropolitan areas within its existing territory, the company expanded into Ohio in 1995.

Growing

Beginning as a class mutual serving Wisconsin farmers only, Farmers Mutual/ American Family gradually evolved to offer a broad spectrum of insurance and financial service products to people in every walk of life. But one group was missing. As late as the 1980s, American Family—and many other insurance companies—did little business in the inner-city neighborhoods of large urban areas like Chicago, Milwaukee, and St. Louis. But political pressure in the mid-1980s forced the insurance industry to reconsider its avoidance of the inner city. Hoping to forestall government intervention and explore an opportunity for expansion, American Family's vice president of marketing Jack Chopp and management development director Bruce Thalacker pushed district managers to recruit more metro agents. But lacking experience in urban markets, district managers found little success. In 1987, Chopp and Thalacker went a step further, establishing the urban agent program.

TODAY'S AMERICAN FAMILY

AMERICAN FAMILY INSURANCE

In May 1996, this vibrantly colored poster debuted on buses and billboards in Milwaukee, Chicago, Minneapolis/St. Paul, and Kansas City.

U.S. Attorney General Janet Reno, flanked by American Family secretary/general counsel Jim Eldridge (left) and civil rights chief Deval Patrick, announces a settlement in a precedent-setting Milwaukee lawsuit that applied the Federal Fair Housing Act to the sale of homeowners insurance. (This Associated Press photo appeared in the media, including USA Today.)

Progress came quickest in Milwaukee. Officials with the Wisconsin Insurance Plan (WIP), a state-sponsored homeowners insurance program for inner-city residents, were pushing to reduce WIP enrollment. Working with WIP representatives, American Family solicited public program enrollees, converting them to American Family coverage. "Extraordinary is how we would describe American Family's efforts in central Milwaukee," said WIP manager Tom Roeder in 1990.

The momentum, however, stalled on July 27, 1990, when the National Association for the Advancement of Colored People (NAACP) filed a lawsuit charging that American Family had violated the Federal Fair Housing Act by refusing to sell insurance to minorities in certain sections of Milwaukee, a practice known as redlining. "We were the largest writer of homeowners insurance in Milwaukee. By the time we reached a settlement, we had more than 35 percent of the inner-city market—a higher percentage than we had in the whole state of Wisconsin," Eldridge said. "It was very frustrating, because we knew we weren't redlining."

But the NAACP had a "smoking gun." A district manager, violating company policy, had urged an agent to stop writing so much life insurance for African-Americans. The NAACP also documented cases in which busy suburban agents didn't respond to inquiries about homeowner's insurance from inner-city residents. Besides vigorously denying that the company redlined in Milwaukee or anywhere else, American Family argued that the Federal Fair Housing Act did not apply to insurance. Given McCarran-Ferguson's barriers to federal intervention in the insurance market, congressional intent to exempt insurance from the Fair Housing Act seemed clear. The issue, however, remained largely untested in the courts, making the Milwaukee case important to the entire industry. The trial judge agreed with American Family's argument, but the Seventh Circuit Court of Appeals in Chicago reversed the ruling, stating that the Fair Housing Act did apply to homeowner's coverage. In 1993, the U.S. Supreme Court refused to hear American Family's appeal, paving the way for the NAACP lawsuit to proceed.

To avoid continuing huge legal fees and to fully implement an aggressive urban marketing program, American Family opted for a negotiated settlement. EVP Jim Eldridge and associate general counsel Chris Spencer led the negotiations for American Family, assisted by others, including assistant general counsel Alice Kissling, and outside counsel in Washington, D.C. Under a 1995 consent decree, the company paid $14.5 million to compensate the plaintiffs and help inner-city residents purchase and repair homes. The settlement also established a number of goals regarding urban market penetration, most of which already were encompassed in the company's urban marketing plan.

With the settlement nearing, Dan DeSalvo, former Colorado state director who succeeded Chopp as vice president of marketing in 1992, stepped up the urban marketing effort. A graduate in psychology from Illinois State University, DeSalvo sold life insurance in Bloomington, Illinois, for Massachusetts Mutual before joining American Family in 1973. Illinois state director Dale Mathwich appointed DeSalvo as a district manager in Rockford in 1976. In 1980, Mathwich brought him to Madison as field training director. He returned to the field as a district manager to help open Arizona in 1985, then moved to Colorado two years later.

For urban marketing to work, the program needed a point person, someone to give it an identity. Dick Adler, director of sales promotion, knew just the

Jerry Rekowski

✛ In 1997, the strategic planning team created a new commercial lines/farm ranch division. The division is decentralized, including all functions except actuarial. Profit is the primary focus for the new organization, with a secondary focus on automation, organizational structure, and growth. The board of directors elected marketing agency director Jerry Rekowski vice president, commercial lines, effective September 1, 1997.

A December 1995 ribbon cutting in Kansas City opened American Family's first metro service center. Pictured from left are Russ Lemons, A. Marie Young, Kazell Pugh, and D. Jeanne Robinson.

In the late 1960s, many states enacted fair access to insurance requirements, or FAIR plans. Funded through assessments on insurance companies, the plans provide homeowners insurance to inner-city residents who can't purchase insurance through commercial companies.

person—Kazell Pugh. A successful sales director in the hotel industry, Pugh grew up in the Watts-Willowbrook area of South Central Los Angeles and earned a football scholarship to the University of Colorado. Drafted by the Philadelphia Eagles in 1980, Pugh returned kick-offs until he was cut just before the Eagles' Super Bowl season. He eventually moved to Palm Springs, California, and worked for Stouffer Hotels and Resorts, where he met Adler.

DeSalvo hired Pugh as American Family's urban marketing director in 1994. Together, they wrote a corporate urban marketing initiative as well as plans for each region. The nearly thirty urban markets in American Family's thirteen geographic states present unique challenges and opportunities. To serve these areas, the urban marketing initiative included new products and services such as the Custom Value Homeowners policy introduced in 1994, support of minority- and women-owned businesses in urban areas, community involvement and investment, more urban offices, a focus on recruiting minority agents and employees, and involvement in government affairs. Support from the regions was vital to the program's success, so Pugh and DeSalvo put urban marketing managers in each region—Harriett Brewer in Midland, Elliott Cohen in Great Lakes, and Theresa Upton in Northwest. In 1997, Jeff Campos was named urban marketing manager in the Mountain Region and Debbie Lacey was appointed to the same post in the Valley Region. Responsible for implementing urban marketing in their regions, these managers coordinated their efforts with Pugh but reported to the regional vice presidents.

Advertising is another essential component of the urban marketing initiative. Although American Family's advertising has never excluded people, urban advertising recognizes that traditional approaches often fail to reach some audiences. Working with a Chicago agency that specializes in minority advertising, Gwen Thompson Jones, senior advertising specialist for urban marketing, develops and places advertising to reach specific groups in each market. "We're doing general image advertising," Jones said. "It's intended to

All of Chicago district manager (DM) Roger Collins' agents qualified for the 1996 All American Convention in Orlando, Florida. Front row (from left): Cliff Surges, David Carter, Clara Rapka, Luis Hernandez, and Tom Ward. Back row (from left): president Harvey Pierce, Mark Heneghan, Andre Howard, DM Lloyd Biddle (former agent in the Chicago district and now a DM), DM Roger Collins, Shamim Tahzib, Jim Kourafas, and CEO Dale Mathwich.

introduce American Family to people who aren't familiar with the company." American Family's first Spanish language ads debuted in 1996. The following year, American Family unveiled a Spanish language television commercial and all-lines brochure.

There is plenty of evidence that American Family is finding fertile ground in urban markets. Among American Family's top agents for 1996 were Dominic Lai and Edward Beavers in Chicago and Charles Vang in Milwaukee. In fact, a dozen of the company's top 100 agents attending the 1996 All American Convention in Orlando sell in Chicago. "If Herman Wittwer were alive today, he would be proud of our involvement in the inner city and the roots we're establishing," Harvey Pierce said. "We have 50 agents in the heart of Chicago. We'll have 200 within five years. It's really fun to be part of that."

Although large cities present exciting opportunities for growth, American Family also is adding new states to its service area. With most of its business concentrated in the Upper Midwest, the company is susceptible to heavy catastrophic storm losses, as happened in 1994 and 1996. This forces American Family to spend millions of dollars each year on reinsurance. Furthermore, the company's strategic plan calls for growing the policy count 7 percent a year—doubling the company's size in ten years.

That ambitious goal is another reason Mathwich and Pierce engineered such a strong financial position. If premium income grows 15 percent, to maintain a proper balance of revenue to surplus then surplus must grow

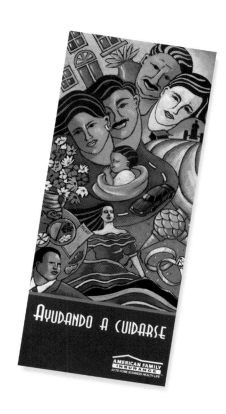

Introduced in 1997, this brochure tells Spanish-speaking people about American Family and describes the company's multiple-lines of insurance protection.

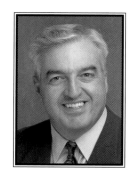

Al Meyer   Dan DeSalvo

Not even the bright sunshine or frigid temperatures could keep president Harvey Pierce (left), marketing vice president Dan DeSalvo (center), and chairman Dale Mathwich from smiling as they prepare to raise the Ohio state flag above American Family's national headquarters, signifying the company's January 1, 1995, entry into the state.

7.5 percent. "So the best way to make sure you can grow is to have a very strong premium to surplus ratio," Mathwich explained. "If we're going to double the policy count in the next ten years, we can't pause every few years to let the surplus catch up."

To prepare for growth, vice president of marketing Dan DeSalvo proposed realigning the regions in 1993. Under marketing's plan, Indiana would leave the Great Lakes Region and join a new state, Ohio, to create the Valley Region. Arizona and Colorado would pull out of Midland to form the Mountain Region, with a new state added in 1998. Responsibility for policy issuing and other support services would remain with the Great Lakes and Midland regions, saving millions of dollars and allowing the new regional vice presidents to focus on sales. The strategic planning team agreed, and on March 1, 1994, the board approved the plan effective January 1, 1995.

Pierce chose Al Meyer to head the Valley Region. Calm and unflappable, Meyer proved his mettle as Missouri East state director during the New Madrid quake scare and the resulting earthquake exposure reduction plan. To lead the Mountain Region, Pierce selected EVP of operations Clayton Nelson. Strong-willed and independent, Nelson had long wanted to return to the field. His experience as a Colorado state director and Northwest regional vice president made him the ideal candidate for the new post.

To open Ohio, Meyer named Wausau, Wisconsin, district manager Pat Maloney as state director in Ohio South Central. Maloney recruited Gregg Antony, Joe Krolikowski, and Tim Miller as district managers. Sales began January 1, 1995. To take advantage of a new law offering a premium-tax break to insurance companies chartered in Ohio, American Family formed two new companies—American Family Insurance Company and American Standard Insurance Company of Ohio—on November 21, 1995.

Expansion into Ohio followed the

Harvey R. Pierce

An Agent of Change in Changing Times

Examining a portable air conditioner at an auction in Fargo, North Dakota, Woodrow Wilson Pierce saw an opportunity for his son Harvey. He bought sixty of the units for $19.95 apiece—$40 below the retail price. "I'll front you the money," Pierce told him. "You and your older brother can sell these as a summer project." Demonstrating a keen understanding of business, Harvey recognized an opportunity himself. He told his older brother and a friend they could keep anything over $39.95 for each air conditioner they sold. "My father never told them what I was paying for the units," Harvey Pierce recalled.

Born January 5, 1942, Harvey Pierce grew up in Willmar, Minnesota. His father, a used-car dealer, taught his daughter and five sons the value of initiative. Rather than give them an allowance, he gave them opportunities to earn money. Meanwhile, Harvey's mother, Farolyn, insisted that her children learn to play the piano. Harvey initially resisted, but the discipline of practice eventually drew him to the instrument, which he still enjoys playing.

Pierce graduated from high school in 1960 and married his high school sweetheart, Delores Petersen. He started selling insurance for Penn Mutual Life Insurance Company and became friends with his auto insurance agent, Rob Larson. In December 1962, Larson's district manager, Arch Schrom, recruited Pierce as a part-time agent for American Family. Recognizing greater opportunities in multiple-line sales, Pierce signed on as an exclusive agent a month later and soon moved to Fairfax, Minnesota, to build an agency.

Three years later, Pierce accepted a district manager position in Windom. The challenging southwest Minnesota district was dominated

President 1990-Present

Harvey R Pierce

by eighteen longterm, part-time and independent agents. Pressure was mounting to develop an exclusive field force, and state director Joe Stephan gave Pierce three years to convert or terminate part-time and independent agents. It was a difficult time for Pierce, whose income dropped steadily, and he often considered returning to agency. But new state director Noel Warren saw great potential in him and spent time with Pierce, teaching him how to recruit, train, and manage agents. Warren's efforts paid off. Pierce became a leading district manager whose agents wrote profitable business.

Pierce and his family enjoyed Windom and the district, prompting him to turn down several promotions. But in 1978, regional vice president Clayton Nelson divided Minnesota

into two operating states and convinced Pierce to lead Minnesota North. Five years later, Pierce succeeded Dale Eikenberry as Midland regional vice president and oversaw American Family's entrance into Arizona in 1986.

In 1988, president Dale Mathwich brought Pierce to the home office as executive vice president of field operations. On January 1, 1990, Pierce became president of the American Family Insurance Group. In this position, he helped engineer the group's dramatic growth and unprecedented financial strength. Pierce also has been American Family's chief proponent of diversifying the company's employee ranks and field force. As an executive, Pierce is both open minded and decisive, airing all sides of an issue before making a decision. Once made, however, there is no room for second thoughts. "When you make a decision, you're committed to making it work," Pierce said.

Family always has been Pierce's number one priority. Two of Harvey and Delores' four children are American Family agents: Susan in Madison, Wisconsin, and Steve in Plymouth, Minnesota. Presiding over more than 6,800 employees and 3,600 agents, Pierce contends that spirituality is essential to success. "You have to believe in something," he explained. Spirituality leads to purpose, which provides focus. As president of American Family, Pierce finds his purpose in striving for profitability in an industry accustomed to operating losses. "I want to be remembered as an agent of change," Pierce said, "as someone who brought true profitability and diversity to American Family."

Pat Maloney

Ralph Kaye

Jean McCarter

Cassandra Ruffin

Don Alfermann

Ranger Duran

Arizona plan, with an emphasis on controlled growth. Maloney and his team focused on a single urban area—Columbus—and started with an aggressive advertising campaign and rates 10 percent below the competition's. Unlike Arizona, the marketing division didn't allow agents to transfer to Ohio, nor did it appoint agents with previous experience. Growth in Ohio was slow but steady. By the end of 1995, Maloney's team had thirteen agents and more than 6,700 policies in force.

Since becoming vice president of marketing in 1992, DeSalvo had proven himself time and again, and in September 1995 the board of directors promoted him to EVP of operations. Four months later, Al Meyer moved to Madison as vice president of marketing. To step in as RVP of the Valley Region, DeSalvo chose Illinois Chicago Metro state director and twenty-four-year veteran Ralph Kaye.

The Ohio plan called for entering a second Ohio market three years after opening Columbus, with additional areas opening every three years. But to take advantage of the company's strong financial position and deep pool of management candidates created by the management development program, DeSalvo proposed opening Ohio Northwest in 1996. The strategic planning team agreed, and Kaye appointed Jean McCarter, American Family's first female state director and former Missouri Central district manager, to begin sales in the Toledo area on January 1, 1996. The pace quickened again in May 1997, when the company announced plans to enter the Cincinnati-Dayton area, beginning January 1, 1998. Kaye appointed Cassandra Ruffin to lead the new Ohio South sales state. An Illinois Chicago Metro district manager, Ruffin became the company's first African-American state director.

While growth in the Valley Region got underway, Nelson returned to Denver as regional vice president and converted the Colorado state office into the new Mountain Region headquarters. Two years later, in May 1997, he retired after more than thirty-five years with the company. To succeed him, DeSalvo chose Colorado state director Don Alfermann as sales vice president. Replacing Alfermann was Colorado district manager Ranger Duran, the first Hispanic-American state director in the company.

Friendly

In 1955, the Farmers Mutual board of directors abandoned the American Agency System with its reliance on independent agents and set exclusive agency representation as its goal. Though hundreds of independent agents left the company and sales stagnated for nearly a decade, time proved the board's decision correct. As competition intensified and insurance products grew more complex, American Family and other exclusive agent companies found strong partners in their field forces. While many carriers served by independent agents skimped on education and lagged in agent automation, exclusive agent companies implemented extensive training programs and invested in computer networks that increased efficiency and reduced expenses. Gradually, exclusive agents captured more of the market from independents. Today, the majority of the personal lines market rests with exclusive agents like those comprising American Family's 3,600-member field force.

In the last decade, competition in the property/casualty field has intensified, straining the industry and rearranging its landscape. Many carriers have downsized, abandoning some lines to focus on others. Some insurers have merged to ensure survival or as a way of entering new markets. Others have sold out to international conglomerates. In this yet unsettled arena, American Family faces new competitors. Since the early 1980s, banks have crept into the insurance field. At the same time, direct writers using 1-800 numbers and the Internet have nibbled away at the market. Without the expense of maintaining a field force, these organizations have competed successfully on price. As the public grows accustomed to doing business over the phone or computer, these companies will likely gain market share.

Cassandra Ruffin (second from left), then an agent in Milwaukee, reviews files with clients Danae and Fred Gordon and their son Kwesi.

Nevertheless, American Family remains committed to selling products through exclusive representatives who can provide people with efficient, friendly service. "The exclusive career agent is the system of survival," Pierce stated with certainty. "When it comes to buying insurance, consumers need advice and direction."

Agents also provide vital service when filing a claim. "No matter how high-tech people become, when they're at a point of crisis—when they're filing a

Beginning in the 1980s, some American Family agents began employing customer service representatives (CSRs). Originated by State Farm, CSRs are highly trained office staff able to carry more of the burden of operating a large agency. Many rural agents employ CSRs to staff satellite offices in distant parts of their territory where local service is essential. To promote the use of CSRs, American Family provides CSR training and credentialing.

Communicating with agents and others challenged American Family in 1996 as the company announced plans to trim agent commissions from 11 percent of premiums to 10 percent over ten years. Pictured here (from left) president Harvey Pierce, executive vice president Dan DeSalvo, marketing vice president Al Meyer, and director of public relations Rick Fetherston sit down for a question/answer session that appeared in employee and agent publications.

claim—most people want to talk to a real person who can think, and be flexible, and help them," Mathwich said. "Once someone tries to handle a claim with a stranger over the telephone or through the Internet, they're going to have second thoughts."

Though the human touch is an essential advantage that American Family has over these new competitors, price remains an important factor—which explains why Pierce continued to hammer on expenses in the wake of record profits. "Every dollar we spend finds its way into our premiums," he said. "If we can get our expense ratio below 30 percent and at the same time emphasize the value of the agent to the customer, no one could compete with us."

With agent commissions and district manager salaries accounting for 40 percent of operating expenses, Pierce knew any cost-reduction effort had to include the field force. "There aren't any sacred cows," he told EVP of operations Clayton Nelson and marketing vice president Jack Chopp in 1990. "We have to look at commissions."

Chopp, however, returned to the field as a district manager in 1992. To replace him, Nelson turned to Colorado state director Dan DeSalvo. Intent on meeting Pierce's demand to squeeze 1 percent out of commissions, DeSalvo took on the issue in 1993. To get field input, he convened an advisory panel of agents, district managers, and state directors. The goal was not to cut agent income but reduce commissions as a percent of premium.

So DeSalvo and the panel proposed dropping commissions 0.1 percent a year for ten years, bringing overall commissions down from 11 percent of premiums

to 10 percent by 2006. Inflation and the natural growth of an agency would more than offset the reduction, meaning agents wouldn't see their incomes decrease under the plan.

"I'm interested in seeing agents' incomes continue to grow and the company having a more competitive expense ratio," Mathwich said. "This plan will achieve both goals."

Nevertheless, the panel felt any change would be viewed as a pay cut. "The agents said we couldn't change their commission without helping them lower expenses," DeSalvo explained. "If we could trade commission dollars for expense dollars, they'd support us 100 percent."

Under the agency expense study, the panel spent nearly a year interviewing agents and analyzing reports. Afterward, they recommended nearly fifty changes to help agents cut costs. Immediate steps included taking television advertising off the co-op plan, saving agents $450 a year, giving them a $75 annual allowance for brochures and other promotional materials, and taking numerous steps to reduce the paper flow that demanded staff time.

Based on agent input, American Family upgraded its computer network, replacing Wang x-terminals, which were limited to running company-installed programs, with new PCs that could run off-the-shelf software. To make the system more user friendly, American Family began migrating from the DOS-based ACCESS system to a Windows-based system called the agency data system (ADS) in January 1997.

Another important project spinning out of the agency expense study is the model agency program. Under the guidance of six vice presidents, with primary responsibility falling to new marketing vice president Al Meyer, the model agency program shares ideas gleaned from the company's top agents on office design, business practices, and technology utilization. Beginning with office design, the model agency team constructed a model agency office in the Great Lakes regional building in January 1997. After receiving feedback from the field, the team completed a model office plan and began sharing it with regional vice presidents. Phase II, beginning in the spring of 1997, focused on

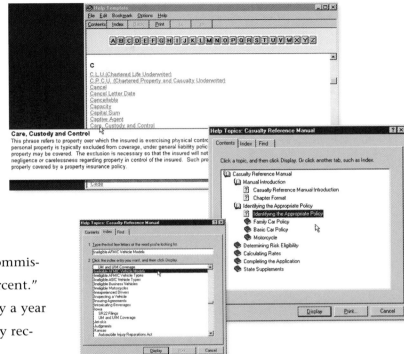

In January 1997, a small group of agents began testing the agency data system (ADS). The new computer program employs a Windows-based point-and-click system that makes it easier for agents and their employees to use.

business operation issues such as developing a business plan, hiring and training staff, and implementing successful underwriting and claims practices. Phase III will examine the most effective uses of technology.

"The model agency program is not only to share best practices but also to give agents a vision of what a successful agency will look like in the future," Meyer explained.

That vision includes continued growth in the size and diversity of American Family agencies. In 1986, the average American Family agent served 1,300 policies. By 1996, the figure had risen to 1,900. Today many large agencies have more than 5,000 policies. In St. Louis, Paul Young's book of business

Around-the-Clock Service in a Twenty-Four-Hour World

Squeezed by the demands of work, family, and outside activities, many people struggle to keep pace with their lives. To make reporting claims more convenient for time-strapped policyholders and claimants, American Family launched a twenty-four-hour claims call center on June 2, 1997. Beginning as a six-month pilot project, the center—based in Madison—provides around-the-clock claims service to people in Arizona. If successful, the service may expand companywide.

"The claims call center was one of the claims 2001 committee's earliest initiatives for changing our claims process," said Bob Kovich, claims administration director. "It's a linchpin for other changes we're considering."

With vigorous support from claims vice president Darnell Moore, American Family put the claims call center on a fast track and had it open after less than a year on the drawing board. Claims center representative Asabi Hayes fielded the first call at 10:18 a.m. opening day. In less than fifteen minutes, Asabi had collected all the information needed to file the claim, helped the policyholder decide the next steps to take, and explained the claim process.

The center employs twenty-nine people, with between two and five employees working each shift. During its first week, the center received 299 calls, with peak times from 8:00 a.m.—noon and 4:00 p.m.—6:00 p.m. Arizona time. Project manager Wendy Clausz expects those peaks to level out over time. "People are calling at times when it is easy to get in touch with their agents," Clausz explained. "As they become aware of the center, we hope they will call immediately after an accident."

Agents have primary responsibility for making customers aware of the claims call center. Most agents put the center's phone number on their answering machines. A few even forward calls to the center, saving the agent time and paperwork. Renewal notice inserts promote the claims call center.

Should the project expand to include all American Family states, Clausz estimates the center will receive more than 2 million calls annually and employ more than 150 people. "We're in the learning phase right now. But if that happens, we'll be ready," she said.

exceeds 9,400 policies, and he is on track to become American Family's first 10,000-policy agent in 1997. "I would like to see an agent with more than 10,000 policies," Mathwich said. "Then two, then three, then a hundred agents with more than 10,000 policies."

To help agents increase their policy count, Pierce and DeSalvo asked advertising director Annette Knapstein, who succeeded Bob Salisbury in 1990, to develop a direct marketing partnership with agents in 1995. The new direct marketing partnership began with a pilot project in Wisconsin, North Dakota, and Missouri, offering Medicare supplement insurance to current policyholders. A complex product that many agents avoid, Medicare supplement was an ideal product for the program, and 825 agents participated. The following year, the direct marketing partnership expanded to all states, beginning with American Family Financial Services information and mini-applications in homeowners renewal notices. The program also offered free multiple-line mailings to new agents in selected "growth" states. In 1997, the direct marketing partnership expanded to include auto and homeowners coverage. Like the company's other direct marketing programs, agent participation is voluntary, and agents receive all commissions and points for the All American competition. In some cases, agents share part of the expense, while in others the company picks up the entire tab.

American Family is experimenting with other avenues of direct marketing. In April 1996, the company went on line with its own home page on the World Wide Web. A year later, the direct marketing partnership piloted a telemarketing program in Ohio. As with all its direct marketing, American Family funnels business from these projects through its agents.

With a few industry observers predicting the demise of the agency system, some American Family agents are leery of the company's foray into direct marketing. Those who have taken a closer look, however, see it as an asset. "We hope agents will see it as a way to increase their book of business and customer retention at minimal cost or effort to them," DeSalvo said.

Further proof of American Family's commitment to its friendly, people-oriented approach to insurance is the company's growing emphasis on training. The agency expense study revealed that agents wanted more sales and automation training. In 1995, the marketing department began stationing

Typically all business, St. Louis-area agent Paul Young takes time out for a little fun. With more than 9,400 policies, Young is on track to become American Family's first agent with 10,000 policies.

Fearing American Family's logo was outdated, the company's strategic research department in 1996 asked employees, agents, current and potential policyholders to give their impressions of the thirty-four-year-old logo. Rather than suggest changing the logo, the responses reinforced that the simple, familiar logo still conveyed strength and comprehensive coverage.

Reinvigorating the Annual Policyholders' Meeting

Excited by the prospect of owning their own auto insurance company, scores of enthusiastic farmers traveled to Madison, Wisconsin, on October 3, 1927, for Farmers Mutual's first policyholders' meeting. The hearty men who had taken a chance on the new company filled the Green Room in the Loraine Hotel with applause as founder Herman Wittwer urged them to "watch us grow and grow with us."

Turnout for the annual meeting tapered off as their company's success became more certain. Soon, even the most vigilant policyholders let the annual meeting pass without a second thought. For years, the annual meeting languished as little more than a glorified board meeting. In 1985, determined to bring policyholders back into the annual meeting, chairman Bob Koch moved the meeting from the board room to a large training room. He invited longterm policyholders to attend, and ninety-two accepted.

Since then, the audience has grown steadily. At the seventieth policyholders' meeting on March 4, 1997, nearly 300 people filled the National Headquarters Auditorium to hear chairman Dale Mathwich recap American Family's progress and hear of plans for the future.

trainers in the field, with a goal of placing two sales trainers and one automation trainer in every sales state. With the company's investment in technology, computers also are playing a larger role in training. In 1995, the field training department and the media production center produced an interactive CD-ROM training package to help agents determine accurate replacement costs.

As American Family focuses on strengthening its agency system, the field management structure is changing. When Harvey Pierce moved to Madison as EVP of field operations in 1987, the optimum size for a district was twenty agents. This was not only a goal but a limitation. Besides recruiting agents, DMs trained, managed, and motivated them. They provided sales training, product training, and computer training. They showed agents how to keep records, staff their offices, and do anything else that would help them succeed. "It had become almost an impossible task," said Al Meyer.

At the 1996 sales management conference, Dan DeSalvo asked district managers to visualize different roles for themselves. With the company offering more sales and technical training, DMs can spend more time sharing best business practices with their agents, helping them lower expenses and maintain profit. And DMs will have more time to recruit new agents and build stronger districts. "The future of the district manager is different," Meyer said. "But it's much brighter."

The four-decade-old role of the regional vice presidents also is changing. In 1996, Mathwich and Pierce began planning for succession in 1999, when Mathwich, EVP of finance Paul King, and EVP of administration Jim Klokner retire. Rather than simply choose successors, Mathwich suggested that he and Pierce reconsider American Family's management structure. With the help of human resources vice president Vicki Chvala and compensation director Gary Gailfus, they developed nearly two dozen management models before narrowing the options to six, then presented those to the four EVPs for their input.

In Pierce's opinion, the regional vice presidents had focused primarily on sales for the last ten years. American Family's stunning growth reinforced that opinion. To continue that trend, American Family has to keep increasing the number and productivity of its agents. With that in mind, Pierce and Mathwich's reorganization relieved the RVPs of responsibility for managing the regional offices and changed their title to regional vice president of sales. With approval from the board, the reorganization became effective March 31, 1997.

"It's another step in our commitment to the agents," Mathwich explained. "By putting a vice president in charge of sales in each region, we're really focusing on quality recruiting, quality training, and quality building of productive agencies."

American Family also remains committed to providing its agents and policyholders with fast, friendly, efficient service. And, American Family's more than 6,800 employees and 3,600 agents remain the foundation of the personal service that sets the company apart from many of its competitors. To maintain that edge, American Family will continue its practice of hiring high-quality people, training them well, and giving them responsibility. Those employees who can be flexible, adaptable, and approach change as an opportunity will always be able to find rewarding careers at American Family.

Into the Twenty-First Century

Entering the twenty-first century, the American Family Group faces dramatic changes and challenges in the form of increasing cost pressures and competition, growing government involvement, and ever-rising consumer expectations. Pierce knows that to succeed in the next century American Family must grow and evolve. "We need to be willing to make the hard choices," he said. "If we believe a change is necessary, we ought to make it with all the confidence that our people will make it work."

American Family's seventy years of approaching change with a conservative yet creative attitude that began with founder Herman Wittwer gives Mathwich confidence in the company's future. "We think things through before we act," Mathwich said. "We avoid jumping on bandwagons that may be headed in the wrong direction. Instead, we try to be creative. Our entire history indicates we're a very creative company that can take advantage of change."

In that sense, American Family's history continues precisely where it began—creating change, confident in its vision of the future.

"Our entire history indicates we're a very creative company that can take advantage of change."

APPENDIX

INTERVIEW PARTICIPANTS

Charles Ambrosavage
Robert Amundson
Ralph Arnold
Arthur Babler
Leone Babler
Phyllis Benitz
Donald Breitenbach
Martin Brewer
Buzz Buchanan
James Caskey
Joseph Chvala
Vicki Chvala
Gerald Cutsforth
James Dallman
Daniel DeSalvo
Norbert Dettman
Rose Detmer

Robert DeVoe
James Eldridge
Silver Everhart
Bradley Gleason
Allan Gruenisen
Richard Haas
Dick Harmeling
Wally Huebsch
Alan Hunter
J. Brent Johnson
Nancy Johnson
Jeff Johnston
Marvin Kammer
Paul King
Thomas King
Edward Kissinger
William Kleinheinz

James Klokner
Marvin Klitzke
Annette Knapstein
W. Robert Koch
Rev. James Kramer
Richard Kuntz
Ruth Kutz
William Lundy
Donald Mahoney
Dale Mathwich
Irving Maurer
Dean McCarthy
Alan Meyer
Paul Miller
John "Pete" Miller
James Mintz
Darnell Moore

Paul Moosmann
Clayton Nelson
M. Joseph Nicolay
Milton Olson
James Pfefferle
Cary Pierce
Harvey Pierce
Robert Powers
Kazell Pugh
John Reed
Gerald Rekowski
Darrell Riley
Thomas Rivers
Robbie Robinson
Bonnie Rostad
Vonnie Ryan
Robert Salisbury

Sterling Schallert
John Scharer
Robert Scott
Elliott Shuler
Richard Smith
JoAnn Sprecher
Barbara Gail Sticha
Gary Switzky
Margie Thalacker
Gwen Thompson Jones
Steven Tingley
Joseph Tisserand
Rita Underhill
Norbert Vanden Heuvel
Arlette Vander Molen
Chuck Webster
Gene Wilpolt

OTHER CONTRIBUTORS

Irene Babler, Lecanto, Florida, for information on Wittwer family genealogy

Lori Belognia, Marshfield Public Library, for help on Marshfield history and Richard Kalbskopf

Marta Cantu, administrative assistant, for help in coordinating activity through President Pierce's office

John Christner, Marshfield, for early photo of the Hotel Charles

Frank Custer, retired reporter, *Capital Times*, for information on Joseph Boyd

Duane DeBower, Northwest regional operations director, for photos and early American Standard brochure

Frank Feivor, retired district manager, for photos and insights

Jim Jordan, University of Wisconsin School of Music, for help depicting Herman Wittwer's musical involvement as a student at the University of Wisconsin

Jeff Kleiman, assistant professor of history, University of Wisconsin-Marshfield, whose history of Marshfield aided our understanding of the town's early years

Dolly Kobs, North Wood County Historical Society (Upham Mansion), Marshfield, for help searching the *Marshfield Daily News* and the *Marshfield Herald*

James Madden, financial analyst, for compiling financial statistics

Steve Schumacher, video/multimedia producer, for providing digital images of archival material

Neil Shively, Page One Communications, for help with Madison details in the 1920s and 1930s

Dick Sorenson, conservator of instruments, Schubert Club, St. Paul, Minnesota, for loan of a vintage clarinet

Jean Staveness, senior administrative assistant, for help in coordinating the flow of information and activity through Chairman Mathwich's office

Jim Sticha for his recollections of Herman Wittwer

Sue Walker, senior executive secretary, for access to corporate records

Lee Weinberger, corporate librarian, for help researching statistics and industry publications

David Wells, assistant to the general manager, Madison Symphony Orchestra, for an early photo of the orchestra

Sources

"The Adequacy of State Insurance Rate Regulation: The McCarran-Ferguson Act in Historical Perspective," by Spencer Kimball and Ronald Boyce, which appeared in volume 56 of the *Michigan Law Review* in 1958

America on Wheels, by Frank Coffey and Joseph Layden

American Epoch: A History of the United States Since 1900 (Volume II), by Arthur S. Link and William Catton

The Automobile in America, by Stephen W. Sears

Automobiles of America, by the Automobile Manufacturers Assoc. Inc.

Fifty Years of Independents: The Story of an American Insurance Revolution, by Charles J. Lorenz at the National Association of Independent Insurers

History of Wood County, Wisconsin, compiled by George O. Jones and Norman S. McVean

Insurance and Public Policy, by Spencer Kimball

James J. Hill Reference Library, St. Paul, Minnesota, for its collection of the *National Underwriter*

Let the Trumpet Resound, by Lawrence G. Brandon

Madison Public Library for its collection of the *Capital Times* and *Wisconsin State Journal*

Monroe High School, Monroe, Wisconsin, for our search of high school records on Herman Wittwer

Monroe Public Library, for information on Green County and for its collection of the *Monroe Evening Times*

Monticello Past and Present, produced by the Monticello Historical Committee

The *National Underwriter*

Only Yesterday and *Since Yesterday*, by Frederick Lewis Allen

State of Wisconsin Blue Book 1991-1992, compiled by the Wisconsin Legislative Reference Bureau

Treasury of Early American Automobiles, by Floyd Clymer

Wisconsin State Historical Society for its photo archives and excellent service

Minnesota Historical Society for its photo archives

University of Wisconsin-Madison Archives for *The Badger 1911* and *The Badger 1912* yearbooks

Zwingli United Church of Christ, Monticello, Wisconsin, for early church records of the Wittwer family

American Family Insurance Group: A Record of Growth*

Year	Assets	Surplus	Revenue
1927	$6,959	$2,240	$7,548
1932	$280,238	$76,059	$209,337
1937	$835,019	$208,192	$1,014,607
1942	$1,948,150	$752,597	$1,806,500
1947	$6,972,799	$1,394,006	$7,539,537
1952	$21,374,050	$7,635,256	$14,574,088
1957	$34,210,503	$12,055,897	$22,401,326
1962°	$53,751,997	$20,686,542	$38,161,871
1967	$109,205,292	$34,673,620	$72,322,454
1972	$264,857,183	$76,665,351	$180,943,353
1977	$596,103,607	$135,956,205	$447,901,259
1982	$1,213,556,603	$307,209,374	$824,890,816
1987	$2,560,148,000	$641,284,000	$1,656,144,000
1992	$4,698,162,000	$1,128,745,000	$2,676,950,000
1996	$6,835,701,000	$2,150,922,000	$3,353,398,000

*Statutory accounting basis. Slight differences may exist between the audited financial statements and highlights reports due to different account groupings.

°1962 figures include assets, surplus, and revenue for Farmers Mutual Automobile Insurance Company, American Family Life Insurance Company, and American Standard Insurance Company with no eliminations for duplication. All figures after that are from the American Family Insurance Group consolidated audited statements.

AMERICAN FAMILY INSURANCE GROUP: A RECORD OF GROWTH

YEAR	EMPLOYEES	AGENTS	POLICYHOLDERS/ POLICIES IN FORCE
1927*	3	236	486
1932	21	800	18,750
1937	50	1,200	50,000
1942	100	1,900	100,000
1947	250	2,500	200,000
1952+	433	3,267	300,000
1957○	637	1,653	533,345
1962	776	1,587	684,388
1967	988	1,648	852,551
1972	1,512	2,020	1,378,867
1977	2,712	2,360	2,329,641
1982	4,331	2,599	3,350,011
1987▲	5,257	2,931	4,178,211
1992	6,376	2,966	5,102,477
1996	6,456	3,489	6,102,994

*Early information on the number of employees, agents, and policyholders is spotty and in many cases based on estimates. Sources often refer to policyholders and policies in force interchangeably.

+Employee figures for 1952 to the present are based on human resources records and field force figures on marketing records.

○Policy statistics for remaining years are derived from group consolidated figures.

▲Beginning in 1987, group consolidated figures refer to policies in force.

AMERICAN FAMILY FINANCIAL SERVICES

YEAR	LOANS	LEASES
1969	$2.5 million	
1972	$15.4 million	
1977	$61.6 million	
1982	$71.6 million	
1987	$78.4 million	$3.9 million
1992	$162.2 million	$7.1 million
1996	$200.4 million	$21.6 million

AMERICAN FAMILY LIFE INSURANCE COMPANY

YEAR	LIFE INS. IN FORCE
1958*	$11.0 million
1962	$120.6 million
1967	$362.8 million
1972	$1.1 billion
1977	$2.9 billion
1982	$6.3 billion
1987	$13.0 billion
1992	$22.8 billion
1996	$35.5 billion

*Six months in operation.

INDEX